Design for Emotion

Design for Emotion

Trevor van Gorp

Edie Adams

AMSTERDAM • BOSTON • HEIDELBERG • LONDON
NEW YORK • OXFORD • PARIS • SAN DIEGO
SAN FRANCISCO • SINGAPORE • SYDNEY • TOKYO

Morgan Kaufmann is an imprint of Elsevier

Acquiring Editor: Meg Dunkerley
Development Editor: Heather Scherer
Project Manager: Danielle S. Miller
Designers: Joanne Blank, Trevor van Gorp, Edie Adams

Morgan Kaufmann is an imprint of Elsevier
225 Wyman Street, Waltham, MA 02451, USA

Library of Congress Cataloging-in-Publication Data
Van Gorp, Trevor.
  Design for emotion / Trevor van Gorp and Edie Adams.
      pages cm
  ISBN 978-0-12-386531-1 (pbk.)
  1. Design—Psychological aspects. I. Adams, Edie. II. Title.
  NK1520.V36 2012
  745.4—dc23
                            2012003885

British Library Cataloguing-in-Publication Data
A catalogue record for this book is available from the British Library.

ISBN: 978-0-12-386531-1

For information on all MK publications
visit our website at *www.mkp.com*

Printed in China

12 13 14 15   10 9 8 7 6 5 4 3 2 1

Typeset by: diacriTech, Chennai, India

Contents

Acknowledgments   ix
Author Bios   xi
Foreword   xiii
Introduction   xv

CHAPTER 1   Why Design for Emotion?   1
Useful, Usable and Desirable   1
     Prioritizing Emotional Needs   3
Emotion, Personality and Meaning   4
     Five Reasons to Design for Emotion   6
     The Creation of Meaning   14
Conclusion   16
References   17

CHAPTER 2   What Is Emotion?   19
Understanding Emotion   21
     Experiencing Emotion   21
     Expressing Emotion   22
     Mental Models   23
The Anatomy and Influence of Emotion   25
     Emotion Is Both Conscious and Unconscious   26
     Emotions Originate in Different Parts of the Brain   28
     Emotion Combines the Mental and the Physical   31
     Emotion, Attention and Information   39
     Emotion Contributes to Flow   41
     Emotion, Motivation and Intention   43
     Emotions, Moods, Sentiments and Personality Traits   45
Conclusion   47
References   49

CHAPTER 3   When Do We Design for Emotion?   51
Measuring Success Through Flow   53
     Goals and Meaning   53
     Association and Meaning   54
     Status, Values and Meaning   55
Attention and Flow   57
     Goals and Attention   57
     Defining Attention   58
     Types of Attention   58

Measuring Attention   60
The Limits of Attention   61
The Senses and Attention   62
The Tactile (Touch)   63
The Visual   64
The Auditory   65
Emotion, Attention and Behavior   66
Emotion and Attention   66
Emotion and Behavior   67
Motivation and Arousal   69
Emotion and Flow   71
Causes, Characteristics and Consequences of Flow   72
Conclusions   79
References   81

CHAPTER 4　**Where Do We Design for Emotion?**   83
Product Personalities   83
Personality and Identity   85
Perceiving Emotion and Personality   85
Aesthetics and Interaction   86
Responses, Experiences and Relationships   89
Emotional Design Models   91
How Do I Love Thee?   94
The Types of Love   97
Three Brains, Three Levels   100
Personality Traits and Design   101
The Traits of a Good Design   102
Gender and Stereotypes   109
Masculine and Feminine   110
Gender in Products   113
The Evolution of Emotion and Personality   115
Dominance in Nature   115
Dominance and Friendliness   116
Dominant or Submissive?   117
Friendly or Unfriendly?   119
Lines Have Feelings, Too   120
The Influence of Color   121
Do Opposites Attract?   123
The Right Personality for Your Product   124
Conclusions   125
References   126

CHAPTER 5　**How Do We Design for Emotion?**   129
Designing Relationships   129
Cutting Through the Jargon   130

A Passion for Desirable Aesthetics 130
The Intimacy of Usable Interaction 132
A Commitment to Useful Function 132
The A.C.T. model 132
Attract 135
Converse 135
Transact 136
Persuading with A.C.T. 137
Using the A.C.T. Model 138
Get to Know Your Users 139
Define Design Goals 140
Understanding the Dimensions of Emotion 141
Guidelines for Emotion 141
What Personality Do I Design? 146
Gender and Personality 147
Communicating Emotion Through Affordances 148
A.C.T. Guidelines 149
Attract 149
Converse 161
Transact 169
Conclusions 170
A.C.T. Model 171
References 173

CHAPTER 6 Interviews and Case Studies 175
Interviews 175
An Interview with Patrick W. Jordan 175
Reference 178
An Interview with Stephen P. Anderson 178
Reference 184
An Interview with Aarron Walter 184
References 192
An Interview with Trish Miner on the Desirability Toolkit 192
Reference 195
An Interview with Marco van Hout on the LEMtool 195
References 199
Case Studies 200
Windows Phone 7 Reference Designs for Metro UI 200
The Emotional Elements of PICO 205
Conclusions 210

Trademarks 211
Index 213

Acknowledgments

Both authors would like to acknowledge the contributions of their friends and colleagues, who went out of their way to provide feedback, encouragement and support. For providing your time and thoughts in interviews, case studies, and offering material, a heartfelt thanks goes out to Stephen P. Anderson, Patrick Jordan, Trish Miner, Marco van Hout, Aarron Walter, Moni Wolf, Shayal Chhibber, Matt Pattison, Damian Smith, Chris Fryer, Smith & Nephew and Bella Martin. For providing the inspiring images from your collection of faces, a big thanks to Jim Leftwich.

We'd like to thank Rachel Roumeliotis, Heather Scherer, Steve Elliot, Danielle Miller, and the staff at Morgan Kaufmann for believing in the book and working closely with us on the design.

And finally, we'd like to thank all of the people who contributed examples and ideas for the book through DesignforEmotion.com. Your examples inspired us to take the book in directions we might not have otherwise imagined. To anyone we've missed, your feedback, comments and support helped make this possible. Thanks so much!

TREVOR VAN GORP

Before a single word had been written, there were people who offered their time to discuss how a book like this might look. Thanks to Lou Rosenfeld for his openness and encouragement. My sincerest appreciation goes out to Michael Nolan for his enthusiasm about the idea, and to Rachel Roumeliotis for recognizing its value. A heartfelt thanks goes out to Ayça Çakmaklı for her inspiring cards.

Thanks to Cassandra Watson for her love, laughter and encouragement, and my parents for their endless love and support.

My deepest thanks goes out to my coauthor Edie, who was enthusiastic about the project from the very beginning. Thanks for bringing your openness, experience, and deep understanding of design to the book. I continue to grow and benefit from the wisdom of your perspectives, and this book is a reflection of that.

Finally, I'd like to thank anyone and everyone who's been involved in the project. You've helped make the thousands of tiny decisions that add up to a book.

EDIE ADAMS

I would like to acknowledge the examples set by my dear friends Anne Focke and Sylvia Wolf, both of whom published works while this book was in progress. Anne's enthusiasm for the project was ever-present, and her support throughout the phases of creating, writing and editing was unwavering. Sylvia showed me through her own work that writing and publishing a book is an attainable and joyful achievement.

Thanks to Brandon Zebold for his deep commitment to my success in this endeavor. Brandon gave me the space I needed for the writing and provided ample opportunities for mental diversion. Dude love rules!

Finally, I would like to thank my coauthor Trevor, who brought an attitude of honest exploration to the writing and discussing of each idea. Early on, we established a way of working that was open and accepting of the breadth our individual experiences. I'm grateful for what I've learned through the mutual pursuit of our goal.

Author Bios

TREVOR VAN GORP, BFA, M.E.DES.

Trevor has spent the last nine years understanding how emotion affects design and how design affects emotion. He's been working in design and visual communications since 1994, and holds a Master of Environmental Design in Industrial Design from the University of Calgary, and a B.F.A. in Graphic Design. Formerly the first employee at nForm User Experience, Trevor helped build the company into a leading Canadian user experience firm.

He is the founder and principal of Affective Design Inc., a trusted user experience consultancy focused on emotional design. Trevor has created information architecture, performed interaction design and conducted user research & usability evaluations for clients like the City of Edmonton, the Edmonton Transit System, Comcast, Ancestry.com, DDB Canada and the Government of Alberta.

Trevor is the author and editor of affectivedesign.org, a popular blog on the intersection of design and emotion that is used by corporations and institutions all over the world to help learn about emotional and affective design. He contributed to *Deconstructing Product Design* by William Lidwell and Gerry Manacsa, and has written articles for *Boxes and Arrows*, a noted industry web magazine.

Trevor has given presentations on the topic of designing for emotion at conferences in Canada, the United States and Sweden. He is a member of the Information Architecture Institute, Design & Emotion Society and the Industrial Designers of America.

You can find him online at:

Twitter: @affectivedesign

Web: http://affectivedesign.com

EDIE ADAMS, M.E.DES., CPE

Edie has made a career of evoking emotion through design. For more than 20 years, she has worked with product teams, innovation groups, and business leadership to develop an understanding of the physical, cognitive and emotional interactions between people and products that drive product success.

Edie's emotional design and research innovations have been recognized with more than 40 US patents. Her design work is included in the Permanent Collection of the Museum of Modern Art in New York and the Chicago Athenaeum. She was also featured in "Fast Forward: Design in the Pacific Northwest" at the Tacoma Art Museum.

To begin her 16 years at Microsoft, Edie led a team researching people's physical, cognitive and emotional interactions with products for the Microsoft Hardware and Strategic Business divisions. She has held numerous research and design manager positions in Windows, including Windows Mobile and Tailored Products, the Windows Hardware Innovation Group, and the Windows Hardware and Emerging Markets Group. In each, Edie has worked with many different types of designers (industrial designers, interaction designers & visual designers), market and user researchers, hardware and software architects, and business development to spur innovation in the PC industry. During her time with Windows Core Operating System Division (COSD), she developed an understanding of the premium mobile consumer market for the Platform and Core Innovation team. Her last posting saw her leading a diverse team of 27 designers, researchers, and writers as the Principal User Experience Manager for the Mac Business Unit (MacBU) at Microsoft.

Edie is trained in occupational ergonomics, product design, and design research. She is a CPE (Certified Professional Ergonomist), and holds a Master of Environmental Design in Industrial Design and a Bachelor of Science (B.Sc.) in Psychology from the University of Calgary, where she has been an Adjunct Professor in the Faculty of Environmental Design.

Edie is past president of the Office Ergonomics Research Committee, past program chair of the Human Factors and Ergonomics Society Consumer Product Technical Group, and past vice chair of the Human Factors Special Interest Section of the Industrial Design Society of America.

Foreword

BJ Fogg, Ph.D.
Stanford Persuasive Technology Lab

Soon I will ask you to stop reading and notice what surrounds you. I want you to search for evidence that you (yes, you!) are a designer of emotions.

In fact, I'm betting you have lots of experience designing for this purpose, more than you realize. What surrounds you reflects choices you've made, often intuitively, to achieve emotional outcomes. Of course, I might be wrong, but let's find out.

Please take my 60-second challenge: Find three ways you've crafted your environment to influence emotions.

Here are some tips:

- Consider the objects around you (pictures of loved ones?)
- Notice what you're hearing (music?)
- Look over what you're wearing (jewelry?)

Are you ready for my challenge? *Okay, please stop reading now.*

Welcome back!

Let me share what I found …

As I look around my home office, I see how I've designed for efficiency—I've got files and drawers and closets. But these efficiency artifacts seem trivial compared to how I've designed my workspace for emotions I seek.

I have a huge collection of books in this room. But I cannot see them. And that's a relief. About two years ago, I covered this frenetic collection with a cloth that has calming images of plants. It's like nature in my office. I expected that this draping—made from two shower curtains—would be temporary. But nope: It's still there.

On the wall in front of me, I've posted two cards I found in a collection for children. One card says "brave"; it has a quirky superhero image. The other card says "peaceful" with a spotted dog at rest; he is smiling calmly. Both look like drawings from kindergarten. I posted those during a tough time in my life. I had too many projects going, and I wasn't sure I would succeed on any of them. Even today, with my life more under control, those cards speak to me: *Be brave, be peaceful, and—above all—don't take yourself so damn seriously.*

As I look over my office for other evidence of emotional design, I realize I've made a big mistake. Along the top of my bookcase, I've placed twelve framed documents. This is a collection of my degrees and awards. Right now, this display strikes me as downright silly. Of course, I'm delighted to have degrees from Stanford. And I'm (sort of) proud of certain awards. But seriously, what's the point of aggrandizing myself to myself? I plan to pack these up tomorrow. Then, as I face the blankness over the bookcase, I can seek a solution that makes me happier.

(Aha! The top of my bookcase would be an ideal spot for my many ukuleles, now languishing in the garage. They will be happier in here with me, and I'll be happier with them at arm's reach, poised for a quick strum.)

We are all emotional designers in our everyday lives. It's a natural human urge. But despite this urge and our experience fulfilling it, few have learned a systematic way to design winning experiences for other people. And that's vital in today's marketplace. If you don't design effectively for emotions, your product will fail. Period.

If I have one hope for you, as a reader, it would be this: By reading this book you will create a foundation so solid that you continue to learn every day how emotions work, simply by observing life around you. In my view, that is the mark of an expert. And the promise of this book is to put you on that winning path.

Introduction

Creative professionals who design consumer products, entertainment, software, websites, marketing and communications are beginning to appreciate the importance of evoking emotions and communicating personality to capture viewers' attention and create satisfying experiences. This book was written to help you create designs that do a better job of communicating emotion and personality to fulfill users' needs.

Just as there are different types of relationships between people, there are different types of relationships between people and products. Throughout the book, when we use the word "product," we're referring to any type of product, including but not limited to: physical products, software applications, websites, and interactive products. By understanding how products communicate emotion and personality, along with the psychology of interaction, you can encourage the formation of relationships between people and the products you design.

Part of what makes designing for emotion difficult is that everyone has his or her own set of personal experiences and learned associations. Although some associations are learned, other associations are part of our evolutionary inheritance. In this book, we explore how to practically apply these unconscious associations to express emotion and personality through design.

Although it's possible to flip to almost any page and pick up useful insights, each chapter builds upon the concepts that were previously covered. Because of this, we suggest reading the book from start to finish to get the most value for your time and attention.

CHAPTER 1

In Chapter 1, we discuss the goals of designing for emotion and provide five reasons that you should be considering emotional responses as part of your design process.

CHAPTER 2

Chapter 2 is a deep dive into the psychology of emotion. By the end of this chapter, you'll understand the basic dimensions of emotion and be able to predict how your design decisions will affect users' emotions. You may also find that having a better understanding of your own emotions will affect more than just the way you design.

CHAPTER 3

This chapter explains why some products become meaningful to users. We explore the importance of attention in creating flow – the state of being fully immersed in an activity. Then we explain how emotions influence intention and motivation to trigger behavior.

CHAPTER 4

In Chapter 4, we examine how design communicates emotion and personality to your users. We'll explore several models of designing for emotion, and we'll look at the different ways people experience the emotion of love to get a better understanding of how to design relationships with products. Next, we'll talk about the two most important distinctions that people make when judging the personality of a product.

CHAPTER 5

Chapter 5 introduces the A.C.T. model, a framework for addressing the users' emotional needs. Based on a comparison between the different models for designing emotion and a model of love, the A.C.T. model describes how to design the *desirable, usable* and *useful* experiences that form relationships. Finally, this chapter summarizes what we've covered throughout the book, and provides guidelines to help guide your designs through each stage in the A.C.T. framework.

CHAPTER 6

Chapter 6 features interviews and case studies from industry leaders researching and applying emotion to design. We interviewed people in the user experience, medical device and smartphone fields, as well as the creators of two different emotional design research methods. This chapter will give you a better understanding of how emotional design has been successfully applied across different design disciplines.

Why Design for Emotion?

1

The ever-changing and ephemeral nature of emotions has led many to believe that it's impossible to consistently trigger emotional responses through design. Over the last three decades, research that examines the relationship between design and emotion has grown steadily. This research has provided new ways to visualize the basic dimensions of emotion, allowing for the creation of models that can help us understand and design for emotional responses. In the upcoming chapters, we'll be describing a number of ways to model and understand how products affect us on different emotional levels.

By the end of this book, you should have a basic understanding of emotion and why users' experiences affect the way they make decisions, become motivated (or unmotivated), behave, and perceive personality. You'll learn when to balance users' emotions through design and you'll be able to predict the emotional level at which you should focus your design efforts. Finally, we'll tie it all together with the A.C.T. framework, along with a set of guidelines for designing more emotional experiences.

USEFUL, USABLE AND DESIRABLE

When Trevor was a teenager, he would go to the traveling car shows that would come to the convention center near where he grew up. The shows would feature famous cars from movies and television shows, like the General Lee from the *Dukes of Hazzard* or the Batmobile from the first *Batman* movie. Occasionally, they would also have what are called "concept cars." Concept cars aren't intended for mass production. Instead, their goal is to showcase new design directions and gauge public reaction to new styling and technology.

Trevor remembers strolling through one of the shows and being entranced with the highlights, sleek lines and gleaming chrome that surrounded him. One vehicle caught his eye, mainly because it had gullwing doors like the car in the *Back to the*

Future movies. He remembers thinking how "cool" it would be to have a car with doors like that, and saying as much to the attendant, seated nearby.

Looking over at him, the attendant asked, "You like this car?" Trevor nodded in the affirmative. "Well," he said, "don't get too excited. It's not like it moves or anything." "Do you mean," Trevor asked in slight shock, "that it has no engine?" Standing slowly, the attendant walked over to the car and put his hand on the door. The windows were tinted, making it almost impossible to see any detail inside. Opening the door to reveal an interior with a very basic steering column and no dash controls, he exhaled deeply and said, "Doesn't really matter how good it looks, if it doesn't move."

FIG. 1.1 Time Machine in the *Back to the Future* Films
Creative Commons

Designers are faced with many considerations when designing interactive products and services.

Designers are faced with many (often conflicting) considerations when designing interactive products and services. For a concept car, the most important requirement is the appearance. From a business standpoint, the concept car needs to be aesthetically pleasing in order to attract public interest. From a viewer or "user" standpoint, the fact that the concept car is beautiful triggers pleasure and creates attraction. In a different context, a need, other than attraction, might be a higher priority for either the business or the users. In a production vehicle, for example, the most important needs would be functionality and usability, rather than appearance and desirability.

Liz Sanders described three categories of product requirements: useful, usable, and desirable (Sanders, 1992). These three categories are intended as a blanket description, covering all the aspects of users' emotional experiences with products.

Useful: Performs the tasks it was designed for
Usable: Easy to use and interact with
Desirable: Provides feelings of pleasure and creates attraction

To satisfy the goals of your clients (i.e., "the business") and the needs of their customers (i.e., "the users"), your design must be **useful**. In other words, it must perform the task it was designed for. It must also be **usable**, or easy to understand and interact with in a predictable and reliable manner. Usability has become a basic business requirement as well as a user expectation. Finally, in order to attract users, your design must also be **desirable**. For many types of products, the pleasure provided by beauty has become an expected part of the experience during purchasing, ownership and use.

Sometimes, a product can be immensely useful, but because it's a new discovery or a new category of products, it's not yet very usable or aesthetically pleasing. The first computers, for example, were bulky terminals that came with command-line interfaces. As the age of a category of products increases, competitors enter the market with products that offer the same functions. Simple functionality becomes the norm (van Geel, 2011).

When the functional quality of a product increases, usability and aesthetics take on greater importance. As the computer industry and the technology matured, usability and desirability became important differentiators. Today, we have beautiful graphic user interfaces on screens that allow objects to be moved around intuitively via touch on elegantly thin devices. In today's competitive environment, products that neglect aesthetics and usability often fail to attract the attention of demanding consumers. This applies not only to physical products, but also to websites, software and other digital products as well.

Designers must balance the goals of the business and the needs of the user with the constraints imposed by the technology.

Prioritizing Emotional Needs

When it comes to most products, websites, and applications, our emotional needs are complex and multilayered. We want our products to work while also being easy to use. Of course, it doesn't hurt if they also look and feel good. Over time, our emotional responses to these criteria can determine whether a product becomes a beloved tool, or a part of the day you simply put up with.

As designers, we must learn to identify the emotional considerations that are most important for the context of use. From there, we can prioritize these considerations by examining how each affects our ability to fulfill important business goals and satisfy crucial user needs. Designers must balance the goals of the business and the needs of the user with the constraints imposed by the technology.

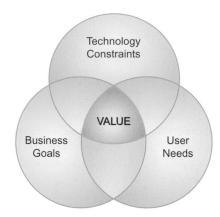

FIG. 1.2 Balancing User Needs With Business Goals and Technology Constraints

© *Trevor van Gorp*

Aesthetics alone won't supply a usable or useful product.

Some of the most successful products have been embraced because they've managed to satisfy the emotional needs that were most important for their context of use. Because the use context for every product is different, your solution may need to focus more on some areas than others. As we saw in the example of the concept car, some things really *only* need to focus on being beautiful. The car with no dashboard controls and no engine accomplishes its purpose in the convention center: to show off new styling and generate excitement. But, it's not much use outside on the street.

With a different product, in a different context of use, desirability alone might not suffice. Aesthetics may satisfy users' simple need for pleasure, but providing aesthetics alone won't supply a usable or useful product. On its own, the concept car, for example, doesn't fulfill the average user's needs for a functional commuting vehicle. It won't actually take you anywhere and if it did, there would be no way to safely control the necessary functions.

EMOTION, PERSONALITY AND MEANING

When we use products, we experience emotional responses that are no different from the responses we experience with real people.

So why should you design for emotion? The short answer is that emotion is an overriding influence in our daily lives (Damasio, 1994). It constitutes our experiences and colors our realities. Emotion dominates decision making, commands attention and enhances some memories, while minimizing others (Reeves & Nass, 1998).

The emotions we feel allow us to assign meanings to the people and things that we experience in life. Most of the time, pleasure means "good" and pain means "bad." When we use products, websites and software applications, we experience complex social and emotional responses that are no different from the responses we experience when we interact with real people in the real world (Desmet, 2002).

Over time, the emotional expressions that we perceive in both people and things can come to be seen as "personality traits" (van Gorp, 2006). We perceive personality in the things in our environment and then form relationships with those things based on the personalities we've given them (Reeves & Nass, 1998). As Donald Norman put it, "everything has a personality, everything sends an emotional signal. Even when this was not the intention of the designer, the people who view … infer personalities and experience emotions. … Horrible personalities instill horrid emotional states in their users, usually unwittingly" (van Geel, 2011).

Our tendency to perceive emotion and personality in things is utilized by marketers and advertisers, who target advertisements for particular brands to the audiences of specific shows. The "personality" of each show—represented by its look, feel, and emotional tone—is known to attract an audience that fits certain demographics and has certain tastes. "Modest people are more likely to watch the blue-collar hero show *Deadliest Catch*, while altruistic people tend to prefer cooking shows like *Rachael Ray* and reality shows with happy endings like *The Bachelor*" (Bulik, 2010).

Because of people's natural tendency to perceive personality in things, they also tend to form **relationships** with those things based in part on the personalities they perceive. Personality traits are powerful factors in design, contributing to what we choose in terms of media (e.g., TV shows, music), the products

We perceive personality in the things in our environment and then form relationships with those things based on the personalities we've given them.

FIG. 1.3 Object Displaying Emotion and Personality
© iStockPhoto.com

we purchase and the story of the brands we embrace or ignore (Govers & Schoormans, 2005).

Five Reasons to Design for Emotion

The information you take in informs your mental model or "map" of the world and reality.

To create better value for both your clients and their customers, you should begin considering your users' emotional responses as part of your design process. Emotions affect key cognitive functions on both the conscious and unconscious levels. Let's take a more detailed look at the reasons that emotion has such a profound influence on the success of a design:

- Emotion is experience.
- All design is emotional design.
- Emotion dominates decision making.
- Emotion commands attention and affects memory.
- Emotion communicates personality, forms relationships, and creates meaning.

Emotion Is Experience

We receive information about the world from our senses. Because we don't have the attention required to process and interpret all the information we receive each day, a lot of the information we encounter is simply screened out (Davenport & Beck, 2001). Our brains then process and interpret the information that has actually made it into our heads. This information is represented and compared to the information we already know.

Together, all this information informs your mental model or "map" of the world and reality. Because no one can be exposed to everything, everyone's map is incomplete. No single person's map can possibly encompass "all" of reality. This inherent limitation naturally leads to some heated debates between people with different "maps" about the nature of existence, god and a number of other interesting questions that we won't attempt to address here.

Emotion is the energy that drives and directs attention.

But let's back up for a minute. What is it that keeps information from being ignored or screened out in the first place? What is it that selects the information that actually gets into our brains and becomes part of our mental models of reality? Attention selects relevant information by focusing on it and deletes information that's considered irrelevant by simply ignoring it. Emotion is the energy that drives and directs attention.

Emotions and other **affective states** like moods, sentiments and personality traits influence every aspect of our interactions with brands, products, and websites (Forlizzi & Battarbee, 2004). This includes our intentions, our plans, and any feedback on whether we achieve success. Our plans are our internal representations of sequences of events, actions, and consequences. Plans provide a link between the goals we envision in our minds and the actual realization of those goals in the physical world.

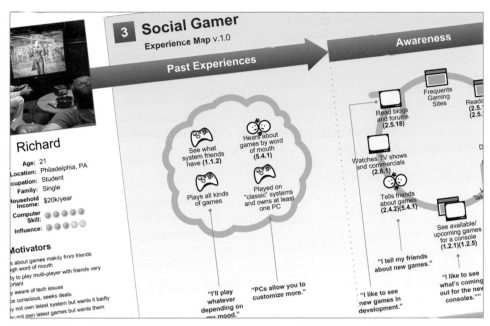

FIG. 1.4 Social Gamer Mental Map

Gene Smith and Trevor van Gorp (2007). Used with permission of nForm User Experience.

Affective states run the range from short-term emotions to long-term personality traits. In this way, affective states act as continuously shifting influences that are always altering perception and triggering the mental processes that lead to behavior.

In emotion research circles, this influence is called "emotional affect" (Russell, 1980). Emotional affect can be envisioned as a lens that constantly colors our realities. This lens is so pervasive and ubiquitous that it's easy to forget that it's there, unless our emotions become intense enough to demand and divert our attention. The color and focus of the lens may change depending on the quality of the emotions we're experiencing, but the lens is always there, subtly influencing how we see the world. We'll be exploring the effects of emotional affect in more detail in Chapter 2.

Emotional affect can be envisioned as a lens that constantly colors our realities.

All Design Is Emotional Design

If your business involves competing in a market in which your customers have to choose between your product and similar products made by your competitors, consider this: individuals without the capacity for emotional response are *unable* to make even simple cognitive decisions such as what clothes to wear in the morning (Damasio, 1994). Simple decisions such as this rely on the emotional feedback provided by our feelings. You're required to make hundreds of seemingly inconsequential decisions each day, and simple emotional responses are likely the deciding factor in those decisions.

Professionals in a large number of industries are now realizing the importance of considering their customers' emotional responses. Security professionals have now realized that they are providing not only actual security but also the feeling or perception of security (Schneier, 2008).

Companies that make the latest video games have recognized that emotional engagement is the real reason that games become hits (Kohler, 2008). One of the results of this is that games have become more cinematic, with multiple characters, frequent scene changes, and epic story lines.

Emotional design is not some rare or sacred thing—it's all around us.

Other gaming companies are focusing on incorporating players' emotional states into gameplay by monitoring their physiology. *Journey to the Wild Divine: The Passage* is a video game that uses biofeedback to monitor emotional arousal by measuring heart rate and skin conductance (Wilddivine.com, 2011). Movement through the game is dependent on the player's ability to regulate his or her arousal levels. Some levels require players to relax themselves and others require the players to increase their energy.

With continuing advances in technology and increasing understanding of the psychology and physiology of affective states, interest in emotion is growing because it makes for good business. Emotional design is not some rare or sacred thing—it's all around us. **All design is emotional design.**

FIG. 1.5 "Kinect Star Wars"
Video games are designed with your emotions in mind.
(Used with permission of Microsoft)

Emotion Dominates Decision Making

When asked about their actions in a certain situation, many people will often claim that they carefully weighed the pros and cons before cautiously making a decision. However, this is often the opposite of how behavior actually takes shape. We tend to make decisions irrationally based on how we feel (or how we anticipate we'll feel) and then justify those decisions rationally (Damasio, 1994).

Emotions dominate decision making because they trigger and motivate behavior. The stronger or more intense (i.e., arousing or stimulating) our emotional experience is, the lower our ability to consciously evaluate the pros and cons of an offer or a situation. All of this makes us easy targets for marketers and advertisers.

A few years ago, Trevor was shopping in a department store in Sweden. While browsing in the men's section, he came across a pair of pants that he liked and decided to try them on. In the fitting room, he put on the pants, his back toward the mirror. Turning around to examine the fit, he was surprised to see the message in Fig. 1.6 greeting him.

FIG. 1.6 Using Flattery/Compliments to Influence Purchase Decisions

Even a compliment from an inanimate object is more affective than no compliment at all.
© Trevor van Gorp

The more intense the emotional experience is, the lower our ability to consciously evaluate the situation.

Compliments and flattery are persuasive devices that influence decision making. Even though Trevor was aware that the message was designed to persuade him to buy whatever he was trying on, it still produced an instant, unconscious emotional reaction. Part of that reaction can be attributed to sheer novelty, because he had never encountered something like this. However, the remainder of his reaction was due to a compliment offered, oddly enough, by an inanimate object.

Flattery has long been recognized as an effective persuasion method. The experience of being flattered is usually a pleasurable one, even when the compliments come from a few impersonal words written on a mirror. Tactics like this can often provide the touch of added influence that triggers a purchase decision.

When shoppers make purchase decisions, brain imaging has revealed that a choice is made between the *pleasure* of purchasing and owning the item and the *pain* of spending the money. Researchers found that they could accurately predict the shoppers' purchase decisions by noting which area of the brain was more active when they considered a purchase (Knutson, Rick, Wimmer, Prelec, & Loewenstein, 2006). Behaviorally, pleasure is linked with the tendency to approach, and pain is linked with the tendency to avoid. We'll be exploring this in more detail later in the book.

It's not just retailers who are using emotion to influence your buying habits. The vast majority of pharmaceutical advertising (95%) relies on some sort of emotional appeal (Frosch, Krueger, Hornik, Cronholm, & Barg, 2007). When people get ill, you might think that they'd be looking for the most up-to-date information to help diagnose their illness and choose the appropriate medication. This would likely include descriptions of symptoms, possible risk factors and probable causes. However, a review of pharmaceutical advertising (Frosch, Krueger, Hornik, Cronholm, & Barg, 2007) showed that:

- 82 percent made some factual claim
- 86 percent made rational arguments for product use
- 26 percent described condition causes and risk factors
- 25 percent described prevalence
- 95 percent made some sort of emotional appeal

Studies found that stimulants worked better when colored red, orange, or yellow.

Ninety-five percent of the advertisements used an emotional appeal. Incidentally, not one mentioned lifestyle change as an alternative to their products. The ads often framed medication use in terms of losing (58%) and regaining (85%) control over some aspect of life (Frosch et al., 2007). Even the pills themselves have been "designed," with studies linking the color of the pill to its perceived effectiveness. A survey of 12 studies found that stimulants worked better when colored red, orange, or yellow and that tranquilizers worked better when colored blue or green (de Craen, Roos, de Vries, & Kleijnen, 1996). Marketers and advertisers in a number of industries clearly understand that emotions dominate decision making. It's time that designers understand this as well.

Emotion Commands Attention and Affects Memory

As mentioned previously, the focus of attention determines which experiences enter consciousness and which ones do not. Attention is also required to make other mental events happen, such as thinking, feeling, remembering and making decisions. It is for this reason that attention has been called "psychic energy" (Csikszentmihalyi, 1990). Like energy in the traditional sense, "without it, no work can be done and through work, that energy is dissipated" (Csikszentmihalyi, 1990, p. 33).

Attention makes work possible by selecting the pieces of information that are considered relevant from the vast amount of information that is available to our senses. We then compare those pieces of information to other information patterns stored in memory. Information enters consciousness either because it is our intention to focus our attention on it or because our attention is commanded due to perceived emotional, biological, or social needs (Csikszentmihalyi, 1990).

Negative experiences tend to demand much more attention than positive experiences.

Emotion demands attention and affects memory. The intensity of emotional experience has been linked with the strength and clarity of memories before, during, and after emotional events (Reeves & Nass, 1998). This link is quite natural when you think about it, because without attention, information doesn't get into our brains in the first place. In discussing the power of stories, Peter Guber puts it succinctly: "emotion bonded with information becomes memorable, resonant and actionable" (Power of Stories, 2011).

We don't assign equal weight to negative and positive experiences. Research has shown that negative experiences tend to demand much more attention and therefore hold much more psychological weight than positive experiences, which results in stronger memories of negative experiences, along with weaker memories of what came afterwards. Emotional experiences also affect the memory of events that occur immediately before them. Individuals have impaired memory of events that occur right before negative experiences when compared to memories of events that occur right before positive experiences (Reeves & Nass, 1998).

Using negative emotion to increase the strength of a memory may seem useful. But, commanding attention in this way can have unintended consequences. Although attention is demanded by negative experiences, it may be drawn to some unintended aspect of those experiences. For example, a negative visual image may demand more attention than the textual message that was actually meant to be the focus. In software, unpleasant error messages can cause people to remember and focus on negative experiences over positive ones, potentially distorting how they think and feel about the application.

Multisensory Experiences

By creating powerful, multisensory emotional experiences, brands can demand user attention and embed strong memories of their product or service in consumers' minds. This produces changes in purchasing behavior and contributes to brand loyalty.

FIG. 1.7 Art Provides a Welcome Distraction in Seattle Children's Hospital
A large sculpture helps direct children's attention away from the environment of the hospital.
Sculpture by Martin Oliver, photo © Edie Adams

Emotional design is about directing the user's attention to the right thing, at the right time.

Many adults in North America have strong memories of being taken to McDonald's as children. McDonald's uses a multisensory approach to make potential customers familiar with their products. Colorful commercial advertising, busy store locations, the special scent and taste of the food, the ubiquitous brand identity, and the toys all combine to create positive memories for children. Through association, the children have been conditioned by these early experiences to desire McDonald's products.

Whether you're designing a product, a website, a software application, or even an environment, emotional design is often about directing the user's attention to the right thing at the right time to create an emotional response. These emotional responses help to form a bond through the creation of experiences that become stories and memories. Understanding the importance of attention (and how emotion commands it) will allow you to use design elements to shift the user's focus in the right way at the right time.

Emotion Communicates Personality, Forms Relationships, and Creates Meaning

The human brain is tuned to perceive emotions. In fact, this tuning is so ingrained that we don't even require other people to perceive them! We perceive the expression of emotion and personality in things in our environment, including products, interfaces and websites. Even though we may consciously know that computers and media aren't animate, don't have feelings and therefore couldn't be expressing emotions, we still respond socially and automatically when viewing, interacting and evaluating them. We unconsciously perceive and interpret emotional expression in things and then form relationships with them based on the personalities we've given them (Reeves & Nass 1998).

When it comes to things that aren't alive, we can think of a personality trait as the long-term expression of a particular emotion. The person who appears sad or sullen the first time you meet is expressing an emotion: sadness. When that same person expresses "sadness" the next 20 times you meet, he or she is likely to be seen as possessing a personality trait: "depressed." Because physical products usually remain the same, any perceived emotional expression will be perceived as a "personality trait" over time.

People can feel happy or sad, angry or passive, relaxed or anxious, proud or ashamed, and motivated or unmotivated through the use of products. Social interactions with things trigger emotional reactions normally reserved for social interaction with other people. Because of this effect, products should be viewed as "living objects with which people have relationships" (Jordan, 2000, p. 7). Regardless of whether you intentionally give your product a personality, people will perceive a personality. Intentionally designing specific personalities requires an understanding of visual and interactive design, as well as specific styles of content creation. It also means that designers need to understand how product/user "relationships" evolve through multiple interactions over time.

In relationships between people, personality traits are an important part of attraction and conversation. They shape our relationships by determining who we like and what we expect from those we encounter. Personality traits also influence how much we trust and get along with others. In this respect, perceived personalities in products and websites are no different.

We perceive the expression of emotion and personality in things in our environment, including products, interfaces, and websites.

FIG. 1.8 **Objects Displaying Emotion and Personality**
© Jim Leftwich

Unlike us, however, product personalities can exist in fictional worlds and be controlled by designers so that they appear at particular times and places. They can often be simpler, more consistent, and more easily identifiable than real personalities, reducing uncertainty and promoting trust (Fogg, 2003). Unfortunately, when designers fail to consider and design the personality they're communicating, the result can be the opposite. The personality appears to be inconsistent, the user feels betrayed and trust is destroyed. In the end, we tend to purchase products that seem to have personalities **similar** to our own (Govers & Schoormans, 2005).

We tend to purchase products that seem to have personalities similar to our own.

Although human personality traits are complex, design researchers have identified a number of traits that can be related to design. Psychologists have grouped product personality traits into categories that have a similar character. They've identified two major dimensions of personality that are readily assigned to products, computers and interfaces by users. We'll be exploring those in more detail later in the book.

The Creation of Meaning

The emotions we feel are created in part by the meaning(s) we give to people, brands and things, rather than the people, brands, or things themselves. Meaning is influenced by the personality that we perceive through appearance and interaction. By enabling new behaviors and actions, objects help to shape the existence of the people who use them. In other words, the things we make, buy, and use help us create our existence and form our identities.

Things that assist us in realizing goals can often be associated with the emotions that result when those goals are achieved. This association imbues these things with meaning. If attention is the energy a person requires to complete tasks and accomplish goals, it's through the investment of attention that we create meaning. By actively cultivating meaning through emotional experiences, we both shape and reflect our larger goals.

We connect how we feel in the moment to the people and things that are in the immediate vicinity.

Even though people can derive a wide range of feelings from their interactions with objects, and attribute a wide variety of meanings to those feelings, the physical characteristics of an object often suggest some meanings over others. Objects can also become personally significant because they cultivate meaning by creating associations through time and experience.

Association

New people or things can also take on meanings that are based on an individual's previous experiences and associations. Association can be a powerful way to connect the emotions and meaning aroused by one object or situation with another object or situation. We connect how we feel in the moment to the people and things that are in the immediate vicinity. In addition, when we encounter objects or experiences that are similar to objects and experiences we already have strong associations with, we sometimes experience the emotions we felt previously, albeit at a lower intensity. The natural human tendency to **associate** feelings with certain events, objects, and people contributes to the "emotional affect" that is an ongoing part of our daily experience.

In some cases, familiarity alone can be enough to create pleasurable emotions. Simple familiarity and positive or even neutral past experiences mean that an object is known and relatively safe. People, objects, and brands that are unfamiliar are unknown are potentially unpleasant. This vague feeling of discomfort is often enough of a negative response to dissuade many people from trying or approaching a new product.

Responses like this are evident when an existing product or system undergoes a major redesign. Even if the new system is a vast improvement in every way, some users will respond negatively. They may be irritated by the inconvenience of learning a new tool or simply fearful of change.

By association, the sensory impressions that lead to emotional responses are compared and linked to similar sensory impressions encountered in the past. Whether emotions are aroused by associations with past experiences or by objects in the present moment, the feelings come from the internal representation of the thing, rather than the thing itself.

As you'll learn in the remainder of the book, association is only one tool in the arsenal of persuasive methods used by designers and marketers to communicate emotion and personality. Through positive and negative associations, these professionals attempt to arouse feelings that nudge you into giving their product a certain meaning and behaving in a certain way.

FIG. 1.9 Google Celebrates the Anniversary of *Sesame Street*

Google celebrated the anniversary of *Sesame Street* and associated their brand with feelings of childhood nostalgia.

http://google.com © Google.com

CONCLUSION

In this chapter, you learned that although some products can be limited in the scope of their emotional requirements (e.g., the concept car), most require a careful balance of emotional considerations. For any consumer product, software application, or website, we need to first identify the context of use and then prioritize the different emotional considerations. These considerations should be prioritized by balancing the goals of the business with the needs of the user. When a product or service needs to function on a number of emotional levels, three categories of requirements can help us describe ideal product characteristics.

Identify the context of use and then prioritize the different emotional considerations.

Each product you design should be:

- **Useful:** Performs the task it was designed for
- **Usable:** Easy to use and interact with
- **Desirable:** Provides feelings of pleasure and creates attraction (Sanders, 1992)

Why Design for Emotion? The answer is simple. If you want your product to be successful, it must be emotional. Emotion dominates our experiences and colors our realities (Damasio, 1994). Because of this, all design is emotional design. Emotion dominates decision making, commands attention and enhances some memories while minimizing others (Reeves & Nass, 1998).

Products, websites, and software applications trigger complex social and emotional responses that are no different from the emotional responses we experience when we interact with real people (Desmet, 2002). Over time, the emotional expressions that we perceive in both people and things can come to be seen as "personality traits." Finally, we learned that the emotions we feel allow us to assign meanings to the people and things that we experience in life, ultimately influencing the relationships we form (Jordan, 2000).

In Chapter 2, we'll explore different ways to model and understand emotion. We'll take a deeper look at the different dimensions of emotion, explore the conscious and the unconscious and examine the different types of affective states.

REFERENCES

Bulik, B. S. (2010). You are what you watch, market data suggests. *Adage.* <http://adage.com/article/news/research-links-personality-traits-tv-viewing-habits/146779/> Accessed 2.13.11.

Csikszentmihalyi, M. (1990). *Flow: The psychology of optimal experience.* New York: Harper Perennial.

Damasio, Antonio, R. (1994). *Descartes' error: Emotion, reason, and the human brain.* Florida: Grosset/Putnam, Inc.

Davenport, T. H., & Beck, J. C. (2001). *The attention economy: Understanding the new currency of business.* Cambridge, MA: Harvard Business School Press.

de Craen, A. J., Roos, P. J., de Vries, L. A., & Kleijnen, J. (1996). Effect of colour of drugs: Systematic review of perceived effect of drugs and of their effectiveness. *BMJ, 313* (7072), 1624–1626.

Desmet, P. R. (2002). *Designing emotions.* Delft: Pieter Desmet.

Fogg, B. J. (2003). *Persuasive technology: Using computers to change what we think and do.* San Francisco, CA: Morgan Kaufmann Publishers.

Forlizzi, J., & Battarbee, K. (2004). Understanding experience in interactive systems. *DIS 2004.* p. 264.

Frosch, D. L., Krueger, P. M., Hornik, R. C., Cronholm, P. F., & Barg, F. K. (2007). Creating demand for prescription drugs: A content analysis of television direct-to-consumer advertising. *Annals of Family Medicine, 5*(1), 6–13.

Govers, P. C. M., & Schoormans, J. P. L. (2005). Product personality and its influence on consumer preference. *Journal of Consumer Marketing, 22*(4), 189–197.

Jordan, P. W. (2000). *Designing pleasurable products.* London: Taylor & Francis.

Knutson, B., Rick, S., Wimmer, G. E., Prelec, D., & Loewenstein, G. (2006). Neural predictors of purchases. *Neuron, 53*(1), 147–156.

Kohler, C. (2008). Interview. Ubisoft's Yannis Mallat wants emotional games. *Wired.* <http://www.wired.com/gamelife/2008/02/interview-ubiso/> Accessed 12.10.2010.

Powerofstories (2011). Storytelling Interview with Peter Guber. < http://www.powerofstories.com/storytelling-interview-with-peter-gruber > Accessed 8.13.2011.

Reeves, B., & Nass, C. (1998). *The media equation: How people treat computers, television and new media like real people and places.* Cambridge, UK. Cambridge University Press.

Russell, J. A. (1980). A circumplex model of affect. *Journal of Personality and Social Psychology, 39,* 1161–1178.

Sanders, Elizabeth B. N. (1992). Converging perspectives: Product development research for the 1990s. *Design Management Journal, 3*(4), 49–54.

Schneier, B. (2008). The psychology of security. <http://www.schneier.com/essay-155.html> Accessed 2.22.2011.

Smith, G., & van Gorp, T. (2007). *Social gamer experience map.* Client deliverable. nForm User Experience 2007.

will take the desired action. Rendering a design element like a button in color, for example, will make it demand more attention than the same design element rendered in gray.

Negative emotional responses encourage us to avoid.

The beeping noise in Trevor's friend's car was purposefully designed to be unpleasant, triggering an urge to avoid. Negative emotional response encourage a particular behavior (i.e., avoidance). As a passenger, the simplest option for avoiding the annoying sound is to just fasten your seatbelt and get on with life. Given that most of us would rather fasten our seatbelts than suffer the inconvenience of walking, the emotional response is a perfect trigger for the behavior the designer is seeking.

In this chapter, we're going to do a deep dive into the concept of emotion to gain a fuller understanding of its dimensions. A lot of the material in Chapter 2 may seem as though it's pure psychology, but the concepts we're introducing here will be used throughout the remainder of the book, so bear with us. By the end of this chapter, you should understand the basic dimensions of emotion and be able to generalize the ways in which emotion affects cognition, the body and behavior. This knowledge will help in understanding and predicting how your design decisions will affect the emotions of the people who use your products. You may also find that having a better understanding of your own emotions will affect the way you design.

FIG. 2.2 Seatbelt Buckle
Your vehicle's seatbelt reminder sound uses negative affect to get you to buckle up.
© iStockPhoto.com

UNDERSTANDING EMOTION

We tend to think we understand emotions. After all, almost everyone has experience with them. But what are emotions? How are they different from moods? What makes satisfaction different from disappointment, and how do you create the conditions that lead to one emotion rather than another? To effectively design for emotion, it's helpful to understand the different ways that emotion can be described or modeled. To help you gain this understanding, we'll introduce you to a few of the models used to tell emotions apart.

Our intent here isn't to provide an exhaustive account of all the ways that researchers have modeled emotion, but to focus on models that we've found helpful in increasing understanding and applicable in terms of generating design guidelines. Each model represents a different perspective on emotion. These perspectives include both the mental and physical components of emotion, as well as the different ways that emotions are expressed, both internally and externally.

> To design for emotion, you'll need to understand the different ways that emotion can be described.

Experiencing Emotion

"Emotion" is a term that's often used to refer to a number of different responses. What we normally refer to as **emotion** or **emotions** are really a number of different mental and physical states. Each of these affective states has different characteristics and different effects on how we invest attention, make decisions, behave, and express ourselves.

We re-present the experiences we have and the objects we encounter in terms of information we receive from our senses: visual; tactile (i.e., touch); olfactory (i.e., smell); auditory (i.e., hearing); gustatory (i.e., taste); and proprioceptive (i.e., the sense of the relative position of parts of the body in space). The brain associates (or connects) this sensory information with the feelings that are experienced as the information is encountered. Repeated over time, associations become conditioning. Together, association and conditioning influence learning and the retention of information (Gagné, 1985).

Many of us will remember being fascinated by the glowing red element on the stove as children. If you finally touched the hot element and cried out in pain, the high arousal of the experience embedded it in your memory. By associating the feelings of pain and pleasure with people, places, and events, we learn to safely make our way in the world. Emotional responses allow us to evaluate our internal and external environments and respond appropriately. They affect how we feel, how we think, what we say and what we do. The effects of emotion directly influence the way we perceive our everyday lives, affecting how we categorize information, make decisions, evaluate risks and solve problems (Isen, 1999).

> We re-present the objects we encounter and the experiences we have in terms of information from our senses.

Triggering an emotional response begins with a stimulus that is "emotionally competent" (Damasio, 2003), or carries emotional weight. This stimulus could be an external object or experience, or an internal thought or feeling. Stimuli in the external environment include people, objects and experiences. Stimuli in the internal environment include internal representations, feelings and memories. Feelings can be triggered by association to past experiences or through conscious deliberation and evaluation. For example, remembering a loved one who has passed on can bring back both positive and negative feelings connected to their memory.

Feelings can be triggered by association to past experiences or through conscious deliberation and evaluation.

With both external and internal stimuli, what generates the emotional response is the way we re-present the object or experience internally, rather than the object or experience itself. Of course, that being said, the properties of the object (also known as the "design") have a lot to do with the signals the user receives and re-presents in their minds.

Expressing Emotion

One way we can tell emotions apart is based on how they are expressed. The public, external signs of emotion manifest as facial expressions and changes in body posture, vocalization, breathing patterns and behavior. The private, internal expressions (i.e., feelings) of emotions can be seen as a type of kinesthetic feedback from the body that has effects on subsequent thinking.

Public expressions of emotion communicate our feelings to others. These expressions include changes in how we appear (i.e., our facial expressions and breathing), what we say (i.e., our conversation or interaction) and what we do (i.e., how we behave). When the same public expressions of emotion occur consistently over time, what was once seen as an emotional response may come to be seen as a personality trait.

We can tell emotions apart based on how they are expressed.

In the Netherlands, the town of Groningen has installed microphones at street level to help monitor emotional expression on the street. The microphones are part of a system that includes acoustic recognition software. The software is capable of analyzing the voices of people on the street for high-frequency vowel sounds and picking up aggressive sounding voices. Police can then be sent to the scene to break up arguments or fights, hopefully before they escalate into larger altercations (van Hengel & Andringa, 2007).

This example illustrates how particular properties of sound can be linked with particular expressions of emotional experience. In other words, the emission of sounds at a particular frequency or volume almost always indicates that the person emitting the sound is experiencing a particular emotional state—in this case, anger. Anger can often lead to violent behavior. In the same way we can connect properties of sound such as frequency and volume to certain types of emotional expression, we can also connect other aesthetic properties to certain dimensions of emotion.

The Feeling of Emotions

Emotions are different from feelings. Feelings are the physiological experience of emotional states. Damasio defines a feeling as "the perception of a certain state of the body along with the perception of a certain mode of thinking and of thoughts with certain themes" (2003, p. 86).

Particular emotions are associated with certain body states, patterns of mental processing and ways of behaving. With all emotional responses, neurological and chemical responses change the viscera, internal organs, and musculoskeletal system of the body in specific ways depending on the nature of the emotion. When your heart rate increases in moments of anxiety or stress, you feel excited or afraid. The churning of the stomach lets you feel disgusted (Norman, 2004).

From these perceptions, the mind creates mental representations or models that describe the state of the body and its parts. Using these models allows the mind to ignore certain aspects of the body when necessary for survival. For example, it may be useful for the mind to ignore the experience of pain in the body when the most urgent need is to flee from danger (Damasio, 2003).

Mental Models

We're constantly inundated with information about the world we receive from our senses. There is more written factual information in one edition of the Sunday *New York Times* than in all the written documents that were available to a reader in the 15th century. Today, more than 300,000 books are released annually worldwide (Davenport & Beck, 2001). Even without books, billions of websites, apps, games, blogs and text messages continually compete with objects in the physical world for our attention.

Emotions and feelings result from the internal representations that we make of thoughts, people, external objects and experiences. What do we mean by representations? For example, an image of a happy face is not actually a happy face, but rather a re-presentation of one. Even though we often mistake our mental images of people, events, objects and experiences for the real thing, they're really only representations. The brain shifts the meaning of these representations based on how we respond emotionally to them over time.

Our emotional responses result from the internal representations that we make of external objects and internal experiences. Externally, the object may stay the same, but internally, the emotional responses and feelings we have towards it may change. On the other hand, our preexisting feelings and emotions also influence how the internal representation takes shape. Almost all representations of objects and experiences cause emotional responses and feelings, but many of these feelings may be too weak to be perceived by the conscious mind (Damasio, 2003).

Because our mental models are really descriptions of how the various pieces and parts of a system work together, they define how we approach problems. Mental models are the unspoken rules that we've intuited from observing people, things and situations. They describe the parts of a system, the relationships between these parts, how we think things work, and the consequences of action (Johnson-Laird, 1983).

The information we take in from both our internal and external environments informs our mental models of particular situations, our immediate surroundings, and ultimately, each individual's "reality."

Our emotional responses result from the internal representations that we make of external objects and internal experiences.

Your mental model can include only the features of reality that you've been exposed to and associated with feelings.

ce n'est pas un visage
heureux on image

FIG. 2.3 This Is Not a Happy Face
Everything is a representation.
© *Trevor van Gorp*

The Map Is Not the Territory

Because no one can be exposed to everything, everyone's mental model of reality is incomplete. Even if someone could somehow be exposed to everything in life, that person's cognitive faculties couldn't process and assimilate all that information. As a matter of course, we regularly screen out or ignore information by selectively focusing our attention (Davenport & Beck, 2001). For this reason, no individual's model of reality can possibly encompass *all* of reality. Your mental model can include only the features of reality that you've been exposed to and associated with feelings. These features become memories. Because of this, all of our mental models of reality might be better described as "maps" (Korzybski, 1933).

Geographic maps represent important features in a landscape, such as roads, mountains, rivers, and forests. Like geographic maps, mental maps describe the important features of a person, object, situation, or context. In the same way that some maps describe more features of a landscape than others, some mental models describe more aspects of a situation or context than others. In the case of a mental model, the features that are judged to be important may vary from person to person, or within the same person at different times. In the same way that some maps are more accurate than others, some mental models are also more accurate than others.

A good model helps you to understand the users' requirements and how the product fulfills those requirements.

Everyone's personal "reality model" is necessarily composed of the information they've consciously or unconsciously focused attention on, absorbed, and incorporated (Korzybski, 1933). This is the information that has drawn their attention, become associated with a strong feeling, and been stored in their memory. Over time, these experiences create the narrative or *story* of people's lives. Stories are one way that people communicate the emotional meanings associated with their life experiences.

The models of emotion presented in this chapter could also be considered "maps." Just as a map shouldn't be mistaken for the territory it represents, a model shouldn't be mistaken for the thing it describes. Because all maps represent a set of important features or a particular perspective on some feature of a territory, they're necessarily limited. But this limitation is also their strong point. By limiting the description to a single set of features or a particular perspective, models make it easier to define the boundaries of a problem.

A good model for understanding how to design:

- Is easy to understand, so that other people can enter the discussion and collaborate
- Helps predict what will occur so that you can adjust your own actions accordingly
- Helps share and communicate ideas that are abstract and can't be seen or touched
- Is easy to apply in the context of the design process

When applied to design, a good model helps you to understand both the users' requirements, and how the product interacts with the user to fulfill those requirements.

THE ANATOMY AND INFLUENCE OF EMOTION

Many people don't believe that an idea with as much subjective meaning as "emotion" can be clearly understood or purposefully "designed." It's true that conscious emotional responses are relatively complex and subjective. Emotional responses based on conscious evaluations or appraisals can vary depending on the current emotional state of individual, the context and a number of other factors.

However, unconscious emotional responses are fairly consistent and often trigger relatively predictable patterns of behavior. For example, the initial emotional effects of a fire alarm are relatively consistent. The irritating high-pitched noise

Unconscious emotional responses are fairly consistent and trigger relatively predictable patterns of behavior.

FIG. 2.4 Fire Alarm
A fire alarm uses negative affect to get you to leave the area.
© iStockPhoto.com

results in an increase in heart rate and anxiety that triggers the urge to avoid. The natural behavior is to leave the area to escape the noise. In the context of a fire, this is the right behavior to encourage. With frequent false alarms, however, our conscious brains override this unconscious response, as we come to associate the alarm sound with little real danger.

Unconscious emotional responses are triggered automatically, without conscious thought.

In order to encourage behavior by triggering emotion, it's helpful to understand several of the models that have been created to describe emotion. These models can help us understand how emotions are triggered, what differentiates one emotion from another and the effects of emotions on information processing. Let's take a quick look at the concept of emotion from several different perspectives:

- Emotion is both conscious and unconscious.
- Emotion originates in different parts of the brain.
- Emotion combines the mental and the physical.
- Emotion affects attention and the processing of information in predictable ways.
- Emotion contributes to flow.
- Emotion influences motivation and behavior.
- Emotion is one type of "affective state"
  (emotions, moods, sentiments, and personality traits).

Emotion Is Both Conscious and Unconscious

When we hear the terms "conscious" and "unconscious," we tend to associate them with being awake or asleep. In this book, we'll be using these terms to refer to the conscious and unconscious (or subconscious) minds and how each processes information and responds emotionally.

The conscious mind is, well, conscious. In other words, we can "hear" it (in the form of thoughts) and participate in its decision-making process. Conscious emotional responses are triggered by our conscious evaluations and appraisals (i.e., the questions we ask ourselves about what we encounter in the world). For example, evaluating and comparing the features of three models of MP3 player is a conscious process.

Unconscious emotional responses can be much easier to design for, as they are relatively consistent.

Unconscious emotional responses are triggered automatically without conscious thought. In other words, we don't usually "hear" the thoughts associated with unconscious processes, possibly because they're occurring too quickly for our minds to verbalize. Unconscious emotional responses range from simple increases in physical stimulation (e.g., increased heart rate) when viewing deeply saturated colors (Fehrman & Fehrman, 2000) to more complex, multilayered, but yet still unconscious judgments (e.g., is that person attractive?). The first is an unconscious physiological reaction to a stimulus and the second is a decision made based on the unconscious processing of a number of stimuli.

When it comes to designing for emotion, unconscious responses are often much easier to design for, as they are relatively consistent, even in the face of mixed conscious emotions. Some simple unconscious responses are automatic and are part of our genetic heritage. For example, barring advanced training in controlling unconscious processes, a saturated red will almost always raise a person's level of physical stimulation or arousal. Deep red is likely stimulating due to its evolutionary associations with blood (Fehrman & Fehrman, 2000). This association means that red draws attention, even in crowded physical and digital environments. That's one of the reasons we chose it as a color for the cover of this book.

Another example of an unconscious reaction is an emotional response to the smell of someone experiencing fear. Research has shown that although people couldn't

FIG. 2.5 Design for Emotion Cover

The book's cover uses color and contrast to unconsciously increase physiological stimulation and grab your attention.
© *Morgan Kaufmann*

detect a difference in the odor, their brains were much more activated when smelling the sweat of someone who had been afraid than the sweat of someone who was calm (Zhou & Chen, 2009).

Other, more conscious acts can also become unconscious responses when learned over time. Driving, for example, begins as a highly conscious act. New drivers are usually very nervous and somewhat awkward behind the wheel. Over time however, driving becomes an unconscious act for most. The experienced driver no longer needs to consider every action, with most common actions moving to the realm of the unconscious. However, when stress rises and demands on attention grow to a level that's impossible to maintain, even tasks that are normally simple and unconscious may become difficult and require conscious thought (Norman, 2004).

Recently, Edie was training a student to race high-performance cars at the track. On an average day, she would describe what she was doing to the student in the passenger seat as she'd drive around the track. But, on this particular day, it was pouring rain. Edie was surprised to find the driving conditions so challenging that she was unable to continue instructing the student verbally. "Normally, I can drive without thinking about it. It was as if my brain could no longer process everything that was going on. I couldn't seem to divide my attention between driving and thinking of what to say next. I had to stop talking and focus on the track."

Emotions Originate in Different Parts of the Brain

Emotional processing occurs in all three brains.

Emotions and other affective states are believed to originate in a number of different parts of the brain. If we examine the traces of evolution left in the physiology of the brain, we can relate them to the conscious and unconscious. McLean (1990) observed that brain structures similar to those seen deep within the human brain were also observed in lower mammals, reptiles, and other vertebrates. The human brain has been described in terms of three brain systems. Scientists have theorized that emotional processing occurs in all three of these "brains" (Norman, 2004). Based on evolutionary biology, the Triune Brain theory (McLean, 1990) describes the function of these three brain systems:

- Reptilian brain
- Mammalian brain
- Neomammalian brain
  (McLean, 1990)

Reptilian Brain

Our most primitive, unconscious emotional responses originate from what some have called the **reptilian brain** (or **old brain**), a brain structure that we share with reptiles and a few other vertebrates (McLean, 1990). The processing that occurs in the reptilian brain is nearly instantaneous and unconscious. This brain is responsible for basic survival and mating instincts, which are required by humans as well as other animals. These primitive instincts govern behavior around basic instincts such as fight, flight, food, and reproduction. The reptilian brain also keeps

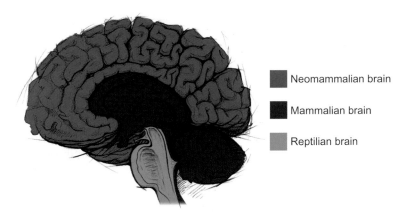

Neomammalian brain

Mammalian brain

Reptilian brain

FIG. 2.6 Triune Brain

The triune brain is made up of the reptilian, mammalian, and neomammalian brains.
Adapted from (McLean, 1990). © alenah - Fotolia.com

all the body's automatic systems (such as breathing and digestion) going even when we are asleep or unconscious (Weinshenk, 2009).

Emotional reactions based on these survival instincts are elicited automatically and unconsciously (in other words, without thinking about them). This explains why physical attraction can be unconscious. You don't usually have to think about whether something is physically beautiful—it just is (or isn't)!

Mammalian Brain

Although emotions have been said to originate in all three brains (Norman, 2004) the **mammalian brain** (or **mid brain**) is often referred to as the "emotional brain." This is the brain structure that we share with other mammals (and some vertebrates). The mammalian brain is involved in our responses to social interaction and generates our emotional responses to things like status, pair bonding and acceptance or rejection by the group (Graziano-Breuning, 2011).

Mammalian social instincts govern our behavior in groups (i.e., packs). These instincts allow us to make subtle judgments about power, status and social hierarchy. These judgments are useful when living in groups with other animals who may be larger or more powerful (Graziano-Breuning, 2011). At this level, feelings of attraction initiated in the reptilian brain can be muted or amplified through further interaction.

Social interactions between humans have been described as exchanges of *power* and *status* (Kemper, 1978) between the members of a group or pack. These interactions are influenced by judgments of power, as well as material, cultural and social status. Although the behavior of packs varies between species and even between packs, most mammals that congregate socially have some form of social ranking system.

The reptilian brain is responsible for basic survival and mating instincts such as fight flight, food and reproduction.

Existing models of social hierarchy derived from evolutionary psychology are based at least in part on measures of relative power and status. Because our lower brain structures are very similar to those of other mammals (McLean, 1990), it's logical to assume that we have been wired to respond in similar ways.

The mammalian brain is involved in our emotional responses to social interaction.

In animal packs, the "alpha" is the animal of either sex with the highest rank among its peers. Generally, the highest status animals are those who are able to physically dominate their group. They are larger, stronger and faster than the others and are usually in early- to mid-adulthood. These traits allow the alpha to best any challengers in a physical confrontation for food, territory or access to mates. Chimpanzee groups show deference to the alpha animal by standing aside and allowing him or her to walk first. The alphas literally *lead* the way for the others. In a gesture that mirrors human social conventions, chimpanzees have also been observed bowing before the alpha. As the "leader" of the group, the alpha also tends to eat first and may take the first choice of mating partners (Darwin, 1877; de Waal, 2007; Mech, 1999).

In human society, the last 40–50 years have seen a reexamination of gender and sexuality that has redefined traditional gender roles. One group that appears to have retained a more traditional, if not exaggerated, approach to gender roles are biker clubs. Like animal groups in the wild, bikers judge power and status by displays of dominance.

People who become bikers tend to be bigger, louder, and stronger (i.e., more physically dominant) than average individuals. After they become part of an official gang, they may also be stronger smelling. This is intentional, as the part of the ceremony for induction into some biker gangs involves the inductee lying on the floor while gang members urinate and defecate on the inductee's patch or colors (Barker, 2007). Scent is a primitive and unconscious marker, and strong scents are difficult to avoid. Some mammals (e.g., primates) use urine and feces to scent mark territory (Johnson, 1973), which suggests some interesting parallels as new members become part of "the territory" of the biker club.

Conscious judgments originate in the neomammalian brain, where we can "hear" our thoughts and participate in decision making.

When your computer crashes, seemingly refusing to perform your requests, you may tell yourself that the source of your frustration is the inability to perform a task that needs to get done. Your conscious mind knows that the computer has no malicious intent. It's not purposefully defying you. Yet you still feel frustrated. Consider that your frustration may be unconsciously fueled by the machines refusal to acknowledge your higher power and status within the "pack."

Neomammalian Brain

Through experience, we learn to pause and evaluate the potential consequences of our actions with our conscious brain structures before responding automatically to situations. In this way, experience and socialization can help us judge whether an emotional response or behavior is appropriate for the situation. These types of conscious judgments originate in the **neomammalian brain** (the **neo cortex** or **new brain**). In the conscious, neomammalian brain, we can "hear" our own thoughts and actively, consciously participate in decision making.

The three brains are closely integrated, with the body providing feedback for emotions through feelings. Together, the three brains and the body operate in a continuous feedback loop. The neomammalian brain can act as a regulator (or an enabler) of urges from the more primitive brains. Meanwhile, the body provides feedback on conscious and unconscious thoughts in the form of feelings. The quality of those feelings then affects subsequent thoughts, emotions and behaviors.

Although we would all like to believe that we consistently make conscious, rational decisions, it turns out that in almost all instances, we consciously rationalize our feelings so that our decisions are congruent with the emotions originating in the reptilian and mammalian brains (Cafferata & Tybout, 1989).

The interaction of these three brains may play a part in the "mixed emotions" we sometimes feel. Our reptilian and mammalian brains may be sending us in one direction, while our neomammalian brain, better able to see the full consequences of taking that path, may tell us it's not the best option. Most of us have experienced the unconscious urge to fight when we feel threatened (reptilian brain), or insult someone when we feel slighted (mammalian brain). Fortunately, most of the time, we're able to hold back from retaliating due to the intervention of our conscious, neomammalian brain.

When we examine the nature of the emotional responses that originate in each of the three brains, we can see several differences between emotions that originate in the unconscious, animal brains and those that originate in the conscious, human brain.

The emotions elicited by *conscious* interaction with products are by their nature:

- Varied, broad and not clearly defined
- Highly subjective
- Changing over time
- Mixed

And the emotional reactions elicited *unconsciously* by interaction with products could be characterized as:

- More clearly defined
- More objective
- Remain consistent over time
- Less mixed
  (Desmet, Ortiz Nicolas & Schoormans, 2008)

> We consciously rationalize our feelings so that decisions are congruent with the emotions from our reptilian and mammalian brains.

Emotion Combines the Mental and the Physical

Pain and pleasure may appear to be the basic dichotomy of emotion and experience. But they're really just one dimension of emotion. The emotions we experience can be described as a combination of two different dimensions. One dimension is comprised of our mental judgments about the **value** of things, which is influenced by our experience of pain and pleasure. The other is our level of physiological stimulation or **arousal** (Russell, 1980).

Everything we experience is either good, bad, or somewhere in between.

When we think about emotions in this way, it can be difficult to envision how these two simple dimensions describe the vast range of human emotions. Luckily, because the facial expressions of specific emotions are consistent all over the world (Ekman, 2003), we can map emotions to the way that they're expressed facially. This also helps us get a better understanding of how the different dimensions map to actual human emotional experiences.

Value

Everything we experience is either good, bad, or somewhere in between. The automatic unconscious brains tend to decide that pleasant things are good and unpleasant or painful things are bad. Consciously, however, we may realize that some painful or uncomfortable things, like exercising regularly, are good for us in the long term. Most of the time, however, we consciously rationalize the urges of our unconscious brains and stay on the couch. These conscious and unconscious judgments of good and bad, based on pain and pleasure, are called **valence** or **value**.

Value Judgments

Value judgments can be conscious or unconscious. Conscious judgments are triggered by **appraisals**. Appraisal theory describes how we make evaluations. There are two kinds of appraisals: primary and secondary. Primary appraisals focus on whether an object, event, or experience helps to achieve an individual's goals (i.e., value).

Value

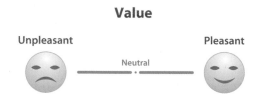

FIG. 2.7 Value (Unpleasant versus Pleasant)

Adapted from (Russell, 1980). © Trevor van Gorp

Secondary appraisals focus on whether an individual has the necessary internal and external resources to address the event, object, or experience (i.e., arousal) (Manstead & Fischer, 2001). This is the secondary dimension of emotion. We make appraisals when we judge a design against a concern we have. The result is an emotional response (Desmet, 2002).

Imagine that your dishwashing machine has just flooded your kitchen. You're not sure what caused the problem, but it could be the fault of the machine, or it could be a problem with the way you loaded it. You evaluate the situation to determine blame. Your initial, unconscious evaluation of the situation finds

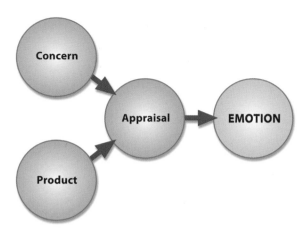

FIG. 2.8 Appraisal Process

Adapted from (Desmet, 2002). © Trevor van Gorp

that the manufacturer must be to blame. Deciding that someone else is at fault, you experience feelings of *relief* and then *anger*. You think to yourself, "Damn dishwashing machine company."

Before calling the manufacturer in a huff, you decide to consciously evaluate the cause of the problem in order to be certain of who is at fault. Upon investigation, you discover that a single utensil (that you previously dropped while rushing to load the dishwasher) fell behind in between the door and the wall of the machine, breaking the seal. Finding yourself responsible, you might experience *guilt*, *sadness*, or *regret*. Although appraisals of the same object or situation may elicit different emotional responses at different times, a similar pattern of evaluation is found in situations that evoke the same emotion (Roseman & Smith, 2001). For example, losing something that was valued results in sadness (Roseman & Smith, 2001).

> **When you find yourself responsible for a mistake, you might experience guilt, sadness, or regret.**

When it comes to applying emotional appraisals in design, it's important to identify the user's primary concern for the situation and then design to satisfy that concern by improving users' emotional responses. If the user's main concern around using a floor mop is that it starts to smell foul after being used several times, alleviating that concern has a number of design implications. While ensuring that the mop adequately clean floors, a designer might also be sure to choose a material that remains hygienic, or in the case of newer floor sweepers, use a disposable cleaning pad that can be thrown away after each use. In this example, designing for emotion involves preventing negative emotional reactions as well as ensuring positive ones.

FIG. 2.9 Floor Sweeper

Newer floor sweepers help prevent the unpleasant odors associated with dirty mops and brooms by using disposable cleaning pads.

© *Trevor van Gorp*

Arousal

Higher levels of arousal focus attention, but too much arousal can lead to tunnel vision.

Our experience of reality is always affected by the state of our bodies. We've all had a bad day when everything seemed to go wrong. The alarm clock was set for PM instead of AM, so you were late getting up for work. There was no milk in the fridge, so you had to skip your breakfast cereal. The car wouldn't start, so you had to take the bus, delaying you even further. By the time you arrived at work, late, angry, frustrated, and wound up into a tight little ball, even the mildest bit of bad news might set you off. On another day, you might respond quite differently. But when you're already highly stimulated in a negative way, that additional piece of bad news might be the straw that breaks the camel's back.

This level of stimulation (also called "arousal" or "stress") is the physiological (i.e., bodily) dimension of emotion. Remember, emotions and feelings influence each other in a circular way. Without proper exercise, rest and relaxation, stress can be cumulative. Our preexisting physical state largely determines how intensely we experience feelings of pleasure or pain (van Gorp, 2006). High levels of physical

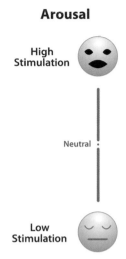

FIG. 2.10 Arousal (Low Stimulation to High Stimulation)

Arousal and stimulation.

and mental stimulation amplify the value of an experience, whether it's good or bad. Low levels of stimulation decrease the intensity.

Arousal is closely related to other concepts such as anxiety, attention, agitation, and motivation. Your arousal level can be thought of as the capacity or load that you can successfully take on. Too little arousal can make someone bored or unmotivated, their attention unfocused. Higher levels of arousal have a focusing affect on attention, but too much arousal can lead to tunnel vision.

Higher levels of arousal narrow focus, increase motivation and make people more intent on reaching their goals.

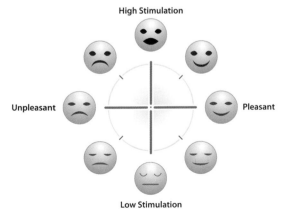

FIG. 2.11 Affective States: Value/Arousal

Adapted from (Russell, 1980). © Trevor van Gorp

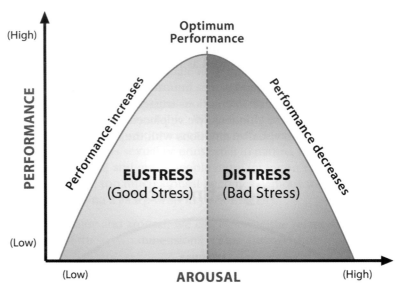

FIG. 2.14 **Yerkes-Dodson Law**

(Yerkes and Dodson, 1908) additions from (van Gorp, 2010). © Trevor van Gorp

Some stress or stimulation is good for performance, but too much damages performance.

Attention can be invested voluntarily or held captive by high levels of emotional stimulation.

Eustress and Distress

In psychology, the Yerkes-Dodson Law (1908) describes how arousal or stress levels affect performance. Most of us are used to thinking of "stress" as a purely negative thing. However, if we define **stress** as physical stimulation, with both high and low levels, we get a more accurate picture. As stress or stimulation rises, so does performance. This positive form of stress is called **eustress**, and it continues up to an optimum point. After this point, as arousal continues to rise, we enter what's commonly called "distress," and performance declines.

From the Yerkes-Dodson Law (1908), we can see that some stress or stimulation is good for performance, but too much damages performance. The amount of stress needed to trigger optimum performance will also differ from person to person and from day to day. Different applications and use contexts will also require different optimal levels of arousal. Entertainment-oriented media should be more highly arousing (i.e., more stimulating) than task-oriented media, for example. People tend to naturally bring a higher level of stimulation to the challenge of task-oriented activities (Novak & Hoffman, 1997).

A good example of this balancing principle is the sound created by the fire alarm. The fire alarm must be loud and irritating enough to raise physiological arousal and motivate you to leave the area, but not so arousing as to push people into feeling

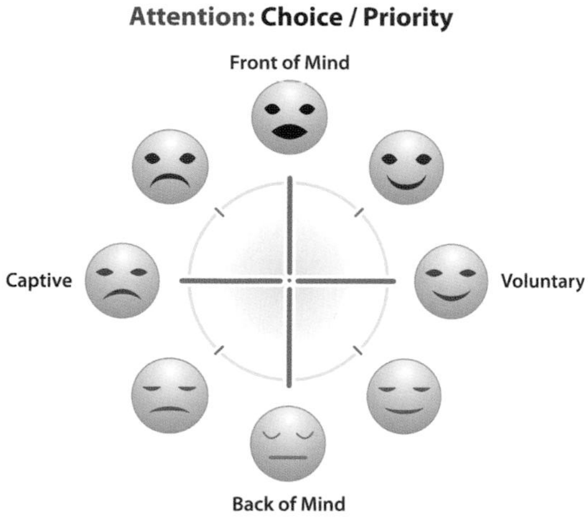

Attention: Choice / Priority

Front of Mind

Captive

Voluntary

Back of Mind

FIG. 2.15 **Attention: Choice/Priority**

Adapted from (Davenport and Beck, 2001). © Trevor van Gorp

overwhelmed. Ideally, arousal is high enough to motivate a quick escape from a hazardous situation.

Emotion, Attention and Information

Attention selects the information that will actually get into our brains and become part of our mental models of reality. In a world where attention is in constant demand, emotional affect changes where and how intensely we focus that attention. Attention selects relevant information by focusing on it and ignores or deletes information that's considered emotionally irrelevant. Emotion is the energy that drives and directs attention. Sometimes, attention is voluntarily invested; other times, attention is held captive by high levels of emotional stimulation. Anything that creates high arousal will be elevated to the top or front of the mind; things that create little or no arousal will naturally fall to the back of the mind.

Emotional Affect

Emotions and other "affective states" like moods influence every aspect of our interaction with brands, products, and websites. As Forlizzi and Battarbee (2004, p. 264) put it, "emotions affect how we plan to interact with products, how we actually interact with products, and the perceptions and outcomes that surround those interactions." This includes our intentions, our plans and any feedback on whether we've achieved success. As we mentioned in Chapter 1, the term used for the way that emotions affect cognition is **emotional affect** (Norman, 2004).

The term used for the way that emotions affect cognition is emotional affect.

"Emotional affect" is the term for emotional reactions that have a high probability of producing changes in awareness, facial expression, body language, physiologyical function and behavior. Affect can be differentiated from cognition because it tends to influence motivation and arouse feelings, whereas cognition is more concerned with facts (Cacioppo & Petty, 1989).

Donald Norman states that emotional affect is:

> the general term for the judgmental system, whether conscious or unconscious. Emotion is the conscious experience of affect complete with attribution of its cause and identification of its object. A queasy, uneasy feeling you might experience, without knowing why, is affect.

(Norman, 2004, p. 11)

Positive affect serves as a signal to continue with one's current behaviors.

Because the lens of emotional affect directly influences much of the way we perceive our everyday lives (affecting how we categorize information, make decisions, evaluate risks, and solve problems) (Isen, 1999), the term "emotional affect" is used extensively throughout this book. The way that emotional affect influences information processing and task performance depends on whether the conditions are perceived as positive (e.g., pleasurable, supportive, caring) or negative (e.g., painful, threatening, punishing) (Hayes-Roth, Ball, Lisetti, Picard, & Stern, 1997).

Affect	POSITIVE	NEGATIVE
Value	Pleasant	Unpleasant
Visual	Smiling faces	Frowning disgusted faces
	Comfortably lit places	Extreme bright or dark
	Objects at safe distance	Looming Objects
	Bright, saturated colors	Faded, dingy colors
	---	Heights
Touch	Rounded objects	Sharp objects
	Warm, temperate climate	Extreme climates
Hearing	Soothing sounds	Harsh sounds
	Repetitive sounds	Abrupt sounds
	Harmonious sounds	Discordant sounds
Smell	Sweet smells	Sour smells
	Fresh smells	Rotting smells
Taste	Sweet tastes	Bitter tastes

FIG. 2.16 **Positive and Negative Affect**

Adapted from (Norman, 2004). © Trevor van Gorp

WHERE ARE YOU GOING?

Where are you going?

FIG. 2.17 **Affect and Personality**

© *Trevor van Gorp*

The Effects of Affect

Positive emotional affect serves as a signal to continue with one's current behaviors; negative emotional affect serves as a signal to adjust thought processes or change physical behavior. Emotional affect influences ongoing evaluations of information and experience. This influence is much more apparent when the information that is appraised is ambiguous in nature (as discussed shortly). The influence of affect on information that already has a strong positive or negative orientation is much smaller (Isen, 1999).

Emotional affect influences us in both individual and social situations. It can alter thought processes, changing how events are perceived and interpreted. It can change how people interact with one another and it can also change how people interact with objects. All of this makes emotional affect an important consideration for interactive products, especially those that are used in stressful emergency situations, where communicating clearly and effectively can be crucial.

In evolutionary terms, positive affect is linked with the tendency to approach and negative affect is linked with the tendency to avoid (Cacioppo, Larsen, Smith, & Berntson, 2004). Emotional affect guides cognition in the same direction as the affect (Cafferata & Tybout, 1989). This is one reason it's so easy to rationalize our decisions. The influence of emotional affect causes us to rationalize our emotional instincts with our conscious human brains.

Negative affect is a signal to adjust thought processes or change physical behavior.

Emotion Contributes to Flow

Most of us have experienced a mental/emotional state where all of our attention is totally focused on an activity. Csikszentmihalyi (1990) named this state "flow" based on how participants in his studies described the experience. In this state of consciousness, people can concentrate intensely and experience feelings of enjoyment, coupled with peak performance. Hours can pass by in what seems like minutes. We tend to enter these states in environments with few interruptions, where our attention becomes focused by a *challenge* that we're confident we can handle with our existing *skills*. Feedback is instantaneous, so we can always get information about the success of our efforts (Csikszentmihalyi, 1990).

Flow occurs at the boundary between boredom and anxiety. You could also imagine it as the optimum point that lies between eustress and distress. When it comes to balancing the users' perception of challenge, think of it this way:

- Too much challenge with too little skill causes anxiety.
- Too little challenge with too much skill causes boredom.

Flow occurs at the boundary between boredom and anxiety.

As the challenges we face increase, we become more anxious and lose flow. Reentering flow involves increasing our skills to match these challenges and reduce anxiety. As we increase our skill level, we become bored unless we increase the challenge to match our greater abilities.

Flow tends to occur in situations with higher levels of challenge and skill. If the challenge is too easy, or user skill levels are very high, arousal can be so low that there is little motivation to do anything. Again, because this is the physiological (i.e., bodily) dimension of emotion, the level of arousal affects how intense any given experience is, and intense emotions demand our attention. In evolutionary terms, it's easy to see why. The more attention your ancestors paid to predators, the more likely they were to survive and reproduce, passing their genes on to their descendants, people like you and me.

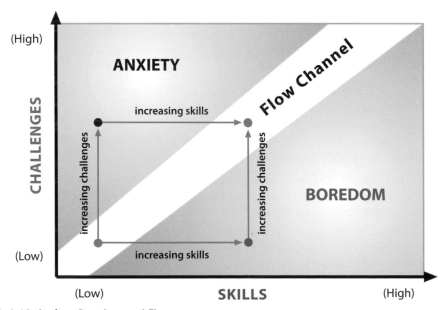

FIG. 2.18 Anxiety, Boredom, and Flow

(Csikszentmihalyi, 1990); captions (van Gorp, 2006). © Trevor van Gorp

FIG. 2.19 Interpersonal Distance and Arousal
How does looking at the picture on the right make you feel compared to the one on the left?
Photo by Curtis Lipscombe

Arousal and Flow

Both pleasant and unpleasant objects and experiences can increase or decrease arousal levels. Frustration and excitement, for example, are both high-arousal emotions. The elements that make up your design can also influence arousal levels as well as value. Large images, bright colors and high contrast all increase arousal and demand attention. Increasing the size of an image and moving anyone within the frame closer will also increase arousal levels (Reeves & Nass, 1998).

> **Both frustration and excitement are high-arousal emotions.**

The key to balancing arousal is to match the perceived challenge to the skill level of the user. Because skill levels differ from one user to the next, interfaces should be very user-friendly for novices, but also allow more advanced users to find challenges appropriate for their skill level. These challenges can include the aesthetic aspects as well as the formatting of the content. To put it simply, everything about a site—including content, information architecture, interaction design and visual design—can and should contribute to flow.

Emotion, Motivation and Intention

The close relationship between emotional affect and behavior means that the body is almost always prepared to respond to a variety of events. Each dimension of emotion affects a different aspect of behavior. Value affects whether we **approach** (i.e., pleasure) or **avoid** (i.e., pain). Arousal affects how motivated we are to either approach or avoid. Low arousal results in low motivation; higher arousal results in higher motivation. Both pleasant and unpleasant experiences can raise or lower arousal levels. For example, fear and excitement are both high-arousal emotions.

> **Value affects whether we approach or avoid. Arousal affects how motivated we are to do either.**

Designers can change the amount of motivation people have by altering the level of physiological arousal. Arousal levels can influence cognition because it's

The level of arousal affects how intensely we experience a given emotion.

easier for people to remember things that occurred when they were in a similar emotional state (Cafferata & Tybout, 1989). The level of arousal affects how intensely we experience a given emotion. The more intense the emotion, the more attention is demanded. This continues to an optimum level (i.e., the balance of flow), after which motivation, attention and performance decrease while arousal increases to distress and anxiety.

Dimensions of Behavior

The lower the amount of motivation and prior knowledge a user has about a product or service, the more that user will rely on unconscious emotional responses to make choices. When prior knowledge and the motivation to consider a choice is high (e.g., making a large investment), people are more likely to rely on their cognitive evaluations and minimize the influence of unconscious emotional responses (Cafferata & Tybout, 1989). In other words, both the difficulty and importance of the task (i.e., challenge) along with our level of knowledge and ability (i.e., skill) influence arousal levels, our level of motivation and perceptions of how difficult the task will be.

With the beeping sound in Trevor's friend's car, the value of the noise was negative (i.e., unpleasant). This unpleasant feeling created the urge to avoid. If the volume of the noise had increased, or the rate of the beeping had sped up, this would have unconsciously increased arousal levels, further increasing his motivation to avoid the noise.

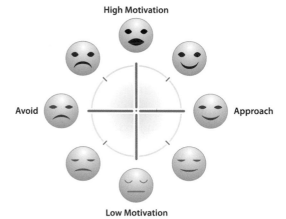

FIG. 2.20 Behavior: Intention/Motivation

The dimensions of behavior.

© Trevor van Gorp

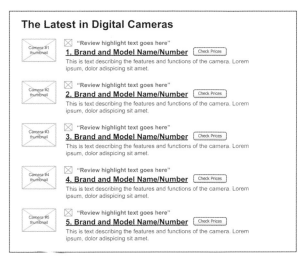
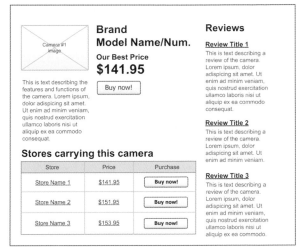

FIG. 2.21 Approaching Online

The design mimics the effect of approaching, as the image appears to grows in size.
© Trevor van Gorp

Shopping online mirrors this real-world approach/avoid experience. For example, when shopping online for a digital camera, we're generally presented with thumbnail images of the available model. If the look, brand, or features of the camera attract us, we decide to "approach" for further investigation and interaction by clicking or selecting the thumbnail image. As we "approach," the size of the camera increases in our view as though we're getting closer to it in space.

> The term "emotion" is used to refer to a number of different experiences.

Emotions, Moods, Sentiments and Personality Traits

To utilize emotion in design, it's important to have an understanding of what actually constitutes an "emotion." As we all know, there are different types of experiences. Some experiences are more emotional than others, and some emotional experiences last longer than others. The term "emotion" is often used to refer to a number of experiences that are actually quite different and specific in nature.

Desmet (2002) differentiates four types of "affective states." This term includes emotions, moods, sentiments and emotional personality traits. As we mentioned earlier, *feelings* are part of the conscious experience of the physiological changes brought on by affective states.

At any given moment, we're always experiencing and/or expressing an emotion, mood, sentiment, or emotional trait. This is emotional affect, in which the current emotional state is always influencing both future cognition and action, while future cognition and action then create further affective states. In addition, emotional states can also be triggered by changes and movement in the body, and by chemical changes caused by the ingestion of food and drugs.

AFFECTIVE STATES	Intentional	Non-Intentional
Acute	Emotions	Moods
Dispositional	Sentiments	Emotional Traits

FIG. 2.22 Affective States

Adapted from (Desmet, 2002, p. 4). © Trevor van Gorp

We can separate affective states in terms of time and intention. We have emotional responses that are intentionally directed towards certain things, but we also have responses that are not intentionally directed towards anything in particular. Our day-to-day lives are the product of minute changes in our affective states throughout the day, with **emotions** changing from moment to moment, **moods** describing the pattern of emotional response over the short term, and **sentiments** emerging as persistent likes and dislikes.

These affective states combine over the long term to create what others perceive as emotional or **personality traits**. All of these affective states can lead to behavior and influence further affective states. In fact, our emotions themselves are likely the number one thing we get emotional about (Desmet, 2002).

Emotions

Emotions themselves are likely the number one thing we get emotional about.

Emotions are relatively short term in duration (i.e., acute), lasting only a short time, ranging from seconds to minutes. They are directed at some thing (Desmet, 2002). They can be triggered by sights, smells, sounds and events in the external environment, or by thoughts and the internal representations of past or future events and experiences.

Moods

Moods are affective states that last longer than emotions, usually for hours or days, but are still considered acute because they last for a limited amount of time. Moods generally have combined causes rather than being elicited by a particular event, so they're considered non-intentional, or not directed at anything in particular. In other words, they're directed at the world rather than towards a particular object or person (Frijda, 1994).

Sentiments

Sentiments are intentionally directed at something and they involve a person-object relationship. They constitute our likes and dislikes as well as our attitudes and standards. So, although you might be afraid of dogs, actually being frightened by a dog is a different emotional state (Frijda, 1994). People also display sentiments towards products and brands. "I love Macs" is an example of a sentiment.

Personality Traits

Emotional traits are personality characteristics that manifest over the long term. In terms of intent, they're like moods, but they persist for a long enough time that people can be characterized by their expression. Thus, emotional traits are often called "character" or personality traits and are generally directed at the world. When an emotional state becomes part of our disposition, we consistently express that state over time (Desmet, 2002). This is the case with both sentiments and personality traits.

Our tendency to perceive emotions as personality traits over time is easier to see in static or physical products than it is in interactive products, because physical products usually don't change forms over time. This means that their "personality" is embodied by the emotions they were designed to express for their useful lives. The important thing is that the personality is appropriate for the task the object was created to perform or the problem the object was created to help solve.

FIG. 2.23 Mike's Corkscrew

Is there anything I can open for you?

© *Trevor van Gorp*

CONCLUSION

In Chapter 2, we first learned that we're all acting on mental models of reality, rather than reality itself. Then, we explored a number of different ways of modeling emotion to enhance our understanding of how design decisions affect users' emotional responses.

What is emotion? We learned that emotion helps us to make our way safely through the world. Emotion is both conscious and unconscious, and it's simpler to design for unconscious emotional responses than for conscious ones. We saw that emotion originates in different parts of the brain, from the most primitive and unconscious, to the most conscious and human.

Positive affect enhances open, creative thought, and negative affect enhances narrow, focused thought.

We learned that emotion can be described as a combination of our levels of physical stimulation (i.e., arousal or stress) and our mental judgments (i.e., appraisals). We also learned that our arousal or stimulation levels determine how intensely we feel an emotion. Then we examined how emotions affect attention and the processing of information. Positive affect expands attention and enhances open, creative thought, while negative affect narrows attention and enhances focused thought.

Next, we learned that balancing arousal levels by matching the perceived challenge to users' skill levels can create a state of both optimum performance and optimum experience called "flow." And finally, we learned to classify the different emotional states according to their intent and duration into emotions, moods, sentiments and personality traits.

In Chapter 3, we'll continue to build on the concepts you've already learned to explore how emotion can be used to direct attention to the task at hand, enhancing performance and creating flow. We'll also examine how certain properties of aesthetics and interaction are associated with different emotions and personality types.

REFERENCES

Ariely, D. (2008). *Predictably irrational*. New York: Harper Collins.

Barker, T. (2007). *Biker gangs and organized crime*. Cincinnati: Anderson.

Cacioppo, J. T., Larsen, J. T., Smith, N. K., & Berntson, G. G. (2004). The affect system: What lurks below the surface of feelings? In A. S. R. Manstead, N. H. Frijda, & A. H. Fischer (Eds.), *Feelings and emotions: The Amsterdam conference* (pp. 221–240). New York: Cambridge University Press.

Cacioppo, J. T., & Petty, R. E. (1989). The elaboration likelihood model: The role of affect and affect-laden information processing in persuasion. In A. Tybout & P. Cafferata (Eds.), *Cognitive and affective responses to advertising* (pp. 69–89). Lexington, MA: Lexington Books.

Cafferata, P., & Tybout, A. (Eds.). (1989). *Cognitive and affective responses to advertising*. Lexington, MA: Lexington Books.

Csikszentmihalyi, M. (1990). Flow: The psychology of optimal experience. New York: Harper Perennial.

Damasio, A. R. (2003). *Looking for Spinoza: Joy, sorrow and the feeling brain*. Orlando: Harcourt, Inc.

Darwin, C. (1859). *The expressions of the emotions in man and animals*. London: John Murray.

Davenport, T. H., & Beck, J. C. (2001). *The attention economy: Understanding the new currency of business*. Cambridge, MA: Harvard Business School Press.

de Waal, F. (2007) (1982). *Chimpanzee politics: Power and sex among apes* (25th Anniversary ed.). Baltimore: JHU Press.

Desmet, P. R. (2002). *Designing emotions*. Delft: Pieter Desmet.

Desmet, P. M. A., Ortiz Nicolas, J. C., & Schoormans, J. P. L. (2008). Personality in physical human/product interaction. *Design Studies, 29*(5), 458–477.

Ekman, P. (2003). *Emotions revealed: Recognizing faces and feelings to improve communication and emotional life*. New York: Henry Holt and Co.

Fehrman, K. R., & Fehrman, C. (2000). *Color: The secret influence*. Upper Saddle River, NJ: Prentice Hall.

Forlizzi, J., & Battarbee, K. (2004). Understanding experience in interactive systems. In *DIS 2004*. Human-Computer Interaction Institute. Paper 46. <http://repository.cmu.edu/hcii/46> Accessed on March 17, 2011.

Frijda, N. H. (1994). Varieties of affect: Emotions and episodes, moods and sentiments. In P. Ekam and R. J. Davidson (Eds.). *The nature of emotion, fundamental questions* (pp. 59–67). Oxford: Oxford University Press.

Gagné, R. M. (1985). *The conditions of learning* (4th ed.). New York: Holt, Rinehart, and Winston.

Graziano-Breuning, L. (2011). *I, mammal: Why your brain links status and happiness*. San Francisco: System Integrity Press.

Hayes-Roth, B., Ball, G., Lisetti, C., Picard, R. W., & Stern, A. (1997). "Panel on affect and emotion in the user interface." In *Proceedings of the 3rd International Conference on Intelligent User Interfaces* (pp. 91–94). San Francisco. <http://portal.acm.org/ ft_gateway.cfm> Accessed July 14, 2005.

Isen, A. (1999). "Positive affect." In Tim Dalgleish & Mick Power (Eds.), *Handbook of Cognition and Emotion.* West Sussex, UK: John Wiley & Sons Ltd.

Johnson-Laird, P. N. (1983). *Mental models: Towards a cognitive science of language, inference, and consciousness.* Cambridge: Cambridge University Press.

Kemper, T. D. (1978). *A social interactional theory of emotions.* West Sussex, UK: John Wiley & Sons Ltd.

Korzybski, A. (1933). "Science and Sanity—A Non-Aristotelian System and its Necessity for Rigour in Mathematics and Physics (pp. 747–761)." Englewood, NJ: Institute of General Semantics.

Manstead, A. S. R., & Fischer, A. H. (2001). "Social appraisal: The social world as object of and influence on appraisal processes." In K. R. Scherer, A. Schorr, & T. Johnstone (Eds.), *Appraisal processes in emotion: Theory, research, application* (pp. 221–232). New York: Oxford University Press.

McLean, P. D. (1990). *The triune brain in evolution: Role in paleocerebral functions.* New York: Plenum Press.

Mech, L. D. (1999). "Alpha status, dominance, and division of labor in wolf packs." *Canadian Journal of Zoology, 77,* 1196–1203.

Norman, D. A. (2004). *Emotional design—why we love (or hate) everyday things.* New York: Basic Books.

Novak, T. P., & Hoffman, D. L. (1997). "Measuring the flow experience among Web users," Nashville: Vanderbilt University.

Reeves, B., & Nass, C. (1998). *The media equation: How people treat computers, television and new media like real people and places.* Cambridge: Cambridge University Press.

Roseman, I. J., & Smith, G. A. (2001). "Appraisal theory: Assumptions, varieties, controversies." In K. Scherer, A. Schorr, & T. Johnstone (Eds.), *Appraisal processes in emotion* (pp. 3–19). Oxford: Oxford University Press.

Russell, J. A. (1980). "A circumplex model of affect." *Journal of Personality and Social Psychology, 39,* 1161–1178.

van Gorp, T. J. (2006). *Emotion, arousal, attention, and flow: Chaining emotional states to improve human-computer interaction.* Master's degree project, University of Calgary, Faculty of Environmental Design.

van Gorp, T. J. (2010). *Design for Emotion and Flow.* 2010 IA Summit, Phoenix.

van Hengel, P. W. J., & Andringa, T. C. (2007). Verbal aggression detection in complex social environments. *Advanced Video and Signal Based Surveillance,* 2007, pp. 15–20. London: IEEE Conference.

Weinshenk, S. (2009). *Neuro Web Design.* Berkeley: New Riders Press.

Yerkes, R. M., & Dodson, J. D. (1908). The relation of strength of stimulus to rapidity of habit-formation. *Journal of Comparative Neurology and Psychology, 18,* 459–482.

Zhou, W., & Chen, D. (2009). Fear-related chemosignals modulate recognition of fear in ambiguous facial expressions. *Psychological Science,* Vol. 20, no. 2, 177–183.

When Do We Design for Emotion?

In Chapter 1, we explored several reasons why emotion should be a consideration in your design process. Throughout Chapter 2, we examined different models of emotion to better understand how the decisions we make as designers affect the different dimensions of users' emotional responses. As you'll see in Chapter 3, emotional states guide decision making and behavior by affecting how we focus attention, altering our intentions and increasing or decreasing our levels of motivation.

When we say "design for emotion," what we're really attempting to design for is an emotional response that increases the likelihood the user will perform a desired behavior. "Behavior is the real medium of interaction design" (Fabricant, 2009). The behavior could be any action: clicking a submit button; dismissing a page on a tablet; closing a door; subscribing for a newsletter; locking the car; or remembering to feed the fish.

Whatever the desired behavior, by applying the principles of emotional design you can guide the user's attention to the right place at the right time to initiate and extend the interaction into a relationship. Because our decisions to behave are based on our emotional responses (Damasio, 1994), it's natural to suppose that you might begin with the emotion itself. However, you may want to start with the desired behavior and work backward.

The behavior you're designing for could be any action.

Let's imagine that we're designing a system to help us remember to feed the fish. You might start by putting a sticky note on the refrigerator. After all, it's bright yellow, which draws a lot of attention. Unfortunately, you've already used this tactic, and your fridge is covered in bright yellow sticky notes, all competing for your attention. At this point, you might want to prioritize the notes on your fridge, because you may have more important things to attend to! But, if feeding the fish is still the top priority, you could apply emotional design principles to increase the amount of attention, intention and motivation you had to get that fish fed.

To grab more of your attention, we could increase the size, or change the color of the sticky note. If it were the only large sticky note on the fridge in a different color, it would stand out against the crowd. Next, instead of using a pen, we could use a black Sharpie marker to write the words "feed the fish" in big, bold uppercase letters. To heighten arousal and attention even more, we could change the text to say something negative, such as "Don't KILL the Fish!" We can make the same kinds of changes in any product, altering size, shape, color, form and language to draw attention and change behavior.

In this chapter, we'll examine the connections between the dimensions of emotion and the dimensions of behavior. We'll look at how emotion affects attention, intention and motivation, and examine how optimizing attention helps to create the conditions for "flow." Finally, we'll explain when to design for flow.

FIG. 3.1 Don't KILL the Fish!
Reminders to feed the fish.
© Trevor van Gorp

MEASURING SUCCESS THROUGH FLOW

From a business perspective, one way to judge the success of our efforts is to measure how often our design solutions lead to the desired user behavior (e.g., number of subscriptions, number of referrals, number of purchases). From the perspective of the user, one metric that's suitable for measuring engagement is the achievement of **flow**.

Businesses want to maintain and maximize employee performance, while users desire experiences that leave them feeling confident, competent and capable. **Flow** is a highly desirable mental/emotional state that combines both optimum performance and optimum experience (Csikszentmihalyi, 1990), satisfying both business goals and user needs.

When people stop to consider what the most rewarding times of their life have been, they often remember times when they successfully tackled a challenge to reach some worthy goal. The mental/emotional state of "flow" is created by focusing attention on a challenge with the appropriate skill set in the right type of environment (Csikszentmihalyi, 1990).

An important part of the flow experience (and user experience) is fostering a sense of accomplishment. In the case of interface design, a sense of accomplishment can be provided by marking the completion of tasks that lead to the realization of goals. If the user's main accomplishment is figuring out how to operate your application, rather than using it to help realize their own goals, they're not likely to be in the flow state.

> "Flow" is created by focusing attention on a challenge that's matched to your skill set.

Goals and Meaning

People attribute a vast range of meanings to the objects with which they interact. These meanings depend in part on the properties of the objects themselves, but also on how those objects help or hinder us in the pursuit of our goals. Objects that play a part in the accomplishment of our goals take on emotional meaning through association.

In this sense, an "object" can be anything. It might be something physical like a tool, or even something virtual like a website, or a piece of software. In either case, we connect the feelings we experience while interacting with the "thing" (e.g., using the tool), to the object or tool itself. The emotions experienced in the pursuit of the goal create (through association) the emotional meaning of the product.

Emotional meaning can generally be associated with either the arousal or value dimensions of emotion. Our levels of emotional arousal effect our levels of motivation, so if your goal is something that you feel passionately about, chances are good that your motivation to reach that goal will be higher. Often, the intensity of motivation (i.e., arousal) connected to goal-oriented activities becomes part of the emotional meaning of the product. These types of conditioned associations are usually unconscious and automatic.

> Emotional meaning can become even more important to the user than the functional meaning.

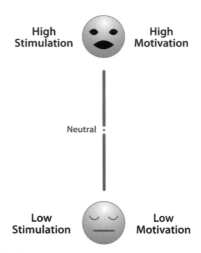

Arousal affects Motivation

FIG. 3.2 **Arousal affects Motivation**

© *Trevor van Gorp*

The physical characteristics of objects often suggest some meanings through association.

Emotional meaning can become even more important to the user than the functional meaning when using the product. In the world of high-end consumer photography, the camera company Leica enjoys incredible dedication from its customers (McGriff, 2011). This dedication and commitment comes about through a deep emotional connection that goes well beyond the features or technical capabilities of the camera, extending to the history, prestige, and authenticity of the brand. Leica fans derive pleasure and status from being associated with Leica and its products.

The psychological and physiological goals that create the emotional meanings when using products can be short-term or long-term. Getting ready for work in the morning, for example, involves completing a number of tasks. Getting out of bed, preparing breakfast, and deciding what clothes to wear for the meeting are all small tasks that contribute to short-term goals. These goals may not be all that meaningful in and of themselves, but their successful completion usually contributes to the fulfillment of a longer-term goal.

The red light at the back of the mouse provided feedback that gave them a sense of control.

Others goals require tools and the long-term investment of attention over time. Gaining a university degree for example, is a long-term goal that requires time, energy, attention, and resources to accomplish. In reaching for, achieving, and sometimes failing to achieve our short- and long-term goals, we search for purpose and direction in life.

Association and Meaning

Even though people can feel a wide range of emotions when interacting with objects, and assign those emotions a wide variety of meanings, the physical

FIG. 3.3 Microsoft IntelliMouse Explorer

Used with permission of Microsoft

characteristics of an object often suggest some meanings through **association**. Whether they are physical or virtual, objects communicate meaning through their own inherent qualities.

For example, a contoured rubber grip on a hand tool might come to mean "control," or "confidence," because the user finds it provides better handling. In the case of the Microsoft IntelliMouse Explorer, users testing early prototypes reported that the red light at the back of the mouse made it seem more responsive and alive. The feedback provided by the red light gave them a sense of control (Ledbetter, 2001). A sense of control is an important aspect of flow experiences, which we'll explore in more detail later in this chapter.

Status, Values and Meaning

The objects that people select, purchase and use are in large part a reflection of the people who chose them. The clothes you wear, the car you drive, the computer you use, and the interior of your home are all expressions of both who you are, and who you aspire to be. The things we choose to surround ourselves with commemorate the goals we've accomplished in the past and symbolize the goals we hope to accomplish in the future. Things also function as symbols that represent and communicate our values to others. Because these things can create possibilities that wouldn't have been available without them, their meaning is related both to their function and the events they make possible (Csikszentmihalyi and Rochberg-Halton, 1981).

> The "things" we buy and use can create possibilities that wouldn't have been there without them.

Every pair of jeans, for example, has a similar function. But, a pair of jeans of a certain brand that fits "just right" may have deeper levels of emotional meaning connected to fitting in with your friends, communicating cultural and material status, feeling attractive and finding a suitable mate.

Brands need to ensure that their products incorporate design features that are consistent with the values of the brand. At a workshop in Sweden, Trevor listened to a car designer from Volvo (Volvo Design, 2005) discuss how the sloping transition between the side panels and the windows of Volvo vehicles is purposefully designed to resemble a "shoulder," helping to communicate a sense of strength. This design feature intentionally symbolizes the brand's core values of safety and security.

FIG. 3.4 Shoulders on a Volvo

The "shoulders" on a Volvo are designed to convey the brand's values of safety and security
© *Trevor van Gorp*

ATTENTION AND FLOW

One of the central ideas proposed in *The Attention Economy*, is that modern society has become driven by the need to capture the attention of consumers. "Anyone who wants to persuade someone to buy something or do something has to invest in the attention markets" (Davenport & Beck, 2001, p. 9). Attention is the link between information received by our senses and our incorporation and understanding of that information.

Most of the software, websites and electronic products we design are created to display and represent information to people. That information could be anything: a company's product list; pictures of your vacation; or an instant message from a friend. In fact, as you're reading this, there's more information available to you than at any other time in history. All this information has a lot of positive effects, but it also creates challenges. "What information consumes is rather obvious; it consumes the *attention* of its recipients … a wealth of information creates a poverty of attention" (Simon, 1971, p. 40-41).

> **"A wealth of information creates a poverty of attention."**

If a product is ignored or fails to draw our attention, the story ends. The potential user goes on living his or her life oblivious to any benefits the product could have supplied. The business loses a potential sale. When a product captures our attention, we may decide to approach and expand the encounter. In this way, the aesthetic qualities of a product attract our attention and begin the interaction. Once engaged, the visual, auditory and tactile qualities of the product interface (i.e., display, controls, touchscreen, sound) may further deepen the interest of the user.

At this stage, the usability of the product becomes more important, determining our ease of interaction and the object's ability to hold our attention over time. Users encountering usability problems often quickly lose interest and abandon products, even if they were initially attracted.

Maintaining attention and building a relationship through many interactions is more difficult. Products that hold our attention over time aren't just aesthetically pleasing; they also help us to accomplish our goals, fulfill our social, cultural, and material needs for status and acceptance, and provoke positive emotions through association and anticipation.

> **Focused attention is the *mental energy* people require to complete tasks and accomplish goals.**

Goals and Attention

To make meaningful progress towards realizing our goals, it takes more than just tools in the form of products or software; it takes *energy*. Focused attention is the *mental energy* a person requires to complete tasks and accomplish goals. Without the investment of attention, nothing that involves information can be accomplished. Attention makes work possible by selecting the pieces of information that we think are relevant from the vast amount of information that's available to our senses (Csikszentmihalyi, 1990). Attention is then used to retrieve and compare those pieces of information to other information patterns stored in memory.

The focus of attention determines which experiences get into our heads and which ones don't. If information enters consciousness, it's either because we've intentionally focused our attention on it, or because our attention was demanded due to perceived biological or social needs, such as safety. How we focus our energy over the course of our lives largely determines who we become, and the kind of life we create for ourselves. That being said, the person we become also shapes how we direct our attention. The direction of attention determines the content of consciousness, which determines the creation and shape of the self, who then directs the focus of attention (Csikszentmihalyi, 1990).

Defining Attention

How we focus our energy determines who we become.

Aside from selecting and comparing information, attention is also required to process other mental events in consciousness, such as thinking, feeling, remembering and making decisions. For this reason, attention is also called "psychic energy." Like energy in the traditional sense, "without it no work can be done and through work, energy is dissipated" (Csikszentmihalyi, 1990, p. 33). In other words, once you invest attention, that attention is gone. But, like currency, if the attention was wisely invested in the creation of flow experiences, there might be a future return in the form of increased skills or a stronger personal identity.

In some ways, attention is a lot like air. Most of us give it little notice until it's not there for our use. Attention has been described as being composed of two dimensions. First, attention is either *voluntary* or *captive* (Davenport & Beck, 2001). Sometimes, we freely choose to invest attention, but sometimes our attention is demanded when we'd rather invest it somewhere else. If you've ever had to take a class you weren't the least bit interested in, you've probably experienced this.

Second, some things demand more attention than others. The level of arousal or stimulation directly affects the amount of attention we have to invest. Most of us know what it's like to have things "on our mind." When a piece of information is especially important, the strong emotions associated with it can propel that information to the top of our working memory, while other information fades back. We can describe the priority of attention as *front of mind* versus *back of mind* (Davenport & Beck, 2001).

Types of Attention

There are three tendencies in the way we employ attention that are important to compensate for in design:

- Selective attention
- Focused attention
- Divided attention
  (Wickens & Hollands, 2000)

Attention: Choice/Priority

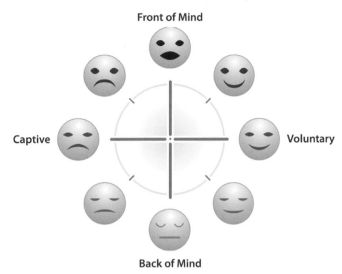

FIG. 3.5 Attention: Choice/Priority

Adapted from (Davenport & Beck, 2001).
© *Trevor van Gorp*

Selective Attention

Selective attention can be a result of higher arousal states. It describes instances in which we consciously or unconsciously choose to focus on information in the environment that may not be appropriate for what we're doing. Selective attention can also be seen as a form of tunnel vision that makes us less open to alternative options (Wickens & Hollands, 2000). If you've ever been searching frantically for your keys, only to find them on the table right in front of you, you've experienced selective attention.

Selective attention can be a result of higher arousal states.

Focused Attention

The focus of attention is easily diverted by emotionally charged information, explaining our tendency to become distracted. Things in the external environment can grab our attention unconsciously by increasing arousal levels, or through conscious evaluations (Wickens & Hollands, 2000).

Divided Attention

Because attention is required for any task to be completed, we can really only invest attention in one thing at a time. People often experience problems when attempting to divide attention between two or more sources of information. We can't actually pay attention to more than one thing at a time. We're limited in our ability to simultaneously process multiple sources of information. Multitasking is really a myth.

FIG. 3.6 Driver on Cell Phone

People using cellphones while driving are as impaired as those who are over the legal blood-alcohol limit.

© *iStockPhoto.com*

What we're actually doing is quickly shifting attention between tasks, rather than working on those tasks simultaneously.

We can't actually pay attention to more than one thing at a time.

Testing found that multitaskers performed worse on all their tasks, possibly reflecting the lack of sustained attention they were able to invest in any one thing (Ophir, Nass, & Wagner, 2011). To underscore just how much multitasking impairs drivers, psychologists at the University of Utah found that drivers talking on a cell phone while driving had the same performance impairments as drivers who were just over the legal limit of 0.08 percent blood/alcohol (Strayer, Watson & Drews, 2010).

Measuring Attention

There are several ways of measuring how much attention our users are investing, although you may not have thought of them in this way before. Direct measures of visual attention include measures like eye tracking, which measures eye positions and eye movement. Services like the 3M Visual Attention Service (3M Visual Attention Service, 2011) can tell you what part of your design people will spend the most time looking at. Indirectly, we can also measure attention on websites through web metrics like the number of visits and actions, time on the site, and conversion rates. Greenier (2011) has divided online emotional engagement into four categories: awareness, attraction, investment, and adoption.

Awareness

We can measure awareness through using metrics like page views, page hits, video views, impressions and click-through rates.

Attraction

We can measure attraction by looking at bounce rates, session lengths, pages per visit, abandonment rates, email opening rates and click-through rates.

Investment

We can measure how invested people are by tracking social network followers, RSS feed or podcast subscribers, email newsletter subscriptions, file downloads, ecommerce conversion rates, purchase line items (both items and amount), community signups and warm leads.

Adoption

We can measure adoption in return customers, unique versus returning visitor ratios, geolocation checkins and participation in "karma" systems (badges, etc.), to name a few (Greenier, 2011).

The Limits of Attention

As a society, we're now so inundated with information that there's no way any one person could possibly process and incorporate all of it. Many of us now live in a state of what's been called "continuous partial attention" (Stone, 2009). We skim the surface of as much data as we can, looking for details that attract our attention by being emotionally relevant. These details can range from the unconsciously processed (e.g., colors, images and contrast) to the consciously processed (e.g., topics, labels and subjects).

FIG. 3.7 Times Square

Competing to capture your attention.
© iStockPhoto.com

FIG. 3.8 **Microsoft Natural Keyboard Elite**

Used with permission of Microsoft

Many of us now live in a state of what's been called "continuous partial attention."

Continuous partial attention is broad but thinly applied. As such, it may lack the necessary depth required for the integration of information that results in knowledge and understanding. However, it is one strategy for determining where to focus attention in a world that's overflowing with information.

Because attention is a finite resource, one way we can reduce the demands on attention is by reducing any physical or psychological discomfort. When Edie worked with Microsoft Hardware to design the Natural Keyboard, awkward wrist postures were identified as one of the main sources of distraction and discomfort for users who spent long periods of time working with computers.

Using flat, standard keyboards created an unnatural wrist position, resulting in increased wrist pressure that caused discomfort and fatigue over time. Discomfort demands users' attention, distracting them from their work and causing fatigue that hampers productivity. The focus of the design solution became the elimination of the chronic wrist deviation that was leading to fatigue and distraction.

THE SENSES AND ATTENTION

Discomfort demands users' attention.

Each of our senses receives information from the world and relays that information to the brain. Our senses have evolved to serve different purposes and receive different types of information.

Both conscious and unconscious emotional responses create changes in the body. The internal expressions of emotions (or *feelings*) are a form of kinesthetic feedback from the body that affects how we invest attention. The kinesthetic sense includes touch and the sense of your body in space, as well any internal feedback from the body in the form of physical pain or pleasure.

The Tactile (Touch)

Although appearance and the visual sense have historically dominated in design, the strongest emotional associations come from the body itself. We feel pain and pleasure in the body, and our brains associate those feelings with whatever appears to have triggered them. Although we can distinguish psychological pain from physical pain, the two are intimately intertwined. An example of this is *takotsubo cardiomyopathy* or "broken heart syndrome." Broken heart syndrome refers to a weakening of the heart muscles induced by emotional trauma or stress, such as the death or loss of a beloved partner (Wittstein et al., 2005). Because of this intimate connection between our psychology and physiology, strong feelings almost always demand our attention.

The amount of the cerebral cortex that's devoted to each body region is directly related to the number of nerves and muscles, as well as the level of sensitivity (Marieb & Hoehn, 2007). Judging by the amount of the brain that's devoted to processing sensory information from certain parts of the body, scientists have created what they call a sensory homunculus. This diagram of a brain shows the size of the body parts based on the amount of brain matter that is assigned to process information from each part.

A large portion of the brain is devoted to processing information from the hands.

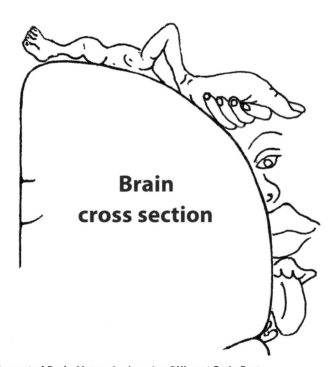

FIG. 3.9 The Amount of Brain Matter Assigned to Different Body Parts
© btarski

From this representation, we can see that the lips, hands, feet, and genitals all have large amounts of the brain devoted to processing their sensory signals. This image also makes it clear why touch devices are so unconsciously engaging. A large portion of the brain is devoted to processing information associated with the hands.

The Visual

Many complex human tasks require the ability to see detail. We see detail in the world through the part of our eye called the **fovea**. The eye can actually see detail in only a very limited range around the fovea (approximately 2 degrees) (Wickens, Gordon, & Liu, 1997). In some ways, this makes visual attention similar to a searchlight.

Things outside the spotlight of attention don't appear to exist.

A searchlight has direction and breadth. When the searchlight of attention "illuminates" something, it can't be illuminating anything else, so those objects never make it into our heads. Our attention is **selective**. Essentially, things outside the spotlight of attention don't appear to exist. Sometimes, there are things we want to process as well as things that we don't want to process that demand our attention. This results in what's called **divided attention** (Wickens, Gordon, & Liu, 1997).

FIG. 3.10 The Spotlight of Attention
© iStockPhoto.com

Our hearing and sight are often sources of things that unintentionally distract or divide attention. The peripheral vision around the fovea is poor for rendering detail, but sensitive to motion, making it ideal for sensing potential threats but also prone to distracting us with unwanted information. As arousal levels increase, the spotlight of attention narrows even further in an effort to reduce the amount of unwanted information (Wickens, Gordon, & Liu, 1997).

The Auditory

Noise is a common source of unwanted information. The auditory sense differs from vision in that it can process input from almost any direction. It's also transient, as most sound disappears shortly after being heard (Wickens, Gordon, & Liu, 1997). Loud sounds increase arousal, while loud, sudden sounds increase arousal and almost *always* demand a shift in attention. The same is true for the sound of our own names. Sounds can also act as feedback indicators when associated with an action and a visual cue. For example, the sound of the keys being pressed on a touchscreen phone adds an element of feedback that mimics the sound of mechanical keys to reduce user uncertainty.

Sounds act as feedback indicators when associated with an action and a visual cue.

FIG. 3.11 **iPhone Keyboard Feedback**
© *Trevor van Gorp*

The engines of electronic vehicles don't make the same sounds as internal combustion engines. They're so quiet that the blind or visually impaired may not notice them. In electronic vehicles, engine sounds are added to offer valuable feedback to pedestrians about oncoming traffic (Motavalli, 2009). We'll explore the emotional properties of sound in more detail in Chapter 4.

EMOTION, ATTENTION AND BEHAVIOR

Emotional affect changes where and how intensely we focus attention. Your existing emotional states and the emotions you're about to experience interact in a subtle and complex way. Your current emotional state affects how you interpret incoming information and your expectations of future events. All of this then influences your unfolding emotional states. In this way, positive emotional states can positively influence future interactions. Unfortunately, negative emotional states can also negatively influence future interactions.

Emotion and Attention

Emotional affect changes where and how intensely we focus attention.

The two dimensions of emotion can be related to the dimensions of attention. Value determines whether attention is *voluntarily* invested (i.e., pleasant) or held *captive* (i.e., unpleasant).

Arousal or stimulation (i.e., the physiological dimension of emotion) is closely connected to other concepts such as motivation and attention. Arousal levels determine whether things move to the front or back of the mind. Remember, because arousal is largely unconscious, it provides an especially powerful channel for designers to influence behavior by commanding attention. When the level of arousal increases, the focus of attention narrows and goes to whatever is causing the stimulation, moving it to front of the mind. Too little arousal leads to unfocused attention as things move to back of mind. Higher levels of arousal have a focusing effect on attention. We'll be exploring different ways to increase arousal through design in Chapter 4.

Value affects Choice

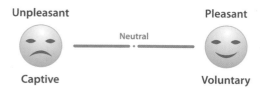

FIG. 3.12 **Value affects Choice**

Adapted from (Davenport & Beck, 2001). © *Trevor van Gorp*

Arousal affects Priority

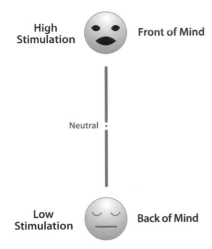

High Stimulation — Front of Mind

Neutral

Low Stimulation — Back of Mind

FIG. 3.13 Arousal affects Priority

Adapted from (Davenport & Beck, 2001). © Trevor van Gorp

Emotion and Behavior

Positive and negative emotional affect influence the two dimensions of behavior: *intention* and *motivation*. *Intentions* guide how we invest voluntary attention and select the information we voluntarily choose and process. All intentional acts require *attention*, whether it's reading a paper, talking with a friend, or interacting with a product. Intentions are structured as a hierarchy of conscious goals, which lead us to *approach* or *avoid* particular types of information. We then interpret this information and add it to our existing mental models.

The value dimension of emotion guides intention. As mentioned in Chapter 2, positive emotional affect is usually connected with the intent to approach, and negative affect is connected to the urge to avoid. Once interaction begins, positive affect serves as a signal to continue with one's current behaviors, and negative affect can be a signal to end interaction.

The value dimension of emotion guides intention.

Approach (Positive Affect)

Positive affect often leads to the further interaction and can increase or decrease motivation (Isen, 1999). At low levels of physiological arousal, positive affect influences thinking and social interaction without interrupting ongoing tasks and concentration (Isen, 1999). Attention is not interrupted, which may explain how low levels of positive affect help facilitate flow experiences. *Excitement* and *joy* for example, both increase arousal, while contentment and relaxation generally lower

Positive affect attracts and encourages approach behaviors.

Value affects Intention

FIG. 3.14 Value affects Intention

The emotional value of a thing affects whether we intend to approach or avoid it.
© *Trevor van Gorp*

arousal. This correlation promotes increased flexibility in thinking and a relaxed, open body. Psychologists have shown that people are better at problem solving and creative thinking when they feel good (Norman, 2004).

In design terms, the implications are that someone who is happy and relaxed is more capable of using creative thought to figure out how to operate a device and overlook minor problems. Considerations like this are even more important for items used in task-based environments in which deadlines and high arousal levels increase emotional intensity and reduce creative thought capacity. Positive affect attracts, encourages approach behaviors and creates positive associations.

Avoid (Negative Affect)

Negative affect triggers higher levels of arousal, promoting focus in the mind and a body that is ready to take action (Norman, 2004). Once interaction begins, negative emotional affect serves as a signal to adjust thinking or behavior. The fact that negative affect commands more attention than positive affect allows us to engage in exploratory behavior while allowing us to stop, avoid, or withdraw from experiences that are considered dangerous (Cacioppo, Larsen, Smith, & Berntson, 2004).

Negative affect promotes focus in the mind.

Why would negative affect demand more attention than positive affect? Imagine our ancestors in the primordial jungle. On a daily basis, they would be called on to make quick decisions about where to focus their attention. In terms of survival, the possibility of danger *should* provoke a stronger response that draws more attention.

From an evolutionary standpoint, this must have proven useful when looking for food in areas where there were many predators. When presented with a choice between a patch of tasty wild berries on the right and a stalking tiger to the left, negative affect caused our ancestors to focus their attention on the tiger. This gave them a better chance of survival, meaning that they were more likely to reproduce and pass down their genes.

Balancing Positive and Negative Affect

One implication of this idea is that products and interfaces designed for fun and entertainment can get away with poorer usability than items and interfaces that are used in stressful or dangerous situations. Because the user's capacity to process information will be reduced, stressful circumstances require more usable products (Norman, 2004). As we mentioned earlier, negative stimuli command more attention and generally evoke stronger cognitive, emotional, and physiological responses than positive stimuli (Cacioppo et al., 2004).

Many situations demand designs that must promote both open, creative thought and more focused, detailed thought. In this instance, all information that is relevant needs to be close at hand and visible. Feedback should remain clear and immediate. When something needs attention, the immediate environment should become more negative to promote a higher level of attention and the focus needed to deal with the problem. One way this can be accomplished is through the use of sound. In this instance, an alarm sound would provoke anxiety and focus. Negative affect causes people to focus on the details (Norman, 2004), which is desirable when things go awry.

> **Negative stimuli command more attention than positive stimuli.**

Here's an example. Carbon monoxide is odorless, colorless, and invisible. But if it builds to a certain level in the air, it can kill you. If you had a fire in your home, you might notice some other signs, such as smoke, or heat, but carbon monoxide displays no such signs until it's too late. To detect the buildup of this poisonous gas, many people install a carbon monoxide detector.

As you would expect, when it detects carbon monoxide, the detector makes an ear-shattering noise and flashes a red light. The negative affect draws your attention and creates the urge to avoid, prompting you to leave the house. However, what's more interesting is that the detector also flashes a green light to confirm that it's powered and that everything is okay. This green flashing light reassures you that the battery hasn't died, and that the detector is actually working, vigilantly guarding your safety. If the detector does go off, you'll be suitably alarmed and ready to behave appropriately by exiting the house. Unlike a fire alarm, the carbon monoxide detector is detecting something that can't be seen, heard, or felt. Without the feedback provided by the green light, it would be easy for the battery to run out without the user noticing.

Motivation and Arousal

Just as value guides the intentional dimension of behavior, *arousal* influences the *motivational* dimension of behavior. We tend to call higher arousal states with a negative tone "anxiety" or "stress." The truth is that both positive and negative states of high stimulation are stressful on the body. Prolonged excitement can be as exhausting as prolonged rage. Still, negative affect commands more attention, causing people to focus on details instead of seeking alternate solutions. For task-based work, someone who's in distress is less likely to be able to come up with creative solutions to any problems that are encountered.

> **Arousal influences the motivational dimension of behavior.**

Arousal affects Motivation

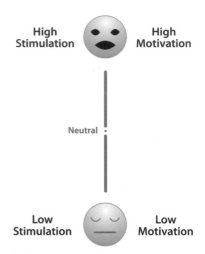

FIG. 3.15 **Arousal affects Motivation**

© *Trevor van Gorp*

The more stimulated we are, the more motivated we are to take action and avoid or approach the thing that's stimulating us. From the image in Fig. 3.15, we might assume that the more we increase stimulation, the more we would increase motivation. But, if we recall the Yerkes-Dodson law (1908) that we mentioned back in Chapter 2; although increasing arousal can improve motivation and performance, after the point of optimum performance has been reached (i.e., the flow area), increasing stimulation leads to decreases in both motivation and performance.

Researchers found that levels of stress hormones which affect human memory performance mirror the upside-down U curve of the Yerkes-Dodson law. The formation of long-term memories is optimal when stress hormone levels are slightly elevated. At the same time, high levels of stress hormones tend to impair long-term memory formation (Lupien, Maheu, Tu, Fiocco, & Schramek, 2007).

If we are to match optimum motivation with optimum performance, we need to carefully consider the user's level of stimulation depending on the likely circumstances of use. Novel, unpredictable, or threatening situations in which the individual is not in control increase arousal or stress. A stimulating message can increase arousal, commanding attention and increasing motivation. If the message is judged as positive, it can trigger approach behaviors like exploration. If the message is judged to be negative, it can trigger avoidant behaviors. Changes in emotional affect are at the root of most persuasive techniques that alter behavior because they influence how we invest attention and process information (Cacioppo & Petty, 1989).

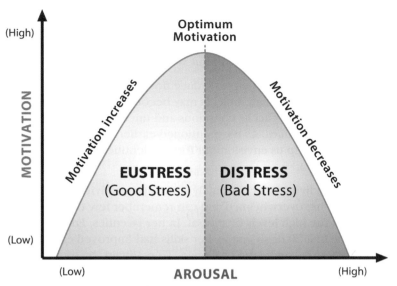

FIG. 3.16 Yerkes-Dodson Law (Motivation)

Adapted from (Yerkes & Dodson, 1908); additions, (van Gorp, 2010). © Trevor van Gorp

EMOTION AND FLOW

Designing for flow doesn't require a new set of tools or skills—only a different way of thinking. If the interface between the human operator and the technology isn't designed to capitalize on human strengths and compensate for human limitations, interaction can be difficult and frustrating, impairing users' efforts to reach flow.

"Flow" describes the state of being completely motivated and totally engrossed in a task, in which time seems to disappear. When people experience a challenge that they feel they can tackle with their existing skills, in an environment with few interruptions, attention becomes focused in the moment and a great sense of enjoyment is experienced, which (Csikszentmihalyi, 1990). called "flow."

Norman (1998, p. 31) has also described this state as "a continual flow of focused concentration" and calls this type of experience "motivated activity." Flow experiences enrich and improve the quality of our lives by creating order in consciousness, increasing our skills, and improving self-confidence (Csikszentmihalyi, 1990).

Flow experiences can occur in the midst of both pleasant and unpleasant conditions, which means that the experience of pleasure or pain is not the determining factor in their creation. People who have survived near-fatal dangers

Flow experiences create order in consciousness, increase skills, and improve self-confidence.

FIG. 3.18 Microsoft Natural Keyboard Elite

Used with permission of Microsoft

Too much challenge with too little skill causes anxiety.

For the Microsoft Natural Keyboard, Edie and her team realized that the distractions caused by fatigue and discomfort were impairing users' ability to achieve flow. Solving this problem meant changing the form of the keyboard to direct the users' wrists into a more natural position. The keys were angled to more closely mirror the natural angle of the wrist while typing, and the keyboard was arced upward in the center. More than ten years after its initial design, the Natural Keyboard is still found in offices all over the world. Edie and her team identified the proper context for their design solution and fulfilled the right emotional need.

The effective use of layout, information design, typography, interaction design, and information architecture all help in balancing the perception of challenge against the users' skill levels. Whatever you're designing, any information it represents should be broken down into manageable chunks that don't overwhelm users cognitive faculties.

When it comes to balancing the users' perception of challenge, think of it this way: too much challenge with too little skill causes anxiety, and too little challenge with too much skill causes boredom. Flow occurs at the boundary between boredom and anxiety. You can picture it as a channel that runs between the two.

As the challenges we face increase, anxiety increases and we risk becoming overwhelmed and losing flow. Reentering flow involves increasing our skills to match these challenges and reduce anxiety. As we increase our skill level, we become bored unless we increase the challenge to match our increased abilities.

Too little challenge with too much skill causes boredom.

It's interesting to note that although the design profession often trumpets simplicity as the primary goal, items that appear too simple are often seen as providing little in the way of challenge and are not perceived as being very powerful. Sometimes, the perception of *complexity* can lead to an increase in the perception of capability or *power* (Norman, 2007). As you'll see in Chapter 5, power is important part of our social perceptions when it comes to building relationships with the things we use.

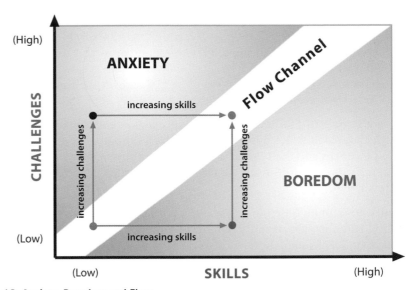

FIG. 3.19 **Anxiety, Boredom and Flow**

Adapted from (Csikszentmihalyi, 1990); captions added (van Gorp, 2010). © Trevor van Gorp

To understand how we can reduce distractions, let's examine the different elements of flow again to see how each can be applied to user experience. The causes of flow have the most implications for designing emotion.

Clear, Evolving Goals

The user navigates through a website or device interface to accomplish a task, like seeking information on a particular topic or surfing for fun. This is an evolving goal that is dependent on the options presented to the user and aided by logical information architecture, intuitive navigation, effective way finding, and clear options for proceeding like information scent, breadcrumbs, meaningful labels, and clear page titles.

Immediate Feedback

The user receives quick, sensory feedback in the form of a visual shift and/or sound from links, buttons, menus, or other navigation items.

Balancing the Perception of Challenge Against Users' Skills

The opportunities for action are balanced with the user's ability. At a basic level, this is accomplished by providing an uncluttered interface and eliminating unnecessary information to limit the user's cognitive load. As the users' skill increases over time, the interface can increase its complexity as well. Adaptive interface technologies allow the user to adjust the complexity of the interface to meet their enhanced skills.

Items that appear too simple may not be perceived as being very powerful.

Flow tends to occur in situations with higher levels of challenge and skill. If the challenge is too easy or user skill levels are very high, arousal levels can be so low that there's little motivation to do anything. Remember, arousal is the physiological (i.e., bodily) dimension of emotion. The level of arousal affects how intensely we experience a given emotion, be it good or bad. Whatever the value, intense emotions demand our attention.

The key to managing arousal is to match the perceived challenge to the users' skill level. Because skill levels differ from one user to the next based on their previous experiences and the type of task, interfaces should be very user friendly but also allow more advanced users to find challenges appropriate for their skill level.

These challenges can include the aesthetic aspects as well as the interaction and functionality. Large images, bright color and high contrast all increase arousal levels (Fehrman & Fehrman, 2000; Reeves & Nass, 1998). As we mentioned in Chapter 2, everything about a product, website, or application, including content, information architecture, industrial design, interaction design and graphic design can contribute to, or impede flow.

Goal-Directed Versus Experiential Use

Whatever the value, intense emotions demand our attention.

Different contexts of product use require different designs to facilitate flow. For example, novice users tended to see the Internet in a playful way, while more experienced users tended to view the Internet as a tool (Novak, Hoffman, & Yung 1998). This leads to an important contextual distinction between experiential and goal-directed use.

Flow tends to occur more often during goal-directed use because of the higher challenge involved. Although the following distinctions apply to website usage, it's likely that we could make the same distinctions with any product, as the emotional reactions would be similar.

Novice Users – Experiential Use
- Less challenging
- More exploratory
- Entertainment-oriented

Experienced Users – Goal-Directed Use
- More challenging
- Less exploratory
- Connected with tasks (e.g., research, work, and shopping)

The lower level of challenge in an entertainment-oriented, experiential product, application, or website means there is a lower level of stimulation or anxiety connected with its use. Someone who is less anxious is more capable of using

FIG. 3.20 Kinect Me

Leisure oriented applications can and should be more arousing since there is little or no task-based challenge involved.
Used with permission of Microsoft

creative thought to determine how to navigate a website and overlook minor problems (Norman, 2004). Motivation here is driven less by the challenge of completing tasks, and more by unconscious arousal triggered by interesting visual elements, bright colors, or high contrast. Experiential products, applications and websites can and should be more aesthetically appealing to demand the greater attention that can lead to flow experiences.

The greater challenge of completing tasks on a goal-directed site stimulates higher arousal. When stress becomes distress, users are less able to think creatively if problems are encountered. When a product will be used in a stressful environment, (such as a hospital operating room), usability becomes crucial. All relevant information needs to be close at hand and visible and feedback should be clear and immediate. A goal-directed product, application, or website can and should be less aesthetically rich so that users already anxious at the prospect of a challenging task are not overwhelmed.

Increasing arousal levels with attractive aesthetics can increase user motivation.

FIG. 3.21 Task Oriented-MSN

An example of a task-oriented site that is less aesthetically rich, with some challenge involved.

Used with permission of Microsoft

FIG. 3.22 MailChimp
The MailChimp site uses attractive visual design and humor to convey an upbeat personality.
http://mailchimp.com © Rocket Science Group

When tasks are particularly unpleasant, we often lack the motivation necessary to complete them. In these cases, increasing the arousal level through the use of aesthetics can actually increase the user's motivation. The MailChimp website uses attractive visual design and humor to convey an upbeat personality that increases motivation and makes email marketing a less onerous task.

CONCLUSIONS

How you apply these ideas depends on your target audience, as well as their internal and external use contexts. Consider the likely emotional state of your users when they encounter your product. Are there loud noises, crowds, brightly colored objects, or other distractions in the user's environment? Is the situation novel, unpredictable, or threatening in some way? Does the individual feel like he or she is in control? All of these factors can increase arousal or stress.

Here are some basic design guidelines that will help to encourage flow:

Does the user feel like they're in control?

    Clear navigation: Whether it's a physical product or an online experience, make it easy for the users to know where they are, where they can go, and where they've been by including signposts such as breadcrumbs, effective page titles and visited link indicators. Giving users a clear sense of the actions they can take next reduces uncertainty to help manage the perception of challenge.

Immediate feedback: Make sure all navigation (such as links, buttons, and menus) provides quick and effective feedback. Offer feedback for all user actions. When this isn't possible, provide an indicator to hold users' attention while waiting (e.g., progress bar).

Reduce distractions: Identify and reduce the distractions that are most likely to interfere with flow. For physical and interactive products, clearly present the information in manageable chunks that don't increase user anxiety.

Balance the perception of challenge with the user's skill levels: Because user skill levels differ, it's up to you to balance the complexity of the visual or industrial design with the number of tasks and features that people can use. Consider whether they're using your product experientially for fun or completing an important task. Tailor your product to your target audience's scenario of use: more aesthetically rich for experiential use, and less so for goal-directed use.

Tailor your product to your target audience's scenario of use.

Allow users to increase or decrease the perceived challenge by choosing how much detail is displayed in one way to create products that encourage flow. Options for information-rich displays can introduce challenge for more experienced users. Clarity helps reduce anxiety for both novices and experts, which is especially crucial in highly stressful situations.

When do we design for emotion? Whenever we need to find the right balance of challenge and skill to help focus attention and create flow. Remember, designing for flow doesn't require a new set of tools or skills; only a different way of thinking. We should design for emotion whenever we need to create engaging and immersive user experiences that build loyalty and encourage the formation of relationships.

In this chapter, we explored the importance of attention and examined its relationship to emotion and flow. Flow is an ideal generalized metric for emotional design because, by definition, it addresses both optimum performance and optimum experience. We explored how the dimensions of emotion affect the dimensions of attention and the dimensions of behavior.

Finally, we looked at how the physiological dimension of emotion (i.e., arousal) affects the creation of flow experiences. Fostering flow helps encourage users to find meaning and create relationships, building trust and brand loyalty.

In Chapter 4, we'll explore how emotions communicate personality over time and how those personalities affect what we choose, the ways we interact with things, and how we form relationships.

REFERENCES

3M Visual Attention Service. <http://solutions.3m.com/wps/portal/3M/en_US/VisualAttentionService/home/> Accessed 11.15.11.

Adams, E. (1990). *A framework for understanding product semiotics.* Master's Degree Project. Calgary: Faculty of Environmental Design, University of Calgary.

Cacioppo, J. T., Larsen, J. T., Smith, N. K., & Berntson, G. G. (2004). The affect system: What lurks below the surface of feelings? In A. S. R. Manstead, N. H. Frijda, & A. H. Fischer (Eds.), *Feelings and emotions: The Amsterdam conference* (pp. 221–240). New York: Cambridge University Press.

Cacioppo, J. T., & Petty, R. E. (1989). The elaboration likelihood model: The role of affect and affect-laden information processing in persuasion. In A. Tybout and P. Cafferata (Eds.), *Cognitive and affective responses to advertising* (pp. 69–89). Lexington, MA: Lexington Books.

Csikszentmihalyi, M. (1990). Flow: The psychology of optimal experience. New York: Harper Perennial.

Csikszentmihalyi, M. & Rochberg-Halton, E. (1981). *The meaning of things: Domestic symbols and the self.* Cambridge: Cambridge University Press.

Damasio, A. R. (1994). *Descartes' error: Emotion, reason and the human brain.* Florida: Grosset/Putnam, Inc.

Davenport, T. H., & Beck, J. C. (2001). *The attention economy: Understanding the new currency of business.* Cambridge, MA: Harvard Business School Press.

Demîr, E. (2008). The field of design: Concepts, arguments, tools and current issues. *METU JFA, 1*(1), 135.

Fabricant, R. (2009). Behavior is our medium. *Interaction Design Association.* ixda09. <http://vimeo.com/3730382> Accessed 09.24.11.

Fehrman, K. R., & Fehrman, C. (2000). *Color: The Secret Influence.* Upper Saddle River, NJ: Prentice Hall.

Greenier, S. (2011). Optimizing emotional engagement in web design through metrics. *Smashing Magazine.* <http://uxdesign.smashingmagazine.com/2011/05/19/optimizing-emotional-engagement-in-web-design-through-metrics/> Accessed 10.23.11.

Isen, A. (1999). Positive affect. In T. Dagleish and M. Power (Eds.), *Handbook of Cognition and Emotion.* West Sussex: John Wiley & Sons Ltd.

Ledbetter, C. (2001). Microsoft IntelliMouse Optical: A mouse for the masses. *In Innovation Yearbook of Industrial Design Excellence,* pp. 61–65. The Quarterly of the Industrial Designers Society of America, Fall 2001. Dulles, VA. IDSA.

Lupien, S. J., Maheu, F., Tu, M., Fiocco, A., & Schramek, T. E. (2007). The effects of stress and stress hormones on human cognition: Implications for the field of brain and cognition. *Brain and Cognition, 65,* 209–237.

Marieb, E., & Hoehn, K. (2007). *Human anatomy and physiology* (7th ed.). San Francisco: Pearson Benjamin Cummings.

McGriff, D. (2011). *Leica new Titanium D-Lux 5.* <http://www.zimbabwemetro.com/29797/leica-new-titanium-d-lux-5/> Accessed 1.5.12.

Motavalli, J. (2009, October 13). Hybrid cars may include fake vroom for safety. *New York Times*. <http://www.nytimes.com/2009/10/14/automobiles/14hybrid.html?_r=2> Accessed 12.20.11.

Norman, D. A. (1998). *Things that make us smart: Defending human attributes in the age of the machine*. Reading, MA: Addison-Wesley Publishing Company.

Norman, D. A. (2004). *Emotional design: Why we love (or hate) everyday things*. New York: Basic Books.

Norman, D. (2007). Simplicity is highly overrated. *Interactions 14*(3). CACM. <http://www .jnd.org/dn.mss/simplicity_is_highly_overrated.html> Accessed 10.24.11.

Novak, T., Hoffman, D., & Yung, Y. (1998). *Measuring the flow construct in online environments: A structural modeling approach*. Working paper, Owen Graduate School of Management, Vanderbilt University.

Ophir, E., Nass, C., & Wagner, A. D. (2011). Cognitive control in media multitaskers. <http://www.pnas.org/content/106/37/15583> Accessed 11.22.11.

Reeves, B., & Nass, C. (1998). The media equation: How people treat computers, television and new media like real people and places. Cambridge: Cambridge University Press.

Simon, H. A. (1971), Designing Organizations for an Information-Rich World. Martin Greenberger, *Computers, Communication, and the Public Interest*, Baltimore, MD: The Johns Hopkins Press.

Stone, L. (2009). Beyond simple multi-tasking: Continuous partial attention. <http:// lindastone.net/2009/11/30/beyond-simple-multi-tasking-continuous-partial-attention> Accessed 3.22.11.

Strayer, D. L., Watson, J. M., & Drews, F. A. (2010). *Cognitive distraction while multitasking in the automobile*. <http://www.psych.utah.edu/lab/appliedcognition/ publications.html> Accessed 11.29.11.

van Gorp, T. J. (2006). *Emotion, arousal, attention and flow: Chaining emotional states to improve human-computer interaction*. Master's degree project, Faculty of Environmental Design. Calgary: University of Calgary.

van Gorp, T.J. (2010). Design for Emotion and Flow. IA Summit 2010, Phoenix. ASIS&T.

Volvo Design. (2005). *Volvo design presentation. Design & emotion*. Gothenberg, Sweden.

Wickens, C. D., Gordon, S. E., & Liu, Y. (1997) *An introduction to human factors engineering*. Upper Saddle River, NJ: Longman.

Wickens, C. D., & Hollands, J. G. (2000). *Engineering psychology and human performance* (3rd ed.). Upper Saddle River, NJ: Prentice Hall.

Wittstein, I. S., Thiemann, D. R., Lima, J. A. C., Baughman, K. L., Schulman, S. P., & Gerstenblith, G., et al. (2005). Neurohumoral features of myocardial stunning due to sudden emotional stress. *New England Journal of Medicine, 352*(6), 539–548.

Yerkes, R. M., & Dodson, J. D. (1908). The relation of strength of stimulus to rapidity of habit-formation. *Journal of Comparative Neurology and Psychology, 18*, 459–482.

Where Do We Design for Emotion?

4

In Chapter 3, we talked about the importance of balancing users' emotional states to command attention and create the circumstances necessary for flow; the experience of being totally immersed in an activity. Flow can occur when people have clear goals and face challenges they know they can handle with their existing skills. When we face these challenges in an environment with reduced distraction and immediate feedback, highly immersive experiences can result (Csikszentmihalyi, 1990). Flow experiences stimulate us to give our best performance while providing us with an enjoyable and rewarding experience. The flow experiences that occur when we interact with products to face challenges can be the foundation for the development of ongoing relationships.

In this chapter, we'll examine how design communicates emotion and personality to your users. We'll demonstrate how design elements express and affect emotional responses and explain how those elements communicate a personality over time. Next, we'll explore several models that describe how to design for emotion and examine the different ways that people experience the emotion of love to get a better understanding of how to design relationships with products. Then, we'll explore the different personality traits that people look for in products. We'll talk about the two most important distinctions that people make when judging the personality of a product, and show you how to create those distinctions. Finally, we'll look at how people form relationships with things based on the emotions and personalities those things express.

Humans are wired to seek out and identify the expression of emotion in their environment.

PRODUCT PERSONALITIES

Previously, we mentioned that humans are wired to seek out and identify the expression of emotion in their environment, especially in things that seem animate (Fogg, 2003). Humans are such social animals that we perceive the expression of emotion in everything, including products, objects and websites.

FIG. 4.1 Poison Symbol

The poison symbol has likely prevented thousands of accidental poisonings. But, because it never changes, its personality is set.

Public Domain

In products, a "personality trait" is the long-term expression of a particular emotion.

Even people who consciously *know* that products aren't animate and don't have feelings, still respond emotionally when viewing, interacting and evaluating them (Reeves & Nass, 1998). In a survey of business professionals (none of whom were employed in technology) conducted by TrackVia (2011), three out of every five people reported yelling at their computers out of frustration. Rather than mere instruments, products should be described as "living objects with which people have relationships" (Jordan, 2000, p. 7). Through their relationships with products, people can experience a wide variety of emotions, including happiness or sadness, anger or contentment, relaxation or anxiety, pride or shame, and motivation or demotivation (Jordan, 2000).

We automatically and unconsciously perceive emotion in the form and content of things. In products, we can think of a "personality trait" as the long-term expression of a particular emotion. Though physical products usually remain the same, interactive and online products change over time as we use them. Because of these changes, the emotions that are communicated can also change over time. In an interactive product, the greater variety of emotional expressions designers can employ makes it possible to create the perception of a much more complex personality.

Every "thing" you've chosen is an expression of who you were, who you are, and who you want to be.

Envisioning the choice, use and ownership of a product in terms of a "relationship" will help you to make better decisions about the type of personality you create, and the way that personality is communicated through design. As we'll see, the same personality characteristics that attract us to other people in relationships are also involved in attracting us to products. In this sense, the products people use are more than just "things." They're closer to characters in the story of your life. Some play minor roles, while others have major parts, helping move the story forward.

FIG. 4.2 Material Goals and Aspirations

Material goals can be symbols of who we aspire to be.
© *Edie Adams*

Personality and Identity

As we mentioned in Chapter 1, although the relationships we have with things may appear to have little lasting impact, these objects are a reflection of the people who've chosen them. Every "thing" you've chosen, purchased, or used is an expression of who you were, who you are, and who you want to be. From the clothes you wear, to the car you drive, to the type of computer you use and the decor in the interior of your home; all of these things are expressions of your former self, your current identity and the potentials you aspire to reach (Csikszentmihalyi & Rochberg-Halton, 1981).

Things that are symbols of past accomplishments help to confirm our identity and sense of self through memory. One way that web applications have been making use of these symbols is through the addition of gaming elements like achievement badges. Sites like Empire Avenue and Foursquare offer trophies and badges to help motivate users by acknowledging their achievements as they happen and allowing them to collect badges as mementos.

Perceiving Emotion and Personality

The perception of emotion and personality is based on the information we receive from the senses of sight, hearing, touch, taste, and smell. These impressions are quick and unconscious (i.e., you don't have to think about them).

FIG. 4.3 Achievement Badges

Badge elements © *iStockPhoto.com*

We perceive product personalities based on the qualities of the same aesthetic and interactive cues that communicate human personality traits. In products, these qualities are communicated through design elements like the use of proportion, composition, layout, color, contrast, images, fonts, feedback sounds, user prompts and navigation. Depending on how all these elements are combined, your product can communicate a number of different personality traits.

> **We perceive product personality based on the same cues that communicate human personality.**

In our relationships with other people, personality traits play an important part in attraction and conversation. They determine both how we get along in the world and who we get along with. Like personality traits in humans, product personality traits communicate information about how attractive, trustworthy, reliable, exciting and innovative products are.

AESTHETICS AND INTERACTION

Aesthetics is the branch of philosophy that deals with sensory judgments of beauty and good taste (Zangwill, 2007). "Aesthetics" doesn't refer just to visual appearance, but also to judgments of what makes a sound, feeling, smell, or taste appealing. Although many companies are aware of the importance of aesthetics in attracting customers, many products are still launched with little attention invested in aesthetic appeal.

When technology staff in large organizations put out RFPs for software and products, aesthetics and ease of interaction may not be priorities for the people who evaluate and purchase the tools. When employees are restricted from using anything other than the approved tools, they simply have to make the best of the situation. Increasingly however, users have a greater number of choices in technology products and tools. As the consumerization of high technology becomes more widespread, users increasingly choose products that are also attractive and fun to use, rather than those that merely "get the job done."

What does this mean? It means that considering how your product "looks and feels" can help attract customers and increase sales. Attraction can also be the beginning of a relationship with the product that can result in long-term brand loyalty.

 "I'm in love! With SCRIVENER. He — sorry, it — has totally changed my life.

I was first introduced to SCRIVENER in an e-mail from my long-suffering Brother. I ignored him — sorry, it — completely. As if a piece of crummy software is going to make any difference to my creativity! I pressed delete.

Fortunately, I got a second chance. A writer friend of mine re-introduced me to SCRIVENER ('Haven't we met?' 'No, I don't think so.' 'I remember! Your brother introduced us! And you totally snubbed me! But fortunately I don't bear a grudge, and you can have me for a 30-day free trial, and then for life for a single payment of around £34.' If only all relationships were so straightforward.)

And now it's love. Proper head over heels. SCRIVENER is amazing. He's — sorry, it's — everything I could dream of in a word processor. Where to even begin? Everything about him — sorry, it — is incredible. Intuitive. Adaptive. User friendly in ways I couldn't ever have imagined from my mispent youth with other computer programmes. I never knew I could feel this way about anything I could download legally. I don't want to nauseate you. I don't want you tutting 'get a study'. But I've never known multiple functions like this before... Truly, he's — sorry, it's — made me into a whole new writer."

— Marie Phillips, **author of** *Gods Behaving Badly*.

FIG. 4.4 Scrivener Love Note/Testimonial

© *Litterature and Latte*

> **Considering how your product "looks and feels" can help attract customers and increase sales.**

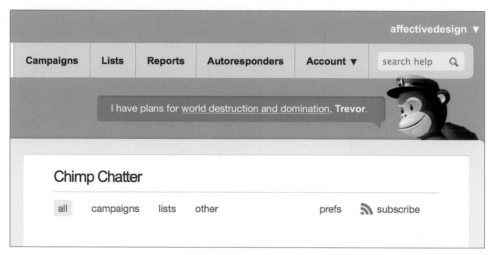

FIG. 4.5 MailChimp

http://mailchimp.com © *Rocket Science Group*

MailChimp is a good example of this. Although other email marketing services offered more features such as integrated surveys (TopTen Reviews, 2011), MailChimp's customer base reached over a million users (MailChimp.com, 2011) by prioritizing the aesthetics and interaction of the application to communicate a friendly and authentic personality.

Without pleasing aesthetics to attract users, the relationship may not begin.

Without pleasing aesthetics to attract the attention of users, the initial stages of the relationship building process may not occur. If the user has the option of purchasing: A) your product or B) a more attractive product with the same ease of use and functionality, you've likely just lost a sale. The quality of the aesthetics and interaction is more important when a product's functionality becomes commoditized, (e.g., vehicles, MP3 players). When many companies offer products that perform the same function, and are all similar in terms of capabilities, users can prioritize aesthetics and interaction over features and functionality.

MP3 players offer an obvious example. Although there were other MP3 players on the market with more features (Van Buskirk, 2003), the iPod, iPod Touch and iPod Nano have became the most widely used MP3 players, capturing 70 percent of the market and selling over 175 million units in the last ten years (Forstall, 2011).

Back in 2003, a CNET reviewer summed it up like this: "It's not the iPod, the operating system, or the iTunes software alone that makes the iPod so smooth to use—it's the way that all three work together seamlessly. Apple has a clear advantage over other portable-device manufacturers because the company controls the operating system, the computer hardware and the product design" (Van Buskirk 2003).

By creating a device that provided users with enough storage space to make their entire music collection portable, while also being attractive and easy to use (with the iTunes ecosystem), Apple managed to command the lion's share of online music sales.

RESPONSES, EXPERIENCES AND RELATIONSHIPS

Designing for emotion isn't just about creating an aesthetically pleasing product, an easy-to-use application, or a high-status brand. Although it could practically include any one of these things, in the end it's about understanding how the different aspects of a design combine to communicate a **personality** over time, and then tailoring that personality to your target audience or user group.

Design, development, and marketing professionals all play a part in communicating an authentic and consistent personality that engenders trust and helps to forge a relationship between the product they create and the person using it. Whether you're designing a website, a software application, or a physical product, you'll need to create appropriate emotional responses across several different levels.

Back in Chapter 1, we mentioned three categories of product requirements that address the different facets of users' emotional needs. As designers, we need to ensure that the products we create are *useful*, *usable* and *desirable* (Sanders, 1992). If the product doesn't *function* as promised, it has very little usefulness, so a relationship is not likely to form. If the product is difficult to *interact* with and unreliable, it's not usable, so any experience the user has will be negative. Finally, if the *aesthetics* of the product are not attractive and appealing to the users' senses, they likely won't find it desirable either.

> The different aspects of a design combine to communicate a personality over time.

Design Goals and Product Elements

Design Goals (Sanders 1992)	Desirable Aesthetically appealing	Usable Capacity to be understood, learned & utilized	Useful Accomplishes what it was designed for
Product Elements	Aesthetics How the product looks and feels	Interaction How the user interacts with the product	Function What the product does
RELATIONSHIP TO OTHER MODELS	← EXPERIENCE OVER TIME →		
Triune Brain (McLean 1990)	Reptilian Brain Unconscious, instant	Mammalian Brain Conscious and unconscious	Neo-Mammalian Brain Conscious, slow, deliberate

FIG. 4.6 **Design Goals and Product Elements**

(Sanders, 1992; McLean, 1990). © *Trevor van Gorp*

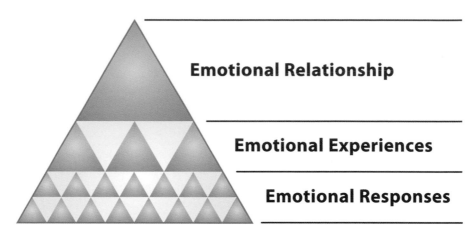

FIG. 4.7 **Responses > Experiences > Relationships**

Adapted from (Demir, 2008). © Trevor van Gorp

In Chapter 2, we learned that emotions originate in different parts of the brain. Triune brain theory describes the human brain as being composed of the reptilian, mammalian, and neomammalian brains (McLean, 1990). Each portion of the brain is responsible for different things. The reptilian brain is automatic and generates unconscious *emotional responses*. The mammalian brain is also largely unconscious and creates our *emotional experiences*. The neomammalian brain is conscious and is where we form *emotional relationships*. Over time, emotional responses combine to form experiences, which combine to create relationships.

Emotional responses combine to form experiences, which combine to create relationships.

Even though aesthetics may be the first thing most people will notice and unconsciously process in the Reptilian brain (e.g., "it's so pretty/ugly!"), frustrations with interaction and usability will provoke status judgments and emotional responses from the mammalian brain (e.g., "why isn't it doing what I tell it to?"). Problems with functionality will provoke conscious emotional responses from the neo-mammalian brain (e.g., "why doesn't this thing do what it says it'll do!"), raising questions about integrity and eroding trust.

Even though discussions of emotion often focus almost exclusively on the aesthetics or desirability of a product, the deeper qualities of usability and usefulness still need to be there. Relationships with products whose designers have only considered only aesthetics are like superficial human relationships based solely on physical attraction—they don't tend to last long. For products where the context of use is a short, hands-off encounter (such as the concept car in Chapter 1), that may be fine. But for products such as software and web applications, or even something as simple as a doorbell, encouraging repeated usage over time is both a business goal and a user need.

FIG. 4.8 Doorbell

© jlcst - Fotolia.com

Emotional Design Models

Like most complex design problems, tailoring design solutions to users' emotions requires a broad understanding of several different perspectives. In order to communicate a few of these different perspectives, we're going to briefly explore three models that have been created to describe the process of designing for emotion. Each model offers a slightly different but valuable perspective on the design of emotions and the formation of relationships.

The three models are:

- Levels of emotional processing (Norman, 2004)
- Types of user benefits (Jordan, 2000)
- Products as objects, agents, and events (Desmet, 2002)

Levels of Emotional Processing

Norman's (2004) model describes the different levels on which users' process emotions and is more reflective of research in cognition and neuroscience. From his studies of emotion, Norman has suggested three levels of brain processing to explain the different emotional reactions we experience:

- **Visceral Level**
- **Behavioral Level**
- **Reflective Level**

Visceral Level

The visceral level is linked to the most primitive part of the brain (i.e., reptilian brain). Having evolved slowly over time, this part of the brain translates sensory information into nearly instant, unconscious judgments about conditions that have been indicators of food, shelter, safety, and mating opportunities throughout our evolutionary history (Norman, 2004).

The visceral level is linked to the reptilian brain.

The main requirement of the behavioral level is feedback.

Behavioral Level

Behavioral design is about the experience of using a product to fulfill needs. It is composed of both usability and performance. Usability measures how easy it is for the user to understand how the product works and utilize its functions. Performance measures how well a product performs the functions it's meant to accomplish (Norman, 2004).

The reflective level extends over time to process self-image and identity.

The main requirement of the behavioral level is feedback. Feedback can consist of information directed at any of the senses, but it is most appropriate when feedback comes from the object of attention. In physical products, for example, feel offers important feedback about materials, construction and the operation of mechanisms and controls (Norman, 2004).

Reflective Level

This emotional level is the most affected by culture, education and experience and can override the other two levels. Reflective design functions at the level of reasoning, interpretation and understanding. Another distinction between the reflective level and the other levels is time. The visceral and behavioral levels function in the present moment, and describe the experiences one has when viewing or interacting with a product. The reflective level extends over time to the past and the future. Self-image and identity are created within the reflective level (Norman, 2004).

Types of User Benefits

Jordan's (2000) model describes the different types of benefits that products can provide to users:

- **Hedonic Benefits**
- **Practical Benefits**
- **Emotional Benefits**

Hedonic Benefits

Hedonic benefits arise from the sensory and aesthetic pleasures.

Hedonic benefits are a result of the sensory and aesthetic pleasures people can experience when interacting with products. This can involve the appreciation of an object for its aesthetic considerations, or the enjoyment of the tactile qualities associated with handling a product.

Practical Benefits

Practical benefits are the benefits that result from completing tasks to realize goals. Finishing a proposal may not realize your goal of creating a successful business, but it's one task in the hundreds of small tasks that will.

Emotional Benefits

Emotional benefits are the longer-term benefits that arise from our relationships with products. Driving a convertible might be exciting and fun, but the accomplishment of owning a convertible might give the user a sense of pride or heightened status (Jordan, 2000).

Products as Objects, Agents, and Events

Desmet's (2002) model describes the types of evaluations or appraisals that users make when forming judgments about products:

- **Products as Objects**
- **Products as Agents**
- **Products as Events**

These are evaluations of value (i.e., good or bad) in relation to a human concern. In this model, our concerns are judged against our *attitudes, standards* and *goals*.

Products as Objects

When our attention is attracted to a product as an object, we are mainly concerned with how aesthetically appealing it is. When the aesthetics match our attitudes

Our concerns are judged against our *attitudes, standards*, and *goals*.

Design Goals and Emotional Design Models

Design Goals (Sanders 1992)	**Desirable** Aesthetically appealing	**Usable** Capacity to be understood, learned & utilized	**Useful** Accomplishes what it was designed for
Product Elements	**Aesthetics** How the product looks and feels	**Interaction** How the user interacts with the product	**Function** What the product does
RELATIONSHIP TO DESIGN MODELS	EXPERIENCE OVER TIME →→→		
Types of Benefits (Jordan 2000)	**Hedonic Benefits** Sensory and aesthetic pleasures	**Practical Benefits** Result from the completion of tasks	**Emotional Benefits** Effects on user's emotions
Type of Appraisals (Desmet 2002)	**Objects** Does it appeal to my attitudes?	**Agents** Does it meet my standards?	**Events** Does it help reach my goals?
Levels of Processing (Norman 2004)	**Visceral** Aesthetic and tactile qualities	**Behavioral** Effectiveness and ease of use	**Reflective** Self-image, personal satisfaction, memories
RELATIONSHIP TO OTHER MODELS	EXPERIENCE OVER TIME →→→		
Type of Reactions (Demir 2008)	**Responses** Automatic	**Experiences** Occur through interaction	**Relationship** Builds over time
Triune Brain (McLean 1990)	**Reptilian Brain** Unconscious, instant	**Mammalian Brain** Conscious and unconscious	**Neo-Mammalian Brain** Conscious, slow, deliberate

FIG. 4.9 Design Goals and Emotional Design Models

Adapted from (Sanders, 1992; Jordan, 2000; Desmet, 2002; Norman, 2004; Demir, 2008; McLean, 1990). © Trevor van Gorp

around what is appealing, we feel pleasure and attraction. Emotional responses like this include positive results like love, negative results like disgust and neutral results like indifference.

Products as Agents

When a product is evaluated as an agent, we are concerned with how well it meets our standards. When we evaluate our experiences with products against our standards, judgments can produce emotions like appreciation and admiration or disappointment and contempt.

When we say we "love" products, what do we really mean?

Products as Events

When we evaluate our relationship with a product as an event, we judge how well the product helps us to realize our future goals. Anticipating the benefits of owning a product creates an emotional response. Owning an expensive car might be perceived as conveying the benefits of higher status to the owner. The anticipation of positive benefits can also make the product more desirable (Desmet, 2002).

How Do I Love Thee?

Throughout our lives, we've all been exposed to different types of relationships, both personally and through the media. We have acquaintances, companions, friends, BFFs (best friends forever), lovers, wives and husbands. Some relationships are short, passionate flings based solely on simple attraction and lust. Some are deep, intimate friendships formed through ongoing interaction and conversation. Others are simple marriages of convenience with commitment but little passion or intimacy.

Even though all of these relationships might seem to be very different, many of the people involved would likely still label the feelings they share as "love." This suggests that, as a culture, we may be using the same term to describe what are really several different emotions, making it difficult to understand what "love" really means. For example, people will emphatically say how much they "love" certain products. But when they say they "love" products, what do they really mean? Is it the same type of love they have for their spouse or their children? What about their pets?

Let's take a look at the different emotions that people call "love" to get a better understanding of how to design relationships with products. Is love the appropriate emotion for every type of product relationship? What other emotions are required to feel love? Examining how the different types of love relate to the different models of designing for emotion will assist us in understanding what they all share.

Forms of Love

Sternberg (1988) described human relationships in terms of three forms of love: Passion, Intimacy and Commitment.

> **Passion:** Aesthetics-oriented
> - Infatuation
> - Quick, unconscious
> - The result of attraction
>
> **Intimacy:** Interaction-oriented
> - Friendship
> - Unconscious
> - The result of connection built through interaction
>
> **Commitment:** Function-oriented
> - Perception of personality based on aesthetics and interaction
> - Conscious
> - The result of trust built through consistent results over multiple interactions

Passion

Passion is based on aesthetics. We're attracted to certain people because of how they look, sound, smell, feel and taste. These aesthetic cues communicate information about health, reproductive fitness, fertility and social status to potential partners (Buss, 2003). We evaluate these cues quickly and unconsciously, without thinking about them.

Passion is based on aesthetics.

This form of love would describe the quick fling or one-night stand. If a relationship had Passion, but lacked Intimacy and Commitment, it would be called infatuation or lust (Sternberg, 1988). Relationships based only on Passion tend to burn out quickly. We tend to be attracted to people who are about as attractive, wealthy and educated as ourselves.

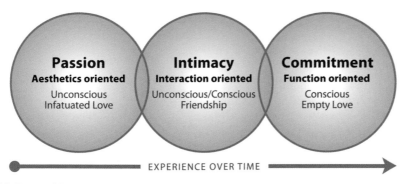

FIG. 4.10 Forms of Love

Adapted from (Sternberg, 1988). © Trevor van Gorp

Intimacy

Sternberg (1988) defines **Intimacy** as friendship, rather than just sexual intimacy. Achieving Intimacy requires conversation and interaction over time. You don't really get to know someone without spending time together in a variety of situations.

Intimacy is friendship.

When we engage in conversation with another person, we make unconscious evaluations of them. We judge whether our styles of interacting are complementary or similar and conflicting. Does the other person constantly interrupt when you're talking? Are you always butting heads over who's in charge? Does he or she give you the amount of respect you feel you require?

If all you had with another person was Intimacy, you'd probably be very close friends. However, you'd likely not feel much Passion or sexual attraction. If someone has ever said "I love you, but I'm not in love with you," it's likely that they were talking about feeling Intimacy without Passion.

Commitment

Without passion or intimacy, commitment is merely empty love.

Commitment is a mutually agreed-upon connection. In marriage, we consciously enter into a public contract with another person. Even in long-term relationships, the majority of couples in the western world still *commit* to an exclusive partnership. Yet, without passion or Intimacy, a Commitment is merely an empty agreement. If the only thing you had with someone was a commitment, without any Passion or Intimacy, you'd have what Sternberg (1988, p. 268) calls "empty love."

Depending on the context, one or more of the three forms of love can occur at different times in a relationship. In the western world, Commitment usually comes after we've had a chance to evaluate our levels of Passion and Intimacy. At that point, we've (hopefully) decided whether the other person's personality is a good fit for our own. In other parts of the world, however, this may not be the case. Arranged marriages are one example of a relationship that begins with commitment, while passion and intimacy are expected to develop later.

Passion (Desirable), Intimacy (Usable), and Commitment (Useful)

You may be wondering how all of this relates to designing emotional experiences that encourage relationships. Well, to start with, we could draw some parallels between the three types of love and the three categories of product requirements that we identified earlier: *useful, usable,* and *desirable* (Sanders, 1992).

Useful, usable, and desirable represent the design goals that the designer has ideally realized in the product. The three forms of love describe users' emotional reactions to the different levels of product experience.

Design Goals and Forms of Love

Design Goals (Sanders 1992)	Desirable Aesthetically appealing	Usable Capacity to be understood, learned & utilized	Useful Accomplishes what it was designed for
Forms of Love (Sternberg 1988)	Passion Infatuated Love	Intimacy Friendship	Commitment Empty Love
RELATIONSHIP TO OTHER MODELS	EXPERIENCE OVER TIME →		
Triune Brain (McLean 1990)	Reptilian Brain Unconscious, instant	Mammalian Brain Conscious and unconscious	Neo-Mammalian Brain Conscious, slow, deliberate

FIG. 4.11 **Design Goals and Forms of Love**

(Sanders, 1992; Sternberg, 1988; McLean, 1990). © Trevor van Gorp

The user is attracted to the product's aesthetics, triggering the *desire* or *passion* to approach. If the user finds that the product is usable and easy to interact with, he or she may begin to feel greater connection or *intimacy* with the product. If the product then reliably and consistently fulfills its purpose, trust and *commitment* can result. At this point, the product has satisfied all the requirements for establishing a highly rewarding relationship. This process then begins again, continuing over time to form deeper relationships. As we mentioned earlier, some products are more disposable in nature and require only a "short-term" relationship. But what about relationships that involve different combinations of the three forms of love?

The three forms of love describe the users' different emotional reactions to a product.

The Types of Love

Just as there are different types of relationships between people, there are different types of relationships between people and products. You can envision every relationship as being made up of some combination of the three forms of love. When we group the forms of love into different combinations, we get additional types. These types describe many of the common relationships we see around us.

Types of Love

- Passion + Intimacy = Romantic Love
- Passion + Commitment = Fatuous or Illusory Love
- Intimacy + Commitment = Companionate Love
- Passion + Intimacy + Commitment = Consummate Love
  (Sternberg, 1988.)

We can visualize the different ways that the three forms of love can be combined over time to create the different types of love.

Many relationships can be described as some combination of three forms of love.

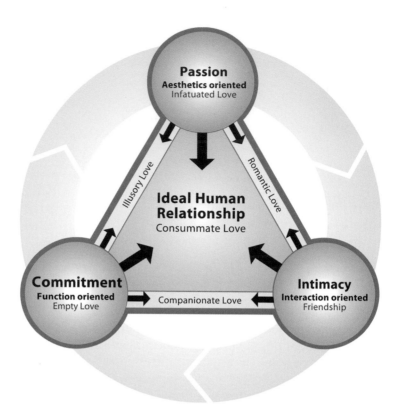

FIG. 4.12 The Forms and Types of Love

Adapted from (Sternberg, 1988). © Trevor van Gorp

Passion (Desirable) + Intimacy (Usable) = Romantic Love

When you combine the attraction of Passion with the interaction and conversation of Intimacy, you get **Romantic Love**. In human relationships, Romantic Love describes sexual attraction, along with a feeling of deep, intimate connection, but no formal commitment.

Virgin Mobile offers attractive, usable phones with no contractual commitment. Its target audience is young and seeks to avoid long-term commitments. Even the tagline of the web page (Why "Go" Beyond Talk?) could be taken as a double entendre for moving to the next (i.e., physical) stage of a relationship.

Passion (Desirable) + Commitment (Useful) = Illusory Love

Combining Passion and Commitment without any Intimacy generally makes a poor foundation for a long-term relationship. This may be why Sternberg (1998) calls this combination **Fatuous** or **Illusory** love. An example of this type of relationship would be a "sugar daddy" relationship, in which one partner is involved purely due to attraction and one is involved purely for commitment.

Marketing that promises more than the actual product delivers is one source of this type of Illusory love. We may commit to a transaction and purchase a product based purely on the marketing only to find that although it looks good and functions, it's difficult to operate and frustrating to use.

Intimacy (Usable) + Commitment (Useful) = Companionate Love

When we combine Intimacy and Commitment, we get a set of good companions, hence the label **Companionate love**. This type of relationship describes a couple who are no longer physically attracted to each other, but remain friendly and committed.

When we think of companionate love, we can imagine more utilitarian products. They're easy to use and reliable and they perform the task they were designed for. But they don't create that spark of attraction, so there's little passion involved. Your hairbrush might be a good example. You don't really think about your hairbrush much when you're not around it. But, like the loss of an old friend, you may only really appreciate it once it's gone.

> **When we think of companionate love, we think of utilitarian products.**

Passion + Intimacy + Commitment = Consummate Love

Occasionally, there are those rare relationships that seem to have it all. Most of us know one or two of these select couples. Such relationships seem to encompass all three forms of love. They've achieved what Sternberg (1988) calls all-consuming or **Consummate love**. They're passionately attracted to one another, have a deep, intimate friendship, and a strong, abiding commitment.

A quick search for the phrase "iPhone love" on Twitter approximately one month after the launch of the iPhone 4S produced a nearly endless stream of tweets. It appears that people may even have Consummate love for their iPhones (and we're no exception to that statement).

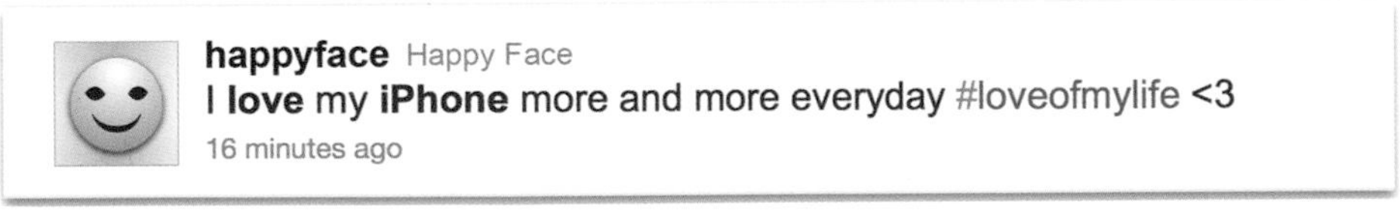

> **It appears that people really do "love" their iPhones.**

happyface Happy Face
I **love** my **iPhone** more and more everyday #loveofmylife <3
16 minutes ago

FIG. 4.13 **Tweet from Search for "iPhone Love" on Twitter**

http://twitter.com. © Trevor van Gorp

Three Brains, Three Levels

When we compare the levels in each of the models, some curious similarities begin to emerge. Each researcher has all come up with a model that describes similar factors, but from a slightly different perspective. Identifying these similarities can advance our understanding of how people relate to products.

Physiologically, we can relate these models to the traces of evolution left in the brain, as some scientists theorize that emotional processing occurs in all three "brains" (Norman, 2004).

As we mentioned in Chapter 2, the Reptilian brain is reputed to control basic survival and mating instincts. The processing that occurs in the Reptilian brain is nearly instantaneous and unconscious. This explains why attraction to aesthetic

Attraction to aesthetic cues can occur without thinking.

Design Goals, Forms of Love and Design Models

	Desirable	Usable	Useful
Design Goals (Sanders 1992)	Aesthetically appealing	Capacity to be understood, learned & utilized	Accomplishes what it was designed for
Product Elements	**Aesthetics** How the product looks and feels	**Interaction** How the user interacts with the product	**Function** What the product does
Forms of Love (Sternberg 1988)	**Passion** Infatuated Love	**Intimacy** Friendship	**Commitment** Empty Love
RELATIONSHIP TO DESIGN MODELS	EXPERIENCE OVER TIME →		
Types of Benefits (Jordan 2000)	**Hedonic Benefits** Sensory and aesthetic pleasures	**Practical Benefits** Result from the completion of tasks	**Emotional Benefits** Effects on user's emotions
Type of Appraisals (Desmet 2002)	**Objects** Does it appeal to my attitudes?	**Agents** Does it meet my standards?	**Events** Does it help reach my goals?
Levels of Processing (Norman 2004)	**Visceral** Aesthetic and tactile qualities	**Behavioral** Effectiveness and ease of use	**Reflective** Self-image, personal satisfaction, memories
RELATIONSHIP TO OTHER MODELS	EXPERIENCE OVER TIME →		
Type of Reactions (Demir 2008)	**Responses** Unconscious	**Experiences** Conscious & unconscious	**Relationship** Conscious
Triune Brain (McLean 1990)	**Reptilian Brain** Instant, automatic,	**Mammalian Brain** Status judgments	**Neo-Mammalian Brain** Slow, deliberate

FIG. 4.14 Design Goals, Forms of Love and Design Models

Adapted from (Sanders, 1992; Sternberg, 1988; Jordan, 2000; Desmet, 2002; Norman, 2004; Demir, 2008; McLean, 1990). © Trevor van Gorp

cues can occur without thinking. You don't have to think about whether something is physically attractive—it either is, or it isn't! At the level of the Reptilian brain, all the models focus on the aesthetic or formal properties of the thing itself. If the aesthetics and sensory properties of the product are appealing, the user responds with pleasure and attraction.

At the level of the Mammalian brain, the focus is on how the product interacts and performs, the benefits that use brings, and how it lives up to our standards.

Our social instincts govern the behavior of mammals in groups or packs. At this level, attraction can combine with intimacy through social interaction. On this level, all the models focus on the interactive properties of the product, the standards we judge them by, and the practical benefits that arise from their use.

Attraction can combine with intimacy through social interaction.

In the Neo-mammalian or human brain, the focus is on what the product says about us (both to ourselves and others), the memories it creates, the emotional benefits it brings, and whether it helps to fulfill our goals. At this level, we can see how each of the previous exchanges between the user and the product has communicated the personality or brand image of the product or service.

If users form relationships with things based on the personalities they perceive, how do we decide what types of personality traits to communicate through design?

PERSONALITY TRAITS AND DESIGN

For many companies creating consumer products, the answer to the question of what personality to design is to portray their products in a neutral way. As you can imagine, by trying to appeal to as many people as possible, these personalities usually fail to trigger much of an emotional response. Although people may not strongly like or dislike bland products, they also don't connect very deeply with them. Before someone can decide whether to connect with you, you have to show that person who you are. There's always a risk of rejection, but the rewards of acceptance can be worth the risk. Strong social connections come from emotional experiences shared between people who play complementary roles during interaction.

Exchanges between the user and the product communicate a personality.

Unless you're dealing with a very homogenous audience, your target user group will likely include a mix of personality types. Generally, large groups are pretty evenly split amongst personality types (Reeves & Nass, 1998). In the same way that no one is liked by everybody, there'll be people that simply don't connect with the personality of your product. However, the good news is that if your product expresses a consistent personality, it will generally be liked more than a product without a clearly identifiable personality (Reeves & Nass, 1998).

If a product's formal properties communicate one personality, but other elements of the design communicate a different personality, the inconsistencies alone can be enough to make people lose trust or question integrity. If the product was a person, people might say "there's something just not right about him."

If your product expresses a consistent personality, people will like and trust it more.

The Traits of a Good Design

Design researcher Ayca Çakmakli from Smart Design identified ideal product personality traits based on the way people judge others as potential mates. Based in evolutionary psychology, Çakmakli's (2010) research identifies seven traits that people look for in products and mates:

- **Attractiveness (sexy, cute, beautiful, graceful)**
- **Status (lifestyle, social class, value system)**
- **Intelligence (smart, adaptive, intuitive, functions well)**
- **Trustworthiness (loyal, safe, trusting)**
- **Empathy (understanding, adaptive, communicative)**
- **Ambitious (innovative, forward thinking, aspiring, motivated)**
- **Exciting (good sense of humor, positively surprising, creative)**

We'll use Çakmakli's list as a framework to discuss each trait.

FIG. 4.15 Trait Framework Cards

Courtesy of (Çakmakli, 2010). © Ayça Çakmakli

Attractiveness (Sexy, Cute, Beautiful, Graceful)

Çakmakli (2010) says that attractiveness is often the most important trait for many males in choosing life partners (Buss, 2003). As we mentioned earlier, aesthetics cause an automatic, unconscious emotional response. From an evolutionary standpoint, attractiveness, and symmetry have been linked to fertility (Buss, 2003). You may notice that the vast majority of products are symmetrical, with each side being a mirror reflection of the other.

In nature, certain waist/hip proportions have been linked with attraction and greater levels of fertility in women (Buss, 2003). Similarly, certain waist/shoulder proportions in men have been judged to be most attractive to women (Horvath, 1981; Dixson, Halliwell, East, Wignarajah, & Anderson, 2003). Both of these numbers are very close to what is known as the Golden Ratio or Golden Proportion (i.e., 1.61803399 or approximately 1.62), a number that is repeatedly found in nature and underlies the design of some of history's most memorable products and architecture (Elam, 2001).

Certain waist/ hip proportions have been linked with attraction and fertility in women.

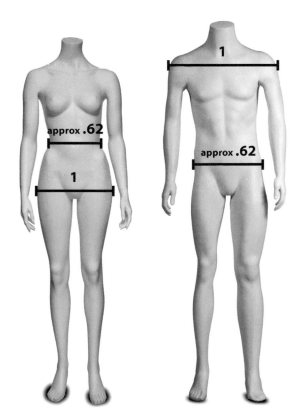

FIG. 4.16 Attractive Proportions

Proportions unconsciously determine attractiveness and can also indicate fertility

© iStockPhoto.com; additions, © Trevor van Gorp

Through instinct and association, the same proportions that cause unconscious responses when we view sexually attractive people cause similar (albeit less intense) responses when we view attractive products. Nature has designed things that are aesthetically beautiful to trigger feelings of pleasure and desire.

Things that are aesthetically beautiful trigger feelings of pleasure and desire.

The more attractive a baby is, the more time adults spend looking at the child (Hildebrandt & Fitzgerald, 1978). Attractive infants are thought to be more competent than less attractive babes by child care providers (Casey & Ritter, 2002). This means that attractive babies are thus likely to receive more attention, beginning a cycle that can continue through life.

When people look at infants (especially attractive ones), the reward centers of the brain are activated. The raising of children requires a huge investment of time, energy, and resources. It is thought that the cuteness of infants increases the likelihood of parental investment and helps ensure infant survival (Kringelbach et al., 2008).

In humans, physical attractiveness affects how well people are liked, trusted, and followed. "All else being equal, attractive people are more persuasive than those who are unattractive" (Fogg, 2003, p. 92). In a similar fashion, products

FIG. 4.17 Attractive Babies Receive More Attention
Attractive infants receive more attention from adults than less attractive babies.
© Anatoliy Samara - Fotolia.com

that are physically attractive are more persuasive than unattractive ones. Physical attractiveness can also lead to other assumptions, like reliability, intelligence, capability and credibility (Fogg, 2003).

Every time you look at an attractive baby (or an attractive product), you feel positive feelings. Over time, this creates an association between the feelings and the baby, that can then affect subsequent judgments. For attractive products, this translates into an unexpected bonus. The more attractive that users found a product, the easier they perceived it was to use (i.e., become intimate with). According to Sonderegger and Sauer (2010), usability and aesthetics have been positively correlated across a range of studies. Attractive things give us feelings of pleasure, which makes us want to continue interacting with them, creating a positive feedback loop.

Physical attractiveness affects how well people are liked, trusted and followed.

FIG. 4.18 Dornbracht Tara Faucet

Using the Tara faucet is both an aesthetic and interactive experience. The water flow is an aesthetically pleasing continuation of the faucet itself, while the feel and performance of the controls evokes a precise lab instrument.
© Edie Adams

Social Status (Lifestyle, Social Class, Value System)

Social status describes how much regard others give to a person.

Social status is highlighted by Çakmakli (2010) as the most important trait many women seek in life partners. The term "social status" describes how much regard others voluntarily give to a person (Kemper, 1978). In the evolutionary sense, status is seen as helping to ensure the survival of any offspring, as a higher-status mating partner will likely have greater access to resources. Status is an important characteristic to consider in the context of product design. Any product that is seen by others can be viewed as a symbol of status.

Social status comes in several forms. Status may be also ascribed or achieved (Foladare, 1969). It can be ascribed due to age, gender, race or state of health, and achieved through accomplishment. It can include both material and cultural status (Jordan, 2000). Possessing products with the mark of expensive brands gives the impression that the owner has material wealth, conferring *material status*.

Having the proper "taste" or knowing which products are "proper" or "cool" within a user's cultural group confers *cultural status* (Jordan, 2000). Most of us are familiar with the cultural status conveyed by owning particular brands. But, maintaining cultural status can also involve minimizing the social stigma involved in dealing with an illness or medical condition.

Social status comes in several forms, including *material* and *cultural status*.

People have both positive and negative associations with the display of status. Although the display of some level of material status may be attractive to our unconscious, Mammalian brains, extreme displays of material status can be perceived as vulgar or lacking in cultural status by our Neo-Mammalian brains. (Jordan, 2000).

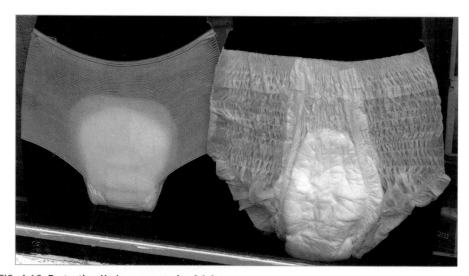

FIG. 4.19 **Protective Undergarments for Adults**

Some medical devices are designed to manage medical conditions in order to help preserve self-esteem and social status.

© *David Shankbone, Creative Commons*

FIG. 4.20 Conspicuous Display of Material Status

Conspicuous displays of *material status* can be perceived as lacking in *cultural status*.
© *iStockPhoto.com*

Intelligence (Smart, Adaptive, Intuitive, Functions Well)

Without minimal intelligence, people have difficulty handling the challenges
of daily life, like work, intimate relationships, children and other obligations
(Çakmakli, 2010). In products, intelligence can be measured by how well
something functions and how easy it is to communicate and interact with.

Intelligence can also be communicated through the features or capabilities of a
product. A clear example of this is the emergence of so-called "smartphones".
These phones possess much greater capabilities than regular cell phones. Because
of this, the natural human tendency is to see the phone as "smarter" or more
intelligent.

Trustworthiness (Loyal, Safe, Trusting)

Çakmakli (2010) describes trust as an important part of all relationships. Trust
is built through the fulfillment of promises. This includes the promises you've
actually made to someone explicitly (e.g., contracts and commitments) as well
promises that that are assumed or implicit (e.g., "this website isn't selling my
data").

Trustworthiness also influences credibility. Credibility is the perception of
believability, a quality that's assigned on the basis of "perceived trustworthiness
and perceived expertise" (Fogg, 2003, p. 123). Products are "likely to be perceived
as credible when they are aesthetically pleasing to users, confirm their positive
expectations, or show signs of being powerful" (Fogg, 2003, p. 135).

**Trust is built
through the
fulfillment of
promises.**

Anticipating and responding to user needs can convey a sense of empathy.

Seller Rating: ⭐⭐⭐⭐☆ **90% positive** over the last twelve months (10, 581, total ratings)

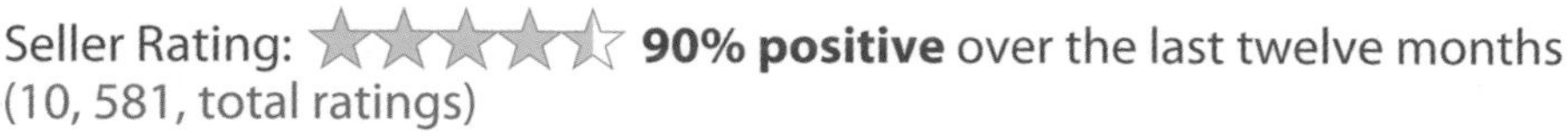

FIG. 4.21 Seller Ratings

Ratings of sellers help you trust them with your information.
© *Trevor van Gorp*

Empathy (Understanding, Adaptive, Communicative)

Çakmakli (2010) describes empathy in the context of design research and understanding user needs. Representing the user's perspective is an example of employing empathy during the design process. In a product, anticipating user needs and offering help right when the user needs it can also convey a sense of empathy. Humor and an open channel for feedback are two ways to help make the user feel that his or her problems are acknowledged and understood.

Exciting (Good Sense of Humor, Positively Surprising, Creative)

Surprise is directly linked to a heightened level of arousal.

In rewarding human relationships, people spontaneously express positive emotions towards each other. Stories of romantic love are filled with unexpected surprises and gifts like flowers and jewelry. Ludden, Schifferstein, and Hekkert (2008) describe positive surprise as a valid strategy in design that both draws attention and reinforces positive memories. When surprised, our heartbeat and breathing rate tends to increase with the excitement.

In products, we can also convey excitement through the use of positive surprise. The John Fluevog shoe company employs humor throughout the company's website, packaging and even on its shoes to help convey an irreverent and offbeat personality that appeals to those who wear its products. The bottom of the sole of a pair of Fluevog Angels is inscribed with the text "Resists alkali, water, acid, fatigue, and Satan!" Positive surprises like this help to form strong positive memories of the product. Fluevog is also a great example of a company that consistently expresses a quirky personality across brand channels. Not everyone loves Fluevog shoes, but those who do *really* love them.

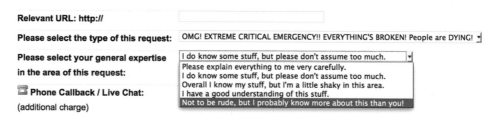

FIG. 4.22 Dreamhost Support Screen

Dreamhost's support screen uses empathy and humor to help the user feel that his or her pain is understood.
© *Dreamhost - New Dream Network, LLC*

Ambitious (Innovative, Forward Thinking, Aspiring, Motivated)

Between two people in a relationship, ambition can create positive, hopeful emotions that are shared between both partners. In products, ambition is expressed through innovation. People want to be associated with products and brands that are embracing new technology and making things better, rather than holding to outdated models (Çakmakli, 2010). One sign of ambition is the creation of new types of products or systems that have never existed before. Sometimes, it doesn't even need to be a new system, but merely a more useful, usable and desirable arrangement of existing components.

Earlier, we mentioned that MP3 players had been around for some time before the launch of the iPod and iTunes. Together, the hardware and software made it easy for technically challenged users to put songs on to their music player. The combination of simple software for getting the music off CDs, a large hard drive, and an easy interface for accessing the music made all the difference.

In products, ambition is expressed through innovation.

GENDER AND STEREOTYPES

Now that we've explored personality traits, let's take a look at the role gender plays in our perceptions of personality. When you begin to practice design with a greater focus on tailoring your product to suit users' emotional needs, you won't be able to ignore the issue of gender for long. It's difficult to have any kind of balanced discussion of gender issues without first talking about stereotypes.

FIG. 4.23 **Women in Technology?**

http://instagr.am © *Lori Cavalluci*

FIG. 4.24 Carlashes
Indicators of gender personalization are showing up in the oddest places.
© *Trevor van Gorp*

The problem with stereotypes and generalizations occurs when they're not based on any kind of verifiable data, or when they're vestiges of past prejudices that are simply no longer applicable (if they ever were). The prevailing view of the last few decades has been that gender and gender roles are culturally constructed and then reinforced by parents, teachers and peers. Recently however, research in neuroscience and evolutionary psychology has shown that gender differences, although undoubtedly influenced by culture, may be based more in biology than was once thought (Harasty, Double, Halliday, Kril, & McRitchie, 1997; Halpern, 2000).

What's needed is a richer, more multifaceted view of gender.

Perhaps what's needed is for us to develop a richer and more multifaceted view of gender that acknowledges and respects the innate differences between the sexes, while also appreciating that each individual should be free to express their gender as they see fit.

Masculine and Feminine

Masculine and feminine stereotypes in the media and popular culture are all around us. Very few of us have the masculinized physique of a pro wrestler or the feminized figure of a Barbie doll. Still, there's no denying that some men seem more stereotypically masculine than others and some women seem more stereotypically feminine than others. Because most men tend to be are relatively masculine in their appearance, speech and behaviors, and most women tend to be relatively feminine in theirs, gender has become associated with the physical and behavioral characteristics

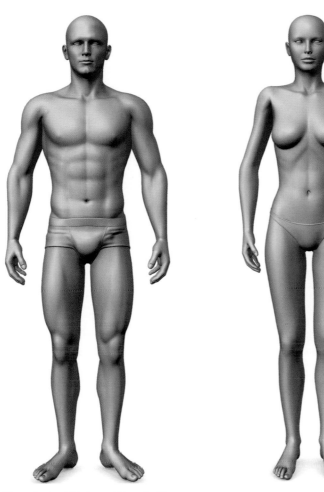

FIG. 4.25 Stereotypical Male and Female Figures

© http://www.hiped.com - Fotolia.com

of each sex (Dutton, 2003). Our tendency, then, is to think that men possess exclusively "masculine" traits, and women possess exclusively "feminine" traits.

Jung theorized that each person's psyche contained a shadow composed of their repressed or unexpressed energies. The shadow is the energy (or part of themselves) that each person is often forced to repress or suppress (von Franz, 1978). For most men, this repressed energy tends to be more feminine in nature and is called the *anima*. For most women, this repressed energy tends to be more masculine in nature and is called the *animus*. The ultimate goal is to successfully incorporate these complementary, yet seemingly contradictory aspects of one's personality to become an authentic individual (von Franz, 1978).

The goal is to incorporate these complementary aspects of personality.

FIG. 4.26 Yin/Yang

The notion of the anima and animus echoes viewpoints seen in other cultures and religions. In Taoist philosophy, for example, the universe and everything in it is interpreted as being composed of complementary yet opposing forces. This idea is symbolized in the form of the Yin/Yang. In this Taoist symbol, the outer circle represents the "whole," and each whole (whatever it may be) is composed of complementary energies that, while opposing in character, are both interconnected and interdependent (Tzu, 2006).

Because of this interdependence, there can be no dark without light and no masculine without feminine. It is only by comparing one to the other that the differences become apparent. Viewing products with this perspective brings a different focus to design. When we move past the stereotypes that "men are exclusively masculine" and "women are exclusively feminine," we can begin to picture each individual as a complex mix of both masculine and feminine traits. Embracing this perspective allows us to imagine product personalities that strike a balance between the qualities of the masculine and those of the feminine, providing clients and their customers with products that fulfill their needs, regardless of gender.

Each product is a complex mix of both masculine and feminine traits.

When the first Macintosh computer appeared in 1984, "Jack Tramiel, the grizzled macho-boss of Commodore, thought it looked like a *girly* device that would be best sold in boutiques" (Naughton, 2011). Now that Apple has established a small empire of boutique-like retail stores all over the world, it appears that Tramiel was right, but not in the derogatory way that he intended.

FIG. 4.27 Apple Macintosh Computer
The Macintosh communicates a mixture of masculine and feminine traits.
© *Schlaier*

With this insight, we can view the personalities of products as reflections of both biology and culture. Like stereotypical people, stereotypical products can be uninteresting and unattractive. Products that merely support rigid stereotypes often wind up failing to serve the needs of their target audience. In our opinion, the best products successfully incorporate both masculine and feminine qualities to create something that's both original and authentic.

Gender in Products

A common strategy for consumer products targeted at women has been to take an existing product designed for men, and then "shrink it, and pink it" (Rockwood, 2009). Strategies like this may be due, in part, to the historically low number of women in the design industry (Femme Den, 2011). Though such approaches may reflect the superficial differences in physical appearance between men and women (e.g., men tend to be generally taller and larger than women of the same age), they often fail to address deeper needs that are specific to each sex.

The best products successfully incorporate masculine and feminine qualities.

The Femme Den at SMART Design is a group of female design researchers, engineers and industrial designers who aim to make gender considerations a standard part of the design process. They consider gender "an untapped design tool that can make a difference in design and business" (Femme Den, 2011).

Good products balance the needs of men and women to the benefit of both.

Women are involved in the purchase of up to 80 percent of consumer goods (Rockwood, 2009). "Good products balance the needs of men and women to the benefit of both. They're not male products masquerading as unisex or—worse—hiding under a coat of pink paint. They don't alienate anyone with overt claims of being women-focused or women-friendly. They just are" (Rockwood, 2009).

FIG. 4.28 Brushing Beauties

This scrub brush offers only a superficial resemblance to the female form.
© *Trevor van Gorp*

THE EVOLUTION OF EMOTION AND PERSONALITY

In the prehistoric world in which humans evolved, there were no computers, websites, or interactive products. If something moved, it was reasonable to assume that it was alive. Your portable music player was the musical instrument you carried on your back, and the musician was you.

In this environment, the humans who survived were the ones who were best able to sense threats in their environment (from other people, predators and the elements) and quickly shift their attention in response. In other words, the people who responded emotionally to threats (i.e., by becoming alarmed and avoiding them) were the most likely to survive and reproduce (Dutton, 2003).

Evidence of this can be seen in the way that people unconsciously pick up the emotional state of those around them (Gallese, 2001; Botvinick, Jha, Bylsma, Fabian, Solomon, & Prkachin, 2005; Lamm, Batson, & Decety, 2007). This ability likely helped early humans form into large, structured groups that worked together for mutual benefit. Sensing and responding to the emotional states of others plays an invaluable role in the formation of relationships.

Size is a powerful cue that another animal could cause you harm.

Dominance in Nature

In the natural environment, relative size is a powerful cue that another animal could cause harm. The animal kingdom contains many different species that instinctively increase their size when confronted in order to intimidate their opponents (Fogden & Fogden, 1974; Darwin, 1872). Other cues that are used in confrontations include sound and touch, as when dogs bark or bite each other to establish what's called a **dominance hierarchy** within a pack of animals (Enger, Ross, & Bailey, 2009). In a group of humans, we'd likely call it a **social hierarchy**.

Because judgments such as these (i.e., bigger, louder, stronger) are relative, they involve comparing one animal or thing to others in a group. Being bigger and stronger than the other animals within a defined pack gives the largest, strongest animal

FIG. 4.29 **Which Vehicle Is Dominant?**

© Trevor van Gorp

"dominant" status. The dominant animal generally has better access to territory, as well as the food and resources within. This can lead to more mating opportunities than animals in the pack with less status (Enger et al., 2009; Cummins, 1996).

Larger, louder, deeper, stronger, and sharper things naturally provoke stronger emotional responses.

So how does all this relate to design? When we think about the unconscious emotional effects of this evolutionary programming on our reptilian and mammalian brains, it's quite natural that larger, louder, deeper, stronger, sharper, and stronger tasting things provoke stronger emotional responses. If another dog in the pack (or another person in your tribe) threatens or attacks you, it's in your survival interest to be able to assess whether they're physically or socially dominant.

Dominance and Friendliness

Every product communicates a personality, but not every designer intentionally created that personality. As we mentioned earlier, users prefer products that express a consistent personality. Although personality traits are complex, psychologists have grouped product personality traits into a small number of categories that have a similar character. They've identified two major dimensions of personality that are readily assigned to products, computers and interfaces by

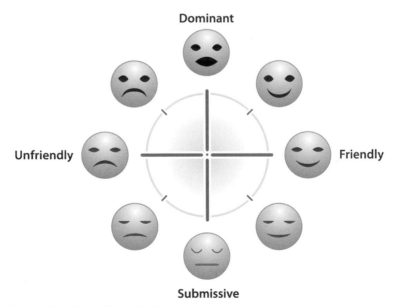

Personality: Friendliness / Dominance

FIG. 4.30 **Personality: Friendliness/Dominance**

Adapted from (Reeves & Nass, 1998). © Trevor van Gorp

FIG. 4.31 **Dominant and Friendly Faces**

© Jim Leftwich

users: dominant versus submissive and friendly versus unfriendly (Reeves & Nass, 1998; Desmet, Ortiz, & Schoormans, 2008).

Take a look at the simple objects in Fig. 4.31. What emotions are they expressing? Because neither object is changing, any emotions they're expressing will remain consistent over time. If the major dimensions of personality are dominance and friendliness, which object do you perceive to be more dominant? Which one do you perceive to be friendlier? Positive emotions are associated with a friendly demeanor, pleasure and approach behaviors, while negative emotions are associated with unfriendliness, pain and avoidance.

The major dimensions of personality are dominance and friendliness.

Dominant or Submissive?

As we mentioned earlier, it's quite natural that larger, louder, deeper, stronger, sharper, and stronger-tasting things provoke stronger emotional responses. Physical characteristics involving larger relative size have been linked to more dominant and aggressive behavior in males (Carré & McCormick, 2008). Aggressive behavior is also usually associated with high arousal emotions.

Dominant visual features could be described as angular, straight, cold or cool, dark, silver, black, hard and heavy, while submissive visual features could be described as rounded, warm, light, golden, soft/delicate and lite (Wellman, Bruder, & Oltersdorf, 2004). When a personality is not represented with overtly dominant visual or interactive characteristics, the tendency is to describe it as more submissive.

Aggressive behavior is associated with high arousal emotions.

The arousal level of the emotions being expressed affects whether we perceive the personality as dominant or submissive. In other words, designs that communicate personality primarily through high-arousal elements will appear as dominant personalities.

Because judgments such as big versus small, or heavy versus light are relative judgments, they're made based on the people (or products) that are part of the group or "pack" that's being judged. When you design a product used for training, that needs to take charge and lead the way, you can use more dominant design to convey that personality. When you design a product to defer to the user and wait for user commands, you can use more submissive design features. This helps ensure that the personality of the product is consistent with its role.

Traits	DOMINANT	SUBMISSIVE
Arousal	High Stimulation	Low Stimulation
Visual	Angular	Curved
	Straight	Round
	Up	Down
	Above	Below
	Bigger	Smaller
	Heavy	Light weight
	Robust	Delicate
	In Motion	At Rest
	Silver	Golden
	Cool	Warm
Text	Uppercase	Lowercase
	Bold	Regular
Tactile	Rough	Smooth
	Hard	Soft
Auditory	Louder	Quieter
	Deeper	Higher

FIG. 4.32 Dominant versus Submissive Characteristics

Adapted from (Wellman et al., 2004). © *Trevor van Gorp*

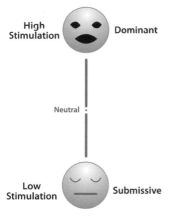

FIG. 4.33 Arousal affects Dominance

© Trevor van Gorp

Friendly or Unfriendly?

The value of the emotion (i.e., pleasant vs. unpleasant) affects whether we perceive the personality as friendly or unfriendly.

Friendly visual features could be described as positive, while unfriendly visual features could be described as negative. Friendliness is determined not only by what is said, but also by *how* it is said. The *tone* of the conversation has as much of an effect as the words that are actually said. Our tendency to assign personality based on the tone of the conversation is easily recognizable in Fig. 4.35. It uses contrast, weight, size and typography to alter the meaning that is conveyed by the words. Just as auditory tone and body language influence the meaning of the words we speak, the aesthetics combine with the words to alter the emotional meaning of the message.

Designs that communicate positive emotions are perceived as friendly.

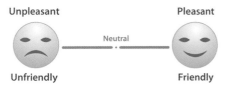

FIG. 4.34 Value affects Friendliness

© Trevor van Gorp

What are you doing?
What are you doing?

FIG. 4.35 Personality Affects Meaning
The more ambiguous the message, the more its meaning will be influenced by design.
© *Trevor van Gorp*

In conversation, someone has to lead, and opposites attract.

Which of the statements in the figure naturally grabs more of your attention? Which one do you feel more *compelled* to "approach" or "avoid"? Which one would you rather be in a conversation with? When it comes to aesthetics, we're attracted to things that we feel are similar to ourselves (Govers & Schoormans, 2005; Reeves & Nass, 1998). But when it comes to conversation and interaction, someone has to lead, and opposites attract (Markey & Markey, 2007).

Lines Have Feelings, Too

Poffenberger and Barrows (1924) had five hundred college students and graduates match 18 different lines to 47 different emotionally themed adjectives. The researchers used two types of lines: curved and angular. For each type of line, there were three size variations: big, medium, and small. For each size variation, there were three directional variations: horizontal, upward, and downward. The researchers found a remarkable amount of agreement around the emotions that some lines symbolize.

The movement of the line imitates the way we express the emotion.

The movement of the line "imitates the motor expression of an emotion... Lines symbolizing states of strong motor expression have short waves and acute angles, and lines symbolizing states of weak motor expression have long and low waves" (Lundholm, 1921, p. 190). Lines with short waves and sharp angles are associated with intense motion and lines with long, low waves are associated with slower, weaker motion.

Color is used as an analogy for physical and emotional states.

A line pointing downward expresses relaxation and a line pointing upward expresses power. A line associated with strength is a line that tends to go upwards, expressing energy, force, ambition and uplifting feelings. Going downwards can be associated with the loss of energy, weakness, relaxation, and depression (Lundholm, 1921).

The direction of each line also matches the arousal level of the emotion it represents. Higher-arousal emotions like *Agitating* and *Furious* are both represented with a line pointing upward, and lower-arousal emotions like *Sad* and *Lazy* are both represented with a line pointing downward.

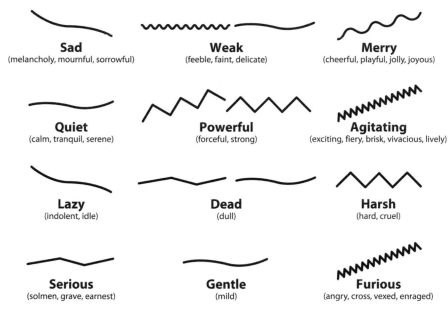

FIG. 4.36 The Feeling Value of Lines

Adapted from (Poffenberger & Barrows, 1924). © *Trevor van Gorp*

The Influence of Color

There are a number of ways that color can influence emotional states, and it's an important aspect of communicating emotion and personality. Color has often been used as an analogy for physical and emotional states. If someone behaves in a cowardly way, they're called "yellow." If someone is feeling good and in the prime of life, we might say they're "in the pink." You might be "green with envy" or get sad and have "the blues" (Fehrman & Fehrman, 2000).

Unconscious Color Associations

Color can be used to convey motion and action. In this respect, red, yellow and orange are considered more dynamic and active. Like movement, dynamic colors increase arousal and attract more attention. These colors may be associated with more aggressive qualities than colors in the blue range, which are considered more passive and have been associated with harmony or tranquility (Fehrman & Fehrman 2000).

Dynamic colors increase arousal and attract more attention.

Due to unconscious associations based on evolution, certain dimensions of color and shape can be linked with certain dimensions of emotion. The saturation and value of a color can be linked with physiological arousal in the body, independent of the hue (Fehrman & Fehrman 2000). What this means is that the saturation of a color is more important in terms of the amount of attention we are able to summon than how much we like or dislike the hue. In terms of arousing attention, it's the intensity or saturation of the color and the contrast against the background that matter. Higher contrast demands more attention and lower contrast levels are less arousing (Fehrman & Fehrman 2000).

The saturation and contrast of a color are more important for attention than the hue.

When Microsoft redesigned and rebranded Live Search to become Bing, they found that simply increasing the saturation of the blue they were using made users feel more confident about the displayed results. What was the bottom line of this emotional insight for Microsoft? An $80 million annual increase in search revenue (Fried, 2010).

The Meaning of Color

The specific meanings of colors are culturally conditioned. Colors are often associated through analogy with objects and events. For example, the color of candy reinforces how sweet we expect it to be. Red is associated with warmth, and blue is associated with cold, especially pale blue (Fehrman & Fehrman 2000). Although colors have different meanings across cultures, we all have our own color biases as well. People's color preferences can often be linked through unconscious association to happy or unhappy memories of past experiences.

FIG. 4.37 Bing's More Confident Color Scheme

Bing's more "confident" color scheme nets Microsoft $80 million more in search revenue annually.

(Used by permission of Microsoft.)

In western culture, red is associated with excitement and activity through fire engines, blood and stop signs. In some eastern cultures, red is associated with celebration. Although the meaning of the color may differ across cultures, you may notice that they are still associated with high arousal emotions. Again, the saturation of the color is more important than the hue in increasing arousal. Although blue is associated with calmness and serenity through the sky and ocean, a highly saturated blue may be more arousing than a less saturated red (Fehrman & Fehrman 2000).

Similarity **plays a vital role in initial attraction.**

Do Opposites Attract?

When it comes to personalities, different things stir our emotions at different stages of a relationship. *Similarity* is the theory that people are more attracted to those with personalities similar to their own, over those who display a different personality (Govers & Schoormans, 2005; Reeves & Nass, 1998). *Complementarity* is the theory that people are attracted to people with personalities that complement their own in levels of dominance (Markey & Markey, 2007; Carson, 1969). It comes down to the old question of whether relationships work better when people are the same or opposite. Do opposites attract, or are we better off with people (and products) that are more similar to us? The answer is "yes."

Researchers found that similarity takes precedence early in relationships, playing a vital role in initial attraction. Participants in a study were lead to believe that another person was either similar, neutral, or dissimilar to themselves. When that person later requested the participant read a short page paper and write a summary, compliance went from 43 percent in the dissimilar group to 77 percent in the similar group (Burger, Soroka, Gonzago, Murphy, & Somervell, 2001). Generally speaking, users are attracted to products that display a personality similar to their own. We're attracted to people and things that look similar to the way we are, or the way we'd like to see ourselves.

Complementarity becomes more important as the relationship develops over time (Vinacke et al., 1988). Two dominant persons may experience conflicts as both attempt to lead, while two submissive individuals may lack initiative, as neither is willing to lead. People in long-term relationships are more satisfied when their partners express more or less dominance than they do (Markey & Markey, 2007). When people display dominance, not only are they bigger, stronger, and louder. They also lead interactions by going first and express more certainty in their statements (Reeves & Nass, 1998).

Complementarity **is more important as relationships develop over time.**

Based on everything we've explored so far, which of the application interfaces below (in Fig. 4.38) is more dominant and which is more submissive? Which is friendlier and which is more unfriendly? Of these two application interfaces, which one naturally grabs more of your attention? Which one do you feel more compelled to "approach" or "avoid"? Some of these questions are easy to answer by responding to aesthetics. But, without actually interacting with either application, it's difficult to say which version of the application you would feel more comfortable using or purchasing from. Which of these applications is a better match for the personality of its target audience?

FIG. 4.38 **Comparing Personalities in Design**

© *Trevor van Gorp*

The Right Personality for Your Product

Apple is a brand whose products communicate a submissive personality. Apple design chief Jonathan Ive has often paid homage to the work of Dieter Rams. One of Rams's famous Ten Commandments of Design is "as little design as possible" (Lovell & Kemp, 2011). In describing the philosophy behind Apple's hardware products, Ive has said, "We have to feel we can dominate them. As you bring order to complexity, you find a way to make the product defer to you" (Isaacson, 2011).

We're attracted to the similar, but we prefer to interact with the complementary.

If you consider the role that the product is playing and tailor the personality accordingly, it's more likely that users will like the personality. Generally speaking, interaction between the system and the user should be complementary, in which the user takes up the dominant role while the product, interface, or service takes on the submissive role by dutifully following user directions. If the product is guiding or directing the user, it may take on a more dominant role.

Roles	DOMINANT	SUBMISSIVE
Friendly	Active helper	Help from a peer
Less friendly	Aggressive instruction	--

FIG. 4.39 **Roles and Personalities**

Adapted from (Reeves & Nass, 1998). © *Trevor van Gorp*

CONCLUSIONS

In this chapter, you learned that emotional expression is perceived as personality over time. Users judge the personality of a product based on the same markers and criteria that they use to judge the personalities of other people. The most significant distinctions that users make when judging product personality traits are whether the product is:

- Dominant versus Submissive
- Friendly versus Unfriendly

We also learned how to intentionally communicate personality types through aesthetics and interaction. Finally, we learned that customers are attracted to things that they perceive have a personality similar to their own. But, over time, they prefer to interact with things that take up a role that is complementary to their own.

Where do we design for emotion? Wherever we need to communicate a personality to the user and create a connection or form a relationship, we should be designing for emotion. In Chapter 5, we introduce the A.C.T. model, a new framework describing how to address the different types of experience necessary to create the *useful*, *usable*, and *desirable* experiences that help to form relationships.

Communicate a personality, create a connection, and form a relationship.

REFERENCES

Botvinick, M., Jha, A. P., Bylsma, L. M., Fabian, S. A., Solomon, P. E., & Prkachin, K. M. (2005). Viewing facial expressions of pain engages cortical areas involved in the direct experience of pain. *NeuroImage, 25*(1), 312–319.

Burger, J. M., Soroka, S., Gonzago, K., Murphy, E., & Somervell, E. (2001). The effect of fleeting attraction on compliance to requests. *Personality and Social Psychology Bulletin, 27*, 1578–1586.

Buss, David. (2003). *The evolution of desire: Strategies of human mating*. New York: Basic Books.

Çakmakli, Ayça. (2010). *A good design = A good mate*. Seventh International Conference on Design & Emotion. Design & Emotion Society. <http://designandemotion.org/library/page/viewDoc/144>

Carré, J., & McCormick, C. (2008). In your face: Facial metrics predict aggressive behavior in the laboratory and in varsity and professional hockey players. *Proceedings of the Royal Society Biological Sciences, 275*, 2651–2656.

Carson, R. C. (1969). *Interaction Concepts of Personality*. Chicago: Aldine.

Casey, R. J., & Ritter, J. M. (1996). How infant appearance informs: Child care providers' responses to babies varying in appearance of age and attractiveness. Journal of Applied Developmental Psychology, 17(4), 495–518. <http://www.sciencedirect.com/science/article/pii/S0193397396900131> Accessed on 11.22.11.

Cummins, D. D. (1996). Dominance hierarchies and the evolution of human reasoning. *Minds and Machines, 6*(4), 463–480.

Csikszentmihalyi, M. (1990). *Flow: The psychology of optimal experience*. New York: Harper Perennial.

Csikszentmihalyi, M., & Rochberg-Halton, E. (1981). *The meaning of things: Domestic symbols and the self*. Cambridge: Cambridge University Press.

Darwin, C. R. 1872. *The expression of the emotions in man and animals* (1st ed.). London: John Murray.

Demîr, E. (2008). The Field of Design and Emotion: Concepts, Arguments, Tools and Current Issues. METU JFA *1*(1), 135.

Desmet, P. R. (2002). *Designing emotions*. Delft: Pieter Desmet.

Desmet, P. M. A., Ortiz, N. J. C., & Schoormans, J. P. L. (2008). Personality in physical human/product interaction. *Design Studies, 29*(5), 458–477.

Dixson, A. F., Halliwell, G., East, R., Wignarajah, P., & Anderson, M. J. (2003). Masculine somatotype and hirsuteness as determinants of sexual attractiveness to women. *Archives of Sexual Behavior, 32*(1), 29–39.

Dutton, D. (2003). Aesthetics and evolutionary psychology. *The Oxford Handbook for Aesthetics*. New York: Oxford University Press.

Elam, Kimberly. (2001). *Geometry of design: Studies in proportion and composition* (1st ed.). New York: Princeton Architectural Press.

Enger, E. D., Ross, F. C., & Bailey, D. B. (2009). *Concepts in biology*. Columbus: McGraw-Hill.

Femme Den. (2011). *About the Femmes*. <http://www.femmeden.com/about/> Accessed 8.20.11.

Fehrman, K. R., & Fehrman, C. (2000). *Color: The secret influence.* Upper Saddle River, NJ: Prentice Hall.

Fogg, B. J. (2003). *Persuasive technology: Using computers to change what we think and do.* San Francisco: Morgan Kaufmann Publishers.

Fogden, M., & Fogden, P. (1974). *Animals and their colors: Camouflage, warning coloration, courtship and territorial display, mimicry.* New York: Crown Publishers.

Foladare, I. S. (1969). A clarification of "ascribed status" and "achieved status." *The Sociological Quarterly 10*(1) 53–61.

Forstall, S. (2011). *Apple WWDC 2011 keynote.* <http://gigaom.com/apple/wwdc-2011-keynote-liveblog> Accessed 11.20.11.

Fried, Ina. (2010). *Behind Bing's blue links.* <http://news.cnet.com/8301-13860_3-20000623-56.html> Accessed 5.12.10.

Gallese, V. (2001). The "Shared Manifold" hypothesis: From mirror neurons to empathy. *Journal of Consciousness Studies, 8*, 33–50.

Govers, P. C. M., & Schoormans, J. P. L. (2005) Product personality and its influence on consumer preference. *Journal of Consumer Marketing, 22*(4), 189–197.

Halpern, D. (2000) *Sex differences in cognitive abilities.* Mahwah, NJ: Lawrence Erlbaum Associates.

Harasty, J., Double, K. L., Halliday, G. M., Kril, J. J., & McRitchie, D. A. (1997). Language-associated cortical regions are proportionally larger in the female brain. *Archives of Neurology, 54*(2), 171–176.

Hildebrandt, K. A., & Fitzgerald, H. E. (1978). Adults' responses to infants varying in perceived cuteness. Michigan State University. <http://www.sciencedirect.com/science/article/pii/0376635778900426> Accessed 8.20.11.

Horvath, T. (1981). Physical attractiveness: The influence of selected torso parameters. *Archives of Sexual Behavior, 10*(1), 21–24.

Isaacson, W. (2011). *Steve Jobs.* New York: Simon & Schuster.

Jordan, P. W. (2000). *Designing pleasurable products.* London: Taylor & Francis.

Kemper, T. D. (1978). *A social interactional theory of emotions.* West Sussex: John Wiley & Sons.

Kringelbach, M.L., Lehtonen, A., Squire, S., Harvey, A. G., Craske, M. G., Holliday, I. E., et al. (2008). A specific and rapid neural signature for parental instinct. *PLoS ONE 3*(2), e1664.

Lamm, C., Batson, C. D., Decety, J. (2007). The neural substrate of human empathy: Effects of perspective-taking and cognitive appraisal. *Journal of Cognitive Neuroscience, 19*(1), 42–58.

Lovell, S., & Kemp, K. (2011). *Dieter Rams: As little design as possible.* London: Phaidon Press.

Ludden, G. D. S., Schifferstein, Hendrik, N. J., & Hekkert, P. (2008). Surprise as a design strategy. *Design Issues, 24*(2), 28–38.

Lundholm, H. (1921). The affective tone of lines: Experimental researches. *Psychological Review, 28*(1), 43–60.

MailChimp. (2011). *One million.* <http://mailchimp.com/million/> Accessed 10.6.11.

McLean, P. D. (1990). *The triune brain in evolution: Role in paleocerebral functions.* New York: Plenum Press.

Markey, P. M., & Markey, C. N. (2007). Romantic ideals, romantic obtainment, and relationship experiences: The complementarity of interpersonal traits among romantic partners. *Journal of Social and Personal Relationships, 24*(4), 517–533.

Naughton, J. (2011, Aug. 27) What made Steve Jobs a giant among the world's greatest communicators? *Guardian.* <http://www.guardian.co.uk/technology/2011/aug/27/steve-jobs-apple-ipod-ipad> Accessed 10.20.11.

Norman, D. A. (2004). *Emotional design: Why we love (or hate) everyday things.* New York: Basic Books.

Poffenberger, A. T., & Barrows, B. E. (1924). The feeling value of lines. *Journal of Applied Psychology, 8,* 187–205.

Reeves, B. & Nass, C. (1998). *The media equation: How people treat computers, television and new media like real people and places.* Cambridge: Cambridge University Press.

Rockwood, K. (2009). Forget "shrink it and pink it": The Femme Den unleashed. Fast Company. <http://www.fastcompany.com/magazine/139/separate-and-equal-femme-den.html> Accessed 8.20.11.

Sanders, E. B. N. (1992, Fall). Converging perspectives: Product development research for the 1990s. *Design Management Journal, 3*(4), 49–54.

Sonderegger, A., & Sauer, J. (2010). The influence of design aesthetics in usability testing: Effects on user performance and perceived usability. *Applied Ergonomics, 41,* 403–410.

Sternberg, R. J. (1988). *The Triangle of Love: Intimacy, Passion, Commitment.* New York: Basic Books.

TopTen Reviews. (2011). Email marketing service review. <http://email-marketing-service-review.toptenreviews.com> Accessed 10.20.11.

TrackVia. (2011). Three in five workers admit yelling at computer. <http://www.market-watch.com/story/three-in-five-workers-admit-yelling-at-computer-2011-12-19> Accessed 12.20.11.

Tzu, L. (2006) *Tao Te Ching: A New English Version* (Steven Mitchell, trans.). New York: Harper Perennial Modern Classics.

Van Buskirk, E. (2003). *MP3 insider: It takes a village to beat the iPod.* <http://reviews.cnet.com/1990-6450_7-5023900-1.htm> Accessed 5.15.10.

Vinacke, W. E., Shannon, K., Palazzo,V., Balsavage, L., et al. (1988). Similarity and complementarity in intimate couples. *Genetic, Social, and General Psychology Monographs, 114,* 51–76.

von Franz, M. L. (1978). "The Process of Individuation". *Man and His Symbols.* London: Dell.

Wellman, K., Bruder, R., & Oltersdorf, K. (2004). Gender designs: Aspects of gender found in the design of perfume bottles. In D. McDonagh & P. Hekkert (Eds.), *Design and emotion: The experience of everyday things.* New York: Taylor & Francis.

Zangwill, N. (2007, Nov. 22). Aesthetic judgment. *Stanford Encyclopedia of Philosophy.* <http://plato.stanford.edu/entries/aesthetic-judgment/> Accessed 11.20.11.

How Do We Design for Emotion?

5

In Chapter 4, we explored the ways that design elements can express and affect emotions, and examined how they communicate personality over time. We looked at several models of emotional design and examined the different ways that people experience love to get a better understanding of how to design for relationships.

Next, we explored the different personality traits that people look for in good products. Then, we identified the two most important distinctions that people make when judging the personality of a product (dominant vs. submissive and friendly vs. unfriendly). Finally, we learned that customers are often attracted to things that have an aesthetic personality similar to their own, but they prefer products that take on a complementary role during interaction.

In this chapter, we'll introduce the A.C.T. model; a framework that describes how to design the useful, usable, and desirable experiences that form relationships. A.C.T. (Attract, Converse, and Transact) provides a new way to think about the design of product relationships that mirrors the different types of love found in human relationships. Finally, we'll summarize what we've learned throughout the book, providing a list of guidelines to help guide your designs through each stage in the A.C.T. framework.

A.C.T. provides a new way to think about designing relationships with products.

DESIGNING RELATIONSHIPS

Although it may seem counterintuitive at first, the idea that we perceive emotion and personality in products is something we can all understand at a basic level. Almost everyone has heard someone curse their computer when it crashed, triggering feelings of betrayal.

Figure 5.1 but why is this the case? Computers and products are nothing more than tools that we use to accomplish tasks. These things have no intent, malicious or otherwise. They're not alive. Your computer didn't crash because it's out to get you (although

FIG. 5.1 Emoticon

Emoticons communicate emotion through a combination of keystrokes that resemble facial expressions.
© *Trevor van Gorp*

you may feel like that's the case). Although you may know all this consciously, your mammalian and reptilian brains are unconscious and automatic, reacting in the moment.

As demands on attention rise, we revert to unconscious, automatic behaviors.

Although it's possible to consciously negate these unconscious effects and treat things purely as tools, it's not our default response. Reeves and Nass (1998) observed people giving complex personalities to line drawings and feeling threatened by photos. As the demands on our attention rise, we're more likely to revert to unconscious, automatic reactions.

Emotional responses occur as a result of quick impressions and associations. Our reptilian and mammalian brains quickly respond not only to highly realistic, virtual environments, but also to cues in very simple types of media, like line drawings, emoticons, and text. "All people automatically and unconsciously respond socially and naturally to media" (Reeves & Nass, 1998, p. 7).

Depending on how the user's interaction with the product progresses, it can mark the beginning (or end) of a relationship. When we use the word "relationship" in the context of people and products, you might envision something quite superficial. After all, we're talking about how people interact with *things*, not other people. And for most products, you're right. Many of the things we interact with on a daily basis are designed for what would appear to be quick, disposable relationships. But, when products will offer multiple interactions over time, we want to place greater emphasis on designing for connection and relationship.

CUTTING THROUGH THE JARGON

When a product is desirable, the urge to approach is triggered.

Back in Chapter 4, we explored the connections between desirable, usable and useful experiences, and several models that help to explain how to design for emotion. Then, we compared those design models to the different forms of love. Now, let's quickly summarize the commonalities between each model at each level. Ultimately, all of these models represent different perspectives on the same things.

A Passion for Desirable Aesthetics

In the first column under *Desirable*, we have *Passion*, which is based on how something looks, sounds, smells, and feels (i.e., aesthetics). When there is only Passion, Sternberg (1988) calls it "Infatuated Love."

Design Goals, Forms of Love and Design Models

Design Goals (Sanders 1992)	**Desirable** Aesthetically appealing	**Usable** Capacity to be understood, learned & utilized	**Useful** Accomplishes what it was designed for
Product Elements	**Aesthetics** How the product looks and feels	**Interaction** How the user interacts with the product	**Function** What the product does
Forms of Love (Sternberg 1988)	**Passion** Infatuated Love	**Intimacy** Friendship	**Commitment** Empty Love
RELATIONSHIP TO DESIGN MODELS	EXPERIENCE OVER TIME ⟶		
Types of Benefits (Jordan 2000)	**Hedonic Benefits** Sensory and aesthetic pleasures	**Practical Benefits** Result from the completion of tasks	**Emotional Benefits** Effects on user's emotions
Type of Appraisals (Desmet 2002)	**Objects** Does it appeal to my attitudes?	**Agents** Does it meet my standards?	**Events** Does it help reach my goals?
Levels of Processing (Norman 2004)	**Visceral** Aesthetic and tactile qualities	**Behavioral** Effectiveness and ease of use	**Reflective** Self-image, personal satisfaction, memories
RELATIONSHIP TO OTHER MODELS	EXPERIENCE OVER TIME ⟶		
Type of Reactions (Demir 2008)	**Responses** Automatic	**Experiences** Occur through interaction	**Relationship** Builds over time
Triune Brain (McLean 1990)	**Reptilian Brain** Unconscious, instant	**Mammalian Brain** Conscious and unconscious	**Neo-Mammalian Brain** Conscious, slow, deliberate

FIG. 5.2 Design Goals, Forms of Love and Design Models

Adapted from (Sanders, 1992; Sternberg, 1988); Jordan, 2000; Desmet, 2002; Norman, 2004; Demir, 2008; McLean, 1990.) © Trevor van Gorp

Norman's *Visceral* level is based on the product's aesthetic properties (sight, sound, smell, touch, and taste). Jordan's *Hedonic Benefits* describe the pleasures a product's aesthetic properties can provide and Desmet's *Object* level describes whether the aesthetics appeal to users' attitudes.

Attraction to aesthetics is processed quickly and unconsciously by the most primitive part of the brain (i.e., the reptilian brain). This explains why attraction to aesthetic cues happens without conscious thought. Products that appeal to our attitudes invoke passionate emotional responses through their aesthetic qualities. The desirability of these products triggers the urge to approach, while a lack of desirability triggers the urge to avoid.

The Intimacy of Usable Interaction

In the second column under *Usable*, we have *Intimacy*, which is based on liking and friendship. When there is only Intimacy, Sternberg (1988) calls it "friendship."

Norman's *Behavioral* level is where the product's ease of interaction and use is processed. Jordan's *Practical Benefits* are the benefits that come from use and the completion of short-term tasks. Desmet's *Agents* level describes whether the product meets up to users' standards throughout the interaction.

Aesthetics combines with interaction to convey personality.

The conversational cues that communicate power and status are processed in the mammalian brain and involve both unconscious and conscious judgments. If a product meets up to our standards for usability by being understandable and easy to use, it offers us practical benefits and can act as an agent of change. The interaction builds attachment and intimacy. Aesthetics combines with interaction to convey personality.

A Commitment to Useful Function

In the third column under *Useful*, we have *Commitment*, which is based on whether the personality that's been communicated through aesthetics and interaction has instilled Passion and created Intimacy to encourage trust. When products reliably fulfill users' needs in a way that's in keeping with their long-term goals, the resulting emotional benefits encourage Commitment. In Sternberg's (1988) model, *Commitment* on its own is "Empty Love." It's only with the addition of Passion and Intimacy to Commitment that we can make all-consuming or "Consummate love."

Norman's *Reflective* level is based on how long-term relationships with things contribute to our self-image and identity. Jordan's *Emotional Benefits* are the benefits that come from longer-term interaction and the realization of goals. Desmet's *Events* level is based on how the product has helped us to complete long-term goals that are also memorable events.

Once the product has communicated a clear and consistent personality, and achieved trust, the user may be willing to consciously commit and engage in transactions with the product. These conscious transactions take place in the neomammalian brain. Repeated transactions that lead to the formation of relationships leave us practically and emotionally satisfied in the long term.

THE A.C.T. MODEL

With all the models we've covered to help you understand the psychology of emotion and personality, you may wonder why we would bother adding another one? The A.C.T. model is designed to help ensure that your design process addresses the three different levels of emotional requirements. The model is based on our research into current models for designing emotion as well as explorations of the nature of love. The idea for a new framework arose in discussions of how to best communicate the underlying concepts behind the models in a way that was easy to understand and apply.

For any human-product relationship to form, attention must be *attracted* through the senses (via beauty, surprise, novelty, volume, size—that is, aesthetics). This triggers a desire to approach, encouraging further interaction. Stephen P. Anderson (2011) has termed the need to make our interactions with products more aesthetically and emotionally responsive as "seductive interactions."

Aesthetics and attraction often receive the lion's share of the attention when people discuss emotional design. This is natural, since aesthetic cues are the most quickly and automatically processed part of the user's experience. But it often means that we neglect the deeper aspects of relationships that depend more on building intimacy and commitment.

Attention must be *attracted* through the senses.

If *Attraction* and *Conversation* succeed in moving the relationship forward, deeper commitments, exchanges and *Transactions* are then possible. A Transaction can be any action, from signing up for a newsletter to making a purchase. The steps in the A.C.T. model may not always occur in the same sequence, but they provide a basic overview of the requirements for creating relationships.

Because interaction between both humans and products follows normal social rules, it might be more meaningful to call it a *Conversation*. The conversations we have in our relationships with other people consist of both dialogues and stories. The conversations we have with products as we're forming relationships are no different. Saari (2005) notes that interaction comes in two different forms: *dialogical* and *narrative*.

When we use a web browser to access a site, for example, we may be looking for a particular piece of information. Moving through the website, clicking different buttons and links, we receive feedback that functions much like a *dialogue*. Users make requests by selecting a button. The button changes in some way and possibly generates a sound to acknowledge that it's been selected. This is similar to the way a person would respond to a verbal request or a touch, changing facial expressions or body posture and replying verbally. Action from the user results in feedback from the product that is similar to a conversation.

Interaction comes in two different forms: *dialogical* and *narrative*.

FIG. 5.3 Dialogical Interaction

Input from the user results in feedback from the interface that is comparable to a dialogue.
© City of Edmonton

Small changes in labeling can have big effects on the usability of information.

All the models in Figure 5.2 phrase their terminology in a descriptive rather than a prescriptive or directive way. In other words, the labels describe a level or stage, but don't *direct* designers as to how they should fulfill the requirements of that stage. This is one area where the A.C.T. model is different. As anyone involved in information architecture or user experience can attest, small changes in labeling can have big effects on the usability of information.

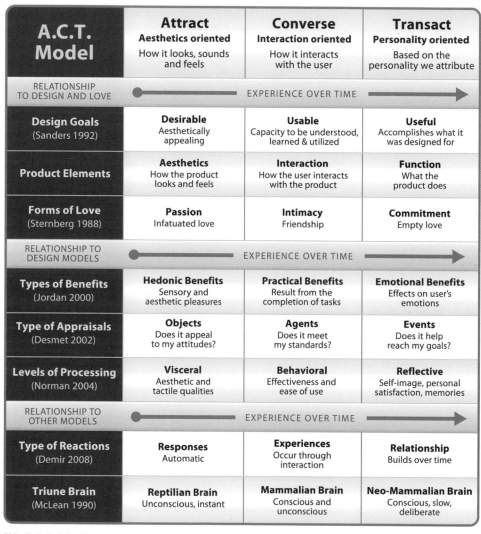

A.C.T. Model	Attract **Aesthetics oriented** How it looks, sounds and feels	Converse **Interaction oriented** How it interacts with the user	Transact **Personality oriented** Based on the personality we attribute
RELATIONSHIP TO DESIGN AND LOVE	EXPERIENCE OVER TIME		
Design Goals (Sanders 1992)	**Desirable** Aesthetically appealing	**Usable** Capacity to be understood, learned & utilized	**Useful** Accomplishes what it was designed for
Product Elements	**Aesthetics** How the product looks and feels	**Interaction** How the user interacts with the product	**Function** What the product does
Forms of Love (Sternberg 1988)	**Passion** Infatuated love	**Intimacy** Friendship	**Commitment** Empty love
RELATIONSHIP TO DESIGN MODELS	EXPERIENCE OVER TIME		
Types of Benefits (Jordan 2000)	**Hedonic Benefits** Sensory and aesthetic pleasures	**Practical Benefits** Result from the completion of tasks	**Emotional Benefits** Effects on user's emotions
Type of Appraisals (Desmet 2002)	**Objects** Does it appeal to my attitudes?	**Agents** Does it meet my standards?	**Events** Does it help reach my goals?
Levels of Processing (Norman 2004)	**Visceral** Aesthetic and tactile qualities	**Behavioral** Effectiveness and ease of use	**Reflective** Self-image, personal satisfaction, memories
RELATIONSHIP TO OTHER MODELS	EXPERIENCE OVER TIME		
Type of Reactions (Demir 2008)	**Responses** Automatic	**Experiences** Occur through interaction	**Relationship** Builds over time
Triune Brain (McLean 1990)	**Reptilian Brain** Unconscious, instant	**Mammalian Brain** Conscious and unconscious	**Neo-Mammalian Brain** Conscious, slow, deliberate

FIG. 5.4 A.C.T. Model: Comparison

Adapted from (Sanders, 1992; Sternberg, 1988); Jordan, 2000; Desmet, 2002; Norman, 2004; Demir, 2008; McLean, 1990.) © Trevor van Gorp

FIG. 5.5 How Not to Attract Customers
Visual overcrowding can make it difficult to focus on any one thing.
© *Trevor van Gorp*

Let's explore how the A.C.T. model makes emotional design easier for both designers and business stakeholders to understand and apply.

Attract

At the level of the Reptilian Brain, all the models focus on the inherent aesthetic and interactive properties of the product, the pleasures they provide, and the senses that allow those properties to enter our consciousness. As we mentioned in the previous chapters, we can relate these models to the traces of evolution left in the brain. Ultimately, attraction comes down to a question of Desirability.

Attraction comes down to a question of desirability.

In the A.C.T. model, we've tried to summarize and simplify all of these perspectives by using a term that is more actionable and meaningful to most people: *Attract*. If your product is something people will see, hear, taste, or touch, it must attract customers and users.

Converse

At the level of the Mammalian brain, the focus is on how Usable the product is. When a product ignores your requests, or fails to perform reliably and consistently (i.e., act with integrity), it becomes less usable and less credible. This includes how well the product performs, the benefits that using it brings, how it meets up to our social standards and the status we perceive it brings us.

You're designing a conversation.

Social cues in conversation and interaction are processed by the Mammalian brain, which governs social instincts around attachment, bonding and status. These instincts govern the behavior of mammals in groups or packs. By responding to the aesthetic and social cues we pick up while interacting with others, we determine the relative *power* and *status* of group members.

In the A.C.T. model, we wanted to indicate the importance of following human social rules during interaction. So, we've summarized these perspectives with the term: *Converse*. When designing how users will interact with your product, keep in mind that you're designing a conversation that consists of both dialogical and narrative elements.

Predictive typing, for example, can be a handy addition to an interface, speeding up interaction and communication—especially when it accurately predicts what you're typing. But when the quality of the predictions is closer to those of a carnival fortune-teller, it can be problematic. It's a lot like when someone is trying to be helpful, but interrupts and cuts you off mid-sentence. Their intentions are good, but they're getting the execution wrong.

Transact

Transactions occur at the level of conscious decisions processed by the Neomammalian brain. At this level of the brain, the focus is on conscious goals, projecting rather than judging status, remembering the past, and anticipating the future.

In this stage of the A.C.T. model, we wanted to capture that moment in time where a decision is made to commit to transaction with the product or service, so we've summarized these perspectives with the term *Transact*. Once you've established trust and credibility through attraction and conversation, you can persuade the user to take action and encourage the formation of relationships.

If you've established enough trust, the user may commit to *Transact* with your product.

In the *Transact* stage, all the models focus on the personality that is communicated through longer-term use of the product. Every exchange between the product and the user contributes to the personality of the product or service. If you've managed to Attract and then successfully Converse with the user, you may have established enough trust and credibility for them to commit to a *transaction* with your product or service. This is where the business goal of the design is accomplished. The user purchases the item, signs up for the newsletter, or downloads the file. Whatever the goal of the business, part of the process involves proving to the customer that your product or service is trustworthy.

If you take the relationship you've built with your users for granted, they will respond emotionally. When Netflix raised the price for their combined DVD/streaming service, and the shortly thereafter separated streaming from the original DVD mail-out service, customers were furious.

For some customers, Netflix was effectively doubling their effort, requiring them to track two separate film lists that had previously been one. As of October 4, 2011, customers had left over 27,000 comments on the CEO blog's, mostly denouncing the changes (Hastings, 2011). Needless to say, customers did not react positively to Netflix unilaterally changing the terms of its previous commitment and the company eventually relented.

Persuading with A.C.T.

Every design is an exercise in persuasion. Whether it's deciding where to go to dinner with your spouse, or what movie to see with your friends, persuasion is a part of every relationship in your life.

Fogg (2003, p. 15) defines persuasion as "an attempt to change attitudes or behaviors or both (without using deception or coercion)." Deception means literally that you tell someone something is true that is actually false. Coercion implies the use of power or force to change behavior. Persuasion is a voluntary change in behavior, attitude, or belief.

With this definition, we can see that many of our daily discussions and interactions have persuasive goals. You may want to persuade your boss to give you a raise based on the quality of your work. Perhaps you want to persuade a great client to work with you. Whatever the relationship, most involve some degree of persuasion.

Designers create products with affordances that persuade users to follow some paths or take certain actions over others (Gibson, 1977; Norman, 1999). Emotion can be an effective tool for persuading us to shift our attention and change our behaviors. This is accomplished by altering the levels of value and arousal through design in two ways. One way is through a conscious, deliberate process of evaluation, while the other occurs through unconscious, automatic evaluations where associations to past experience produce an emotional response. Unconsciously triggered emotions can produce changes in attitudes and behaviors without any conscious thought. These emotions affect attention levels to improve or reduce memory, affect trust and change behavior when purchasing and interacting with products (Saari, Ravaja, Laarni, Turpeinen, & Kallinen, 2004).

Persuasion in Relationships

Fogg (2003) differentiates between two classes of persuasion in interactive products: *microsuasion* and *macrosuasion*. Microsuasive goals help to guide the user's attention to particular actions at the appropriate times. Microsuasive elements "can be designed into dialogue boxes, icons or interaction patterns between the computer and the user" (Fogg, 2003, p. 18). These are the small tasks that help the user realize the macrosuasive goal of the product. Offering praise or a reward is one example of a microsuasive technique that encourages users to work harder to complete subsequent tasks. You can think of the microsuasive goals as contributing to the *Usable* and *Desirable* parts of the product relationship.

Macrosuasion describes the overall goal of the product, application or tool. You can think of the macrosuasive goal as the *Useful* part of the product relationship.

Every design is an exercise in persuasion.

Emotion can be effective at persuading us to change our behaviors.

USING THE A.C.T. MODEL

At its core, the A.C.T. model is about how we can use emotion to persuade people to invest attention in the right things at the right time. This helps create relationships between products and the people who use them. By artfully combining image, form, contrast, color, materials, information design and interactive design, you can Attract your users and Converse with them in a way that fosters credibility and trust, communicating a consistent personality to forge relationships.

Consider how emotions affect people at different stages in the relationship.

We've assembled a list of guidelines that you can use to help affect emotions and guide attention. The guidelines discuss ways to influence the emotions of your users through changes in design elements at each stage of the relationship.

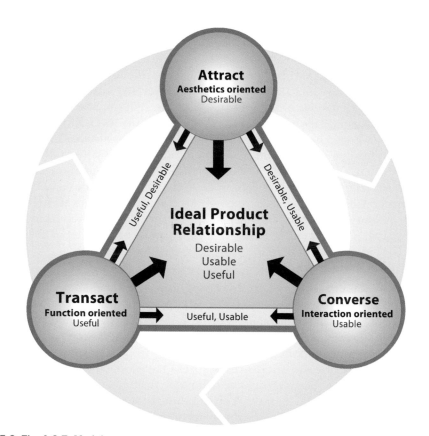

FIG. 5.6 The A.C.T. Model

© Trevor van Gorp

Get to Know Your Users

Getting to know your users is the first step in deciding what personality will fulfill their wants and needs. By considering how emotions affect people at different stages in the relationship, you can tailor your product's aesthetics and interaction to their context of use. Begin by identifying and considering:

- The context in which the design will be used
- The demographics of the target user group
- The emotional state and personality of the target user group
- The intentions and motivations of the target user group

Tailor your product's aesthetics and interaction to the context of use.

The Context in Which the Design Will Be Used

The context may offer clues to the user's current emotional state. For example, when a fire alarm goes off, everyone experiences higher levels of negative arousal. For a timid individual, this may have different effects on behavior than for a more dominant person.

Because your users bring their existing emotional state to whatever they do, there is no way to guarantee that they'll experience a specific emotional reaction. If they're already in a highly stimulated state, their reaction will be much more intense than if they were at a lower level of stimulation, regardless of what that reaction is. Similarly, if they were already in a low state of stimulation, their reaction will be less intense.

The Demographics of the Target User Group

Is your target audience a broad group? Is their behavior driven by a specific subset of users that can be defined by certain factors like age, income or lifestyle? Is there a critical subset of this group that needs to be satisfied? Answers to questions like this can help you to make decisions about what personality traits to design and how to best tailor interactions to your target user group.

The Likely Emotional State and/or Personality of the Target User Group

Is your product employed in high-arousal situations? Are your users under a lot of stress when they interact with it? Is the target user group a well-defined market with clearly established preferences? If so, this makes it much easier to use personas and other design research tools to profile your users and create a personality that is tailored to their wants and needs.

What intentions and motivations do your target users bring?

The Intentions and Motivations of the Target User Group

What intentions and motivations do your target users bring to the product? Do they want to save time? Do they want to project a professional image?

Define Design Goals

Once you've gotten to know your users, you can begin defining the specific goals of the product you're designing and the personality that best fulfills those goals. Will it be friendly or unfriendly? Will its behavior be dominant or more submissive?

- Identify the target personality of your product.
- Define the macrosuasive goal of the product.
- Define and prioritize the microsuasive goals necessary for the user to reach the macrosuasive goal.
- Define the microsuasive goals for each task.

Identify the Target Personality of Your Product

The product's personality should align with broader brand values.

The target personality should align with and convey broader brand values as well as communicating the values of your product. You can use tools like the product personal, style guides and content strategy to help you envision and align your target personality across channels.

Define the Macrosuasive Goal of the Application

Decide on a macrosuasive goal for the product. What function is it meant to perform? What are users meant to do with it? What emotional benefits will the product provide to the users over time through many uses? What emotional state would lead to the appropriate user behavior? Because of the large number of variables involved, it's difficult to guarantee that a series of microsuasive goals will lead to the completion of a macrosuasive change in behavior. However, it's still a worthwhile goal to pursue.

Brand Traits

FUN *but not childish*

FUNNY *but not goofy*

POWERFUL *but not complicated*

HIP *but not alienating*

EASY *but not simplistic*

TRUSTWORTHY *but not stodgy*

INFORMAL *but not sloppy*

FIG. 5.7 MailChimp Personality Traits

http://aarronwalter.com/design-personas/
© Rocket Science Group

Define and Prioritize the Microsuasive Goals Necessary to Reach the Macrosuasive Goal

Decide on the microsuasive goals for each screen or set of tasks. For example, a microsuasive goal might be to have the user select a language (for a translation program). The designer could accomplish this in a number of ways. The language selection button might have the highest contrast, for example, drawing the user's attention. The button could also be placed in a prominent position to facilitate scanning, or rendered in a color that increases arousal.

UNDERSTANDING THE DIMENSIONS OF EMOTION

Understanding how changes in the two dimensions of emotion (i.e., value and arousal) cause shifts in emotional states is the crucial first step for designers. Creating shifts in value and arousal to command attention and create the conditions for flow is the foundation for all the other guidelines.

> Understanding how to cause shifts in emotions is the first step for designers.

Guidelines for Emotion

Good Versus Bad (Value)

The first appraisals made by users will always be of *value* (i.e., good vs. bad or positive vs. negative) (Reeves & Nass, 1998). Value is a fundamental distinction that is connected to our evolutionary past. We are hard-wired to make judgments of value very quickly. Once made, these evaluations can influence how we think, what we pay attention to and how we behave.

The Negative

The evaluation of good and bad is important, but we don't assign equal weight to both ends of the value scale. Negative experiences hold much more psychological weight than positive ones. Psychologists call this the "Law of Hedonic Asymmetry" (Reeves & Nass, 1998, p. 119). Negative experiences are unpleasant, demand more attention, and cause greater shifts in how we store and use information. Negative emotions and feelings increase arousal and tend to have a greater influence on behavior change.

Information processing is also changed after a negative experience. Experiences that occur right after negative events are remembered better than those that come after positive events. Negative events may enhance memory of what comes after them, but they impair memory of experiences that come before them. The higher levels of attention demanded by negative experiences shift our focus to the negative event, removing it from the previous consideration.

> Negative experiences hold much more psychological weight than positive ones.

This means that the sounds and pictures associated with negative information are better remembered. This applies to both accuracy and speed of recognition. Because negative messages demand more attention, people take longer to react to stimuli that comes after a negative message. Negative responses

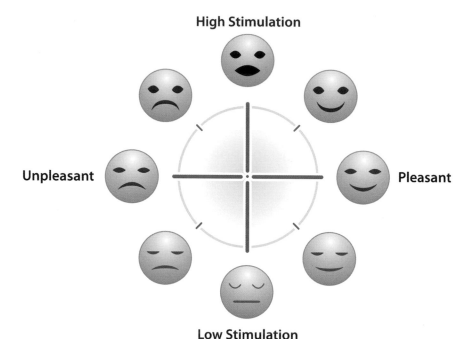

Affective States: Value / Arousal

High Stimulation

Unpleasant

Pleasant

Low Stimulation

FIG. 5.8 Affective States: Value/Arousal

(Adapted from (Russell, 1980.) © Trevor van Gorp

and experiences have a greater influence than positive ones, making it more important for product teams to fix problems (i.e., remove the negative) before adding new features (i.e., adding the positive).

Guidelines for Value

Users:

Remove the negative by fixing problems before adding the positive in the form of new features or functions.

- Do not like negative media
- Pay more attention to negative media than to positive media
- Remember negative media better than positive media
- Have better memory for information that comes after negative media than for information that comes after positive media
- Have worse memory for information that comes before negative media than for information that comes before positive media
  (Reeves & Nass, 1998)

Using negative emotion to increase the strength of a memory may seem useful, but it can have unintended consequences. Attention can be drawn to some unintended

FIG. 5.9 Clicky Error Screen

The Clicky outage screen adds a bit of humor to help mitigate any user frustration.
© Roxr Software Ltd.

aspect of that experience. For example, large images with negative content may overwhelm the text that was intended to communicate the message. Unpleasant error messages from software can cause people to remember negative experiences over positive ones, potentially skewing their overall assessments.

Emotional Arousal

Though good versus bad is our primary judgment, the amount of arousal or stimulation is also important. Arousal influences both attention and the intensity of emotional and cognitive responses. If good and bad had a volume level, you could change that volume by increasing or decreasing arousal.

Judgments of good or bad determine whether a person avoids or approaches a stimulus. But the level of arousal also determines the amount of energy and motivation with which they do so. When there's too little arousal, we lack motivation, while too much arousal can impair functioning.

As with negative experiences, highly arousing events are more easily remembered. In fact, as events become more arousing, they also tend to take on greater value

Arousal levels influence the intensity of good and bad experiences.

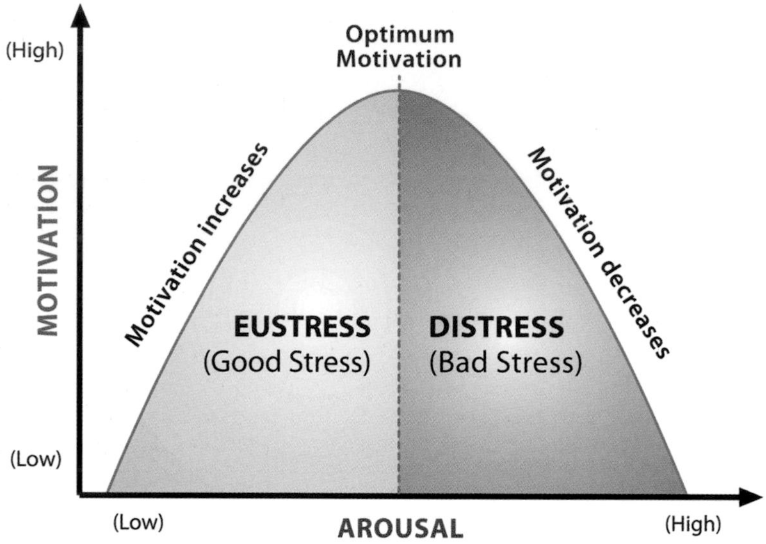

FIG. 5.10 Yerkes-Dodson Law (Motivation)

(Yerkes & Dodson, 1908; additions, van Gorp, 2010) © Trevor van Gorp

one way or the other. It's hard to think of a highly arousing, neutral experience (Reeves & Nass, 1998).

All types of content can trigger emotional reactions, albeit at different levels of arousal. Because arousal has as much capacity for enhancing memory as negative experiences do, highly aroused, positive emotions also enhance memory of events that occur during and after them.

Highly arousing events are more easily remembered.

A good example of this is graduation day. Those who've graduated from high school or university will likely tell you that it's a memory they're unlikely to forget. The combination of ritualized clothing, receiving an award in a large ceremony, and a crowd of people makes for a highly arousing and memorable event.

Guidelines for Arousal

Users:

- Pay more attention to arousing information
- Remember more arousing information better than less arousing information (up to an optimum point)
- Have better memory for information that comes after something arousing than for information that comes before something arousing
- Have impaired memory of information that comes immediately before something arousing
  (Reeves & Nass, 1998)

Because arousal occurs in the body and can carry forward cumulatively, the same experiences may not always elicit the same emotional reaction. In other words, an individual who moves from one highly arousing situation to another does not instantly become relaxed. They bring much of the physiological arousal elicited by previous stimuli to any new situation. Arousal can also be increased and sustained by experiences of different value. So a highly arousing positive experience might be followed by a highly arousing negative experience.

Most of the time, we're seeking to keep users in the balanced state of arousal that comes when they are tackling a worthwhile challenge that they know they can handle with their existing skills. Maintaining this level of arousal assists in the creation of flow. Flow occurs when the level of physiological arousal is balanced between anxiety (i.e., higher stimulation) and boredom (i.e., lower stimulation). Attention can become completely focused on solving challenging tasks to realize goals in an environment with few interruptions (Csikszentmihalyi, 1990).

Because negative responses demand more attention than positive responses, an individual in the flow state can handle fewer negative responses than positive ones. Negative experiences can increase arousal, demand more attention and break the flow.

Flow occurs when the level of physiological arousal is balanced.

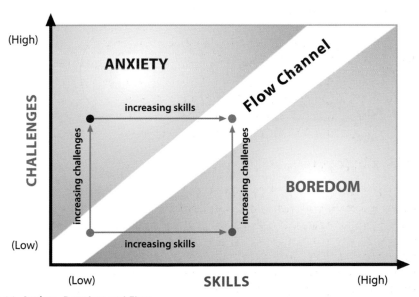

FIG. 5.11 Anxiety, Boredom and Flow

(Csikszentmihalyi, 1990; captions, van Gorp, 2010) © Trevor van Gorp

WHAT PERSONALITY DO I DESIGN?

Before diving into the guidelines for each level of the A.C.T. model, we want to talk a bit about personality. As we mentioned in Chapter 4, people perceive a number of personality traits in products, but the ones that are the most important are related to the distinctions we make between the dimensions of emotion. The first is *friendly* versus *unfriendly*, which is related to our judgments of good versus bad (i.e., value). The second is *dominant* versus *submissive*, which is related to our judgments of arousal levels.

Wearing a suit communicates a different impression than wearing a sweatshirt.

The aesthetic aspects of a product can be used to communicate how friendly the product is as well as the level of dominance. Wearing a business suit communicates a different impression than wearing a hooded sweatshirt. In the same way that a person's clothes will immediately lead to certain assumptions about that person's personality, we quickly form first impressions of product personalities. In the

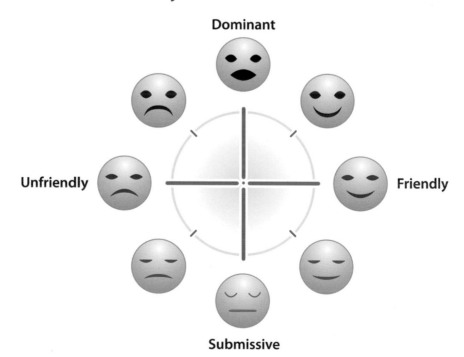

Personality: Friendliness / Dominance

FIG. 5.12 Personality: Friendliness/Dominance

Adapted from (Desmet, 2002; Reeves & Nass, 1998) © Trevor van Gorp

end, the aesthetics and interaction style of the product need to communicate a personality that the user can trust. As Steve Jobs put it, "a great brand means one thing only; it means **trust**" (Isaacson, 2011).

Gender and Personality

The aesthetic aspects of product personality are linked to generalizations about the physical differences between men and women. Products targeted at either gender often reflect these somewhat superficial differences. Despite this, women can still be drawn to so-called masculine product characteristics, depending on their personality and preferences, just as men may be draw to more submissive characteristics. See Chapter 4 for more information on specific aesthetic qualities that are considered dominant or submissive.

As we stated earlier in the book, we believe that when a product's personality is designed to conform to rigid stereotypes, it often winds up failing to serve the needs of its target audience. The best products successfully incorporate both masculine and feminine qualities to transcend stereotypes and create something that serves user's emotional and practical needs in an original and authentic way.

See Chapter 4 for more on specific aesthetic qualities that are considered dominant or submissive.

FIG. 5.13 Men's and Women's Watches
The size difference in these watches reflects superficial differences between the sexes.
© Trevor van Gorp

Communicating Emotion Through Affordances

If every design problem were as simple as reminding yourself to feed the fish, designing for emotion would be simple. In reality, each design context is unique, and the behavior that you're attempting to trigger will inevitably change.

Affordances are clues that suggest how something can be used.

In design and user experience, affordances are those qualities of a product (whether it's an application, website, or physical product) that indicate or suggest to the user what the product can do (Gibson, 1977; Norman, 1999). In other words, affordances are clues that suggest how something can be used. They offer hints about the product's capabilities and functionality, as well as communicating power, status and personality.

In both digital and physical interface design, for example, some buttons need to be designed to afford pressing or clicking. In other words, they need to look like something we'd naturally assume is a button. Other buttons are designed to be used less frequently, and not engaged accidentally. They need to be recognizable as buttons, yet still not be easy to press or click. The design problem (i.e., creating a button that triggers an event) is the same, but the goals, emotions and behavior that you're designing for are different.

Affordances offer hints about capabilities and communicate power, status and personality.

The black keyboard buttons on the MacBook Pro are designed to draw more of the users' attention, *persuading* users to press them. The recessed power button, on the other hand, is designed to *dissuade* users from accidentally shutting off the computer. Both designs persuade or dissuade through the *affordances* of the button (Gibson, 1977; Norman, 1999). In the MacBook Pro example, the black keyboard buttons protrude from the laptop and suggest or "afford" clicking,

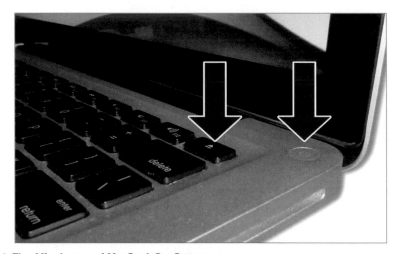

FIG. 5.14 The Affordances of MacBook Pro Buttons

© Trevor van Gorp

while the circular power button is set flush with the surface and does not. Affordances are one way that we can suggest emotional meaning in the things we design.

A.C.T. GUIDELINES

People are strongly oriented toward both social relationships and environments with predictable rules and feedback. We expect products to behave in a manner that mirrors the general rules of human social conduct. Understanding and applying this idea has several benefits. Since most of us have been learning the rules of human social interaction since birth, we already possess these skills. Applying these rules to human-product interactions makes usage more predictable and enjoyable. Product interactions become part of a relationship, with the resulting feelings of trust, attachment, accomplishment and competence.

Reeves and Nass (1998) built a collection of social rules for smart products by researching them in person-to-person interactions, and then applied the results to human-computer interactions. We'll refer to these rules when discussing the guidelines in the A.C.T. model. By applying the natural rules of human interaction to our interactions with products, we can make the relationships we have with them more rewarding and fulfilling.

We expect product behavior to mirror the rules of human social conduct.

Attract

When given a choice, consumers make decisions based largely on their emotions. To be chosen and purchased, your product must first *Attract* its potential owner in some way. Whether it's a coat on the rack at the department store, or a website that users judge in a matter of seconds, your product needs to be attractive to the customer or user.

Unless you're designing a product where the intended behavior is avoidance (like a fire alarm), attraction is usually the beginning of the relationship building process. It occurs largely unconsciously, based on the specific aesthetic properties of the object itself (i.e., size, proportion, composition, color, contrast, shape, movement, sound and feel). In other words, the person experiencing attraction doesn't have to think about it. It simply happens (or it doesn't). The unconscious nature of attraction makes it an especially powerful channel for designers.

Attraction is usually the beginning of the relationship building process.

Attracting the attention of users can be accomplished in a number of ways. People are generally attracted to things that display appealing aesthetic properties and are similar in personality to how they would like to see themselves. Objects that we find attractive trigger the desire to approach and begin interaction and conversation.

In Chapter 4, we mentioned that positive emotions are associated with a friendly personality and negative emotions are associated with an unfriendly personality. Similarly, high-arousal emotions and experiences are associated with dominant personality traits, while lower-arousal emotions (relatively speaking) are associated with more submissive or passive personality traits.

But what about something a bit more subtle? For example, how would we apply these ideas to make an organization's website more attractive? After years with no central authority, the City of Edmonton's web presence was visually crowded and lacked clear organization. Inconsistent navigation confused users and poorly differentiated content competed for users' attention. Overcrowding can increase arousal, but in a negative way that leads to avoidance behavior.

Visual overcrowding can increase arousal, but in a negative way.

The target audience for a website representing a city of approximately one million people is broad, with a wide range of skill levels. Design changes were intended to lower the perception of challenge to accommodate users with lower levels of computer literacy. Reducing the number of items on the home page decreased the demands on attention. The layout was reorganized around the city's communication priorities, with priority placement for the most popular content, which changes throughout the year as users' information needs change. Further reductions in the level of challenge were accomplished by moving to a simpler, more consistent navigation structure and information architecture.

A feed of the news from every city department is updated throughout the day. This element of constantly updating content helps maintains a sense of novelty and excitement as users visit the site day after day.

Smooth transitions increase arousal and attract attention through movement.

Once the challenges around accessing information were reduced, it was time to increase attraction and arousal in order to motivate the user to approach and interact. Introducing visual hierarchy into the design helped to focus attention on important areas. On the home page, large images with stories about the city occupy the primary real estate. These images cycle through using smooth transitions that increase arousal and attract attention through movement. The larger size and more prominent position of the images means an increase in positive attention. All together, these changes to the aesthetic and interactive qualities of the site allowed it to demand more attention, and become more attractive, usable and memorable for users.

When we attract users, we trigger approach behavior that can initiate interaction, which can then evolve into a relationship. Pleasant experiences make people approach; unpleasant experiences make people avoid. High-arousal experiences have been connected to high levels of motivation; low-arousal experiences have been connected to low levels of motivation.

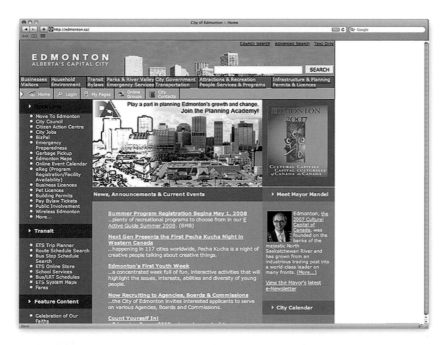

FIG. 5.15 City of Edmonton: Redesign Based on Attract Principles

(user experience design by Affective Design Inc.; visual design by Yellow Pencil Inc.)

© *City of Edmonton*

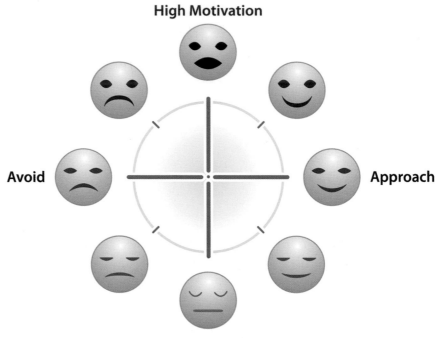

FIG. 5.16 **Behavior: Intention/Motivation**

© *Trevor van Gorp*

Guidelines for Attraction

Attractive products and interfaces are more credible than unattractive ones.

Communicating personality through design involves the use of aesthetics that communicate both an emotion and personality that the user finds attractive. People are generally attracted to products that are *similar* in some way to themselves or how they would like to see themselves:

- Attractive products and interfaces are more persuasive than unattractive ones.
- Attractive products and interfaces are judged as more credible than unattractive ones.

People are more easily persuaded by products and interfaces that they perceive are similar to themselves in some way (Fogg, 2003).

The Aesthetics of Personality

Generally speaking, if an aesthetic element is considered positive, it can be used to communicate a friendly personality. If an aesthetic element is considered negative, it can be used to communicate an unfriendly personality.

If an aesthetic element produces higher arousal, it can be used to communicate a more dominant personality. If an aesthetic element reduces arousal, it can be used to communicate a more submissive personality. Keep in mind that the best products are those that combine dominant and submissive characteristics in ways that, while internally consistent, are authentic and original.

If an aesthetic element is considered negative, it can communicate an unfriendly personality.

Color

One way to match personality through appearance is with color. The hue of the color is judged in terms of value, while the saturation level has effects on physiological arousal.

We can connect color to friendliness and unfriendliness by looking at the behaviors that are associated with different colors and hues. In western society, for example, red is strongly associated with "stop," or avoidance behaviors. Green is associated with "go," or approach behaviors.

Traits	DOMINANT	SUBMISSIVE
Arousal	High Stimulation	Low Stimulation
Visual	Angular	Curved
	Straight	Round
	Up	Down
	Above	Below
	Bigger	Smaller
	Heavy	Light weight
	Robust	Delicate
	In Motion	At Rest
	Silver	Golden
	Cool	Warm
Text	Uppercase	Lowercase
	Bold	Regular
Tactile	Rough	Smooth
	Hard	Soft
Auditory	Louder	Quieter
	Deeper	Higher

FIG. 5.17 Dominant versus Submissive Traits

Adapted from (Wellman, Bruder & Olsterdorf, 2004) © Trevor van Gorp

RED	GREEN
Reject	Accept
Disagree	Agree
Incomplete	Complete
No	Yes
Off	On
Down	Up
Remove	Add
Bad	Good
Low	High
Fail	Succeed
Closed	Opened
Offline	Online
Cancel	Save
Unavailable	Available
Negative	Positive
Dislike	Like

FIG. 5.18 Red versus Green Color Table

Color associations can reinforce the meaning of words used in interfaces.

Adapted from (Kissmetrics, 2009) © Trevor van Gorp

The saturation level has effects on physiological arousal.

Be careful when using the hue of a color to evoke an emotional response because color associations can vary among cultures. In China for example, red is associated with wealth, celebration and luck, all of which may trigger approach behaviors. In both cultures, the meanings associated with red involve high-arousal emotions. Only the value of the association is different. This reflects the unconscious nature of arousal.

Because it's connected to arousal levels, color saturation can be used to automatically draw attention to different portions of a product or interface. Some general rules for color include the following:

- We pay attention to colors we like and ignore those we don't.
- In terms of hue, orange and red increase arousal and attract the most attention.

FIG. 5.19 Werther's Candies

Werther's uses gold foil to make their candies seem more precious and valuable.
© Trevor van Gorp

- Colors with a higher saturation affects arousal independent of the hue (i.e., higher saturation = higher arousal).
- The contrast of a color against its background affects arousal (i.e., higher contrast = higher arousal).
- Red, yellow and orange are considered more aggressive, dynamic, and active than colors in the blue range, which are considered more passive and calm (Fehrman & Fehrman, 2000).

We can use color associations to increase the perception of value.

We can use color associations to increase the perceived value of something. For example, Werther's candies use a gold foil wrap to make each candy seem more precious and valuable.

Line and Form

As we learned in Chapter 4, line and form are primitive visual cues connected through association to the physical expression of different emotions. For this reason, line and form unconsciously exert a profound influence on perceptions of emotion and personality. Lines pointing or moving upwards express strength, energy, force, ambition and uplifting feelings; lines pointing downwards express weakness, a lack of energy, relaxation, or depression (Lundholm, 1921).

Furious
(angry, cross, vexed, enraged)

FIG. 5.20 Furious (angry, cross, vexed, enraged)
Line with small or medium angles, pointing up.
(Poffenberger & Barrows, 1924) © Trevor van Gorp

Line and form are primitive visual cues connected to the expression of different emotions.

The directional tendency of a line expresses arousal levels:

- Lines pointing in an upward direction are perceived to be higher arousal.
- Lines pointing in a downward direction are perceived to be lower arousal.

The directional tendency of a line affects perceptions of power:

- Lines pointing in an upward direction are perceived to be more powerful.
- Lines pointing in a downward direction are perceived to be less powerful.

The shape of a form will affect perceptions of personality:

- Angular forms are perceived to be more dominant.
- Rounded forms are perceived to be more submissive.

The perceived hardness or roughness will affect perceptions of personality:

- Hard forms are perceived to be more dominant.
- Soft forms are perceived to be more submissive.

The perceived weight of a form will affect perceptions of personality:

- Heavy forms are perceived to be more dominant.
- Lite forms are perceived to be more submissive
  (Reeves & Nass, 1998).

Size is one of the most important and primitive visual cues.

Image Size

Size is one of the most important and primitive visual cues. Size helps us determine what's close or far away, as well as what's coming towards us. Because people and objects that are larger than us may pose a threat, larger things generally increase our level of emotional arousal. If you've ever visited the

FIG. 5.21 Remember Your First Visit to the Mountains?

(Photo courtesy of Hailey O'Hara)

mountains, you're not likely to forget them for their sheer size and the sense of awe they inspire.

Increased emotional arousal means enhanced memory, so large objects are also more easily remembered. Although we may know consciously that a large object on a screen is not actually large, we still react as if that object were real.

Larger images are:

- More arousing than smaller ones
- Better remembered than smaller ones
- Better liked than smaller ones
  (Reeves & Nass, 1998)

Screen Size

Screen size also plays a role in judgments of image size. Devices with very small screens are likely to be less arousing than those designed with larger screens.

A larger screen means your eye will be able to focus on only a limited portion of the screen at any given time. This area of focus is called **foveal vision**. Movement outside of foveal vision in our peripheral vision demands a great deal of attention (Wickens & Hollands, 2000). With smaller screens, this is usually not an issue because the entire screen is within the field of view. This is one reason that devices with smaller screens are less stimulating.

- Larger screens increase emotional arousal.
- Close-ups shown on large screens increase arousal levels.
- Close-ups shown on small screens increase arousal levels to create a more intimate and immersive environment.
(Reeves & Nass, 1998)

High levels of arousal can be counter-productive to learning and performance.

Larger screens mean increased arousal, improved memory, and more positive feelings toward the content. Consideration of image size is important, especially if the content will be displayed at different screen sizes. For example, images that appear much larger than their actual size because of a large screen should be framed differently than images that will be displayed on the screen of a cell phone.

Large, highly arousing images (although great for enhancing emotional experience), should not be so arousing as to demand all attention in learning contexts. High levels of arousal can be counterproductive when one needs to learn content or perform tasks. It may be only the large image that's remembered, rather than the actual content. In entertainment contexts, the size of images has been steadily increasing as movie and television screens become larger. Entertaining ourselves often doesn't present much of a challenge, so arousal levels can be higher.

FIG. 5.22 Image Size and Framing

Electronics © Cobalt - Fotolia.com Photo by Curtis Lipscombe

FIG. 5.23 Interpersonal Distance in Photos

Photo by Curtis Lipscombe

Distance in Images

Many products display images of people. Everyone has their own comfortable level of interpersonal space, even though the size of that space may vary across cultures. The meaning of social behavior changes as people change the distance between them. Violating someone's personal space can produce feelings of discomfort and hostility. The less attracted you are to someone, the worse it is to have that person close to you.

However, when people are invited into your personal space, close distances can produce extremely positive reactions:

- Viewers pay more attention to close-ups of people.
- Viewers remember people in close-ups better.
  (Reeves & Nass, 1998)

If a face fills our visual field, it's unconsciously interpreted as a face that is very close to us, instead of a large image on a screen. The person is perceived to be either very large in size or very close to the viewer.

Altering the distance between two people changes the intensity of the emotional response for everyone involved. Close interpersonal distances can be positively or negatively arousing. In either case, arousal focuses attention and enhances memory. The body becomes ready for action. The focus is on the intentions of the other person, which can usually be anticipated from reading aesthetic cues.

When invited, close interpersonal distances can produce extremely positive reactions.

Motion

Motion alerts us and demands our attention, especially if it occurs within our peripheral vision where we're not focusing. This is an evolutionary mechanism, designed to allow us to respond more quickly to possible unknown threats. Attention is higher during sequences with movement, and enhanced memory follows enhanced attention.

FIG. 5.24 Old TV Proportions vs. New TV Proportions

Flat screen @ Cobalt - Fotolia.com, Television @ ksiuha - Fotolia.com Photo by Curtis Lipscombe

Newer television screens, especially widescreen monitors, closely resemble the aspect ratio of the human field of vision. In the normal human field of vision, more field of view is available to the left and the right than above or below. Most of the field of view is composed of peripheral vision, where fidelity is not high. On a horizontal screen, more action occurs in peripheral vision so more arousal is produced. However, the movement that draws attention in peripheral vision may not contain the content that the viewer was intended to remember.

Slow, smooth motions can enhance immersion and characterization.

- Viewers will orient their attention to visual surprises.
- Motion demands more attention than no motion.
  (Reeves & Nass, 1998)

Images or information that are presented slightly (about one second) after motion begins are better remembered than those that appear during movement (Reeves & Nass, 1998). The quality of the motion, whether it is fast or slow, smooth or jerky, has implications as well. Slow, smooth motions can mimic the processes of nature, thereby enhancing immersion and characterization. One example of this is the power light on Apple computers. When the computer is put "to sleep," the power indicator light pulses gently in a rhythmic motion that mimics the breathing rate of a sleeping human.

Scene Changes

In software and portable computing, scene changes are commonplace. These cuts indicate new screens and new sets of available actions or functions.

Changing to a different application or moving between tasks usually means some form of cut. Cuts change the frame and meaning of content by shifting the scene to a completely different view. Cuts demand the same levels of attention that motion does. Like motion, images or information that are presented slightly (about one second) after the cut are better remembered than those that appear closer to the cut (Reeves & Nass, 1998).

- Visual cuts demand user's attention.
- Cuts between related segments are less intrusive than cuts between unrelated segments.
- Increased cuts translate to more favorable evaluations of people in scenes.
- The more cuts, the higher the attention (up to an optimum point).
  (Reeves & Nass, 1998, pp. 228–233)

A higher number of cuts in a segment with a person translates into a better evaluation of that person's personality. More cuts equal a more stimulating visual style, which translates into the perception of a more dynamic personality. Traits such as perceived honesty, trust, intelligence, open-mindedness, and sincerity were all affected (Reeves & Nass, 1998). Too many cuts will actually decrease attention. When we're unable to process all the cuts that are happening, we tune out. With either too many or too few cuts, attention decreases.

Cuts demand the same levels of attention that motion does.

Cuts can also use transitions to help establish their relationships. An example would be the "Genie" effect on the Mac OS X operating system. In this effect, icons morph into full windows and then back into icons, making the relationship between the icon and the application clear.

To be used effectively, cuts should simulate the ways in which people view scenes in real life. Long shots should move into closer shots, as they would in real life. Cuts should function as signals that a unit of information is finished and another has begun. In this sense, cuts are a form of chunking, allowing related information to be contained within a specific unit or chunk.

Converse

According to Kemper (1978), studies of relationship dynamics have shown that most interactions can be understood in terms of two dimensions: power and status. Social exchanges depend not only on the content of the interaction, but also on the form of that content. Take another look at this image from Chapter 2. Can you see how power and status judgments come into play in our reactions to design? Which line of type do you perceive to be more powerful? Which has higher status?

WHERE ARE YOU GOING?

Where are you going?

FIG. 5.25 **Power, Status and Meaning**

@ Trevor van Gorp

Users' experiences are the result of unconscious power and status judgments. User frustrations can be unconsciously triggered by a product's seeming refusal to submit to the user's greater power or acknowledge what the user thought was his or her higher status.

Power

Power can be seen as "the chance of a person or a number of people to realize their own will … against the resistance of others" (Kemper, 1978, p. 35). Historically, realizing one's will against the resistance of others has often required the use of force or coercion. In design, we are attempting to make changes in attitudes and behavior through persuasion, which is a voluntary change.

> **Products need to strike a dynamic balance between simplicity and complexity.**

In design, the perception of power can be communicated through aesthetics or things like feature lists or capabilities. Simple products can be seen as lacking power or capability. Many customers purchase products marketed with extensive feature lists because they perceive these products to be more powerful. It's only later, when actually using the product, that they're often upset at the lack of usability (Norman, 2007).

Products need to strike a dynamic balance between simplicity and complexity in order to appear powerful enough to complete the task, yet still below the user in the social pecking order. As we mentioned in Chapter 4, head of Apple design Jonathan Ive has said about products, "we have to feel we can dominate them" (Isaacson, 2011). The dynamic nature of this balance is related to the dynamic balance between power and status, and the dynamic balance of challenge and skill.

Status

Status is the level of honor or prestige connected to one's position in society. If an individual has status, it means that another individual must give him or her that status. Status is a type of reward that's given voluntarily, rather than through the use of coercion or power. The voluntary nature of status is one of the things differentiates it from rewards acquired through the use of force or coercion.

> **Different types of status being are more important to some groups than others.**

Status can be measured in a number of ways, with different types of status being more important to some groups than others. People are often given **ascribed status** based on their age, race, gender or economic situation. **Achieved status** requires the acquisition of honors through the display of superior skill or ability (Foladare, 1969). **Material status** describes status based on displays of wealth, and **cultural status** can describe taste or style (Jordan, 2000).

We can also give ourselves status in the form of self-esteem, based on how we judge our own behavior. When our performance meets up to our expectations, we experience pleasure and satisfaction, which reduces arousal and the motivation to act. When our performance fails to meet our expectations, we experience displeasure, dissatisfaction and higher arousal levels, which increase the motivation to act.

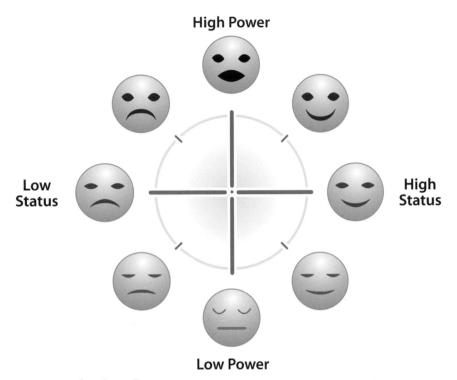

Interaction: Status / Power

High Power

Low Status

High Status

Low Power

FIG. 5.26 **Interaction: Status/Power**

(Adapted from Kemper, 1978) @ Trevor van Gorp

When the user can't complete tasks with a product, they may feel inadequate or lose some self-assigned status. Because we unconsciously treat our interactions with products as social interactions, the user may interpret his or her errors for a lack of power or status.

The relationship between power and status can also be illustrated. The diagram of social interaction relates to the diagram of emotional states. Here, we can see the relative levels of power and status overlaid on to the different levels of value and arousal.

Emotions like embarrassment can result from a perceived lack of cultural or material status. Users may feel ashamed of their lack of technical knowledge, or fearful of looking or feeling stupid. Having inaccurate expectations can also lead to social failures and a loss of status. Self-conscious emotions include fear, shame, guilt, vanity, embarrassment and pride (Thoits, 2004).

The user may interpret his or her errors for a lack of power or status.

If you view the product as a human being within the social pecking order, the user would then be submitting to the product. Unless the product is taking a dominant position by guiding or leading the user, the product should submit by giving the user higher *power* and *status*. The product can accomplish this by being easy to interact with, offering quick feedback, deferring to the user, and offering rewards at the end of sequences of action to motivate the user along the way.

Guidelines for Conversation

When we engage a product or an interface in "conversation," we are unconsciously applying power and status judgments to the interaction. We judge the product or interface based on human social rules. Does it respond when a button is pressed? "Why is this product insulting me by ignoring me? How dare this thing make me wait? Doesn't it know who I am?"

Why is this product insulting me by ignoring me?

One aspect of designing conversation that doesn't get the attention it deserves is the content itself. Content strategy helps the product communicate successfully by identifying and planning for the required content. Failing to provide the content necessary to form accurate expectations and complete tasks can result in frustration or anger. Without a solid content strategy, it's hard to guarantee that the experience of any kind of knowledge-based product will be relevant and *useful*, not to mention *usable* or *desirable*.

All product conversations should follow four principles that govern human conversations. Whether it's another person or a product, violations of these principles are perceived as socially offensive. When we apply these principles to content, we can see how failing to follow them could cause frustration in users.

> **Quality:** Content should be factually correct.
> **Quantity:** The amount of content should be appropriate for the conversation.
> **Relevance:** The content should be relevant to the purpose of the conversation.
> **Clarity:** The relevance of the content that's presented should clear.
> (Reeves & Nass, 1998)

Users bring different emotional states to the interaction.

When we design products to converse with our customers, we need to be aware that users bring different emotional states to the interaction. The tone of the content in a help screen, for example, should reflect the fact that the user might be confused. Content in a success message should have a more celebratory tone. Depending on what part of the product we're designing, we'll need to provide different types of emotional experiences. MailChimp's online style guide, "Voice and Tone" (Rocket Science Group, 2011) contains a set of guidelines for creating content that is suited to the emotional context of the user's situation while also maintaining a consistent personality for the application. By customizing interaction styles to the context of the design, conversation can be used to communicate a personality that establishes connection and trust.

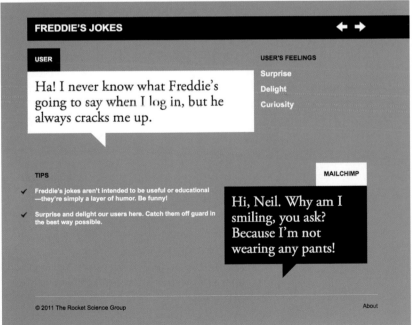

FIG. 5.27 Voice and Tone: Success Message and Freddie's Jokes

http://voiceandtone.com @ Rocket Science Group

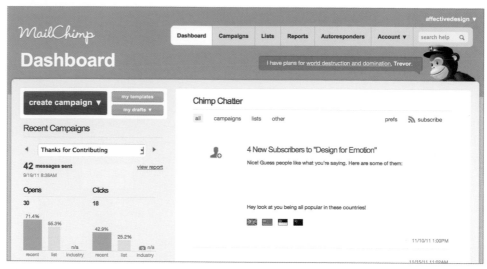

FIG. 5.28 MailChimp

The MailChimp interface mixes dominant and submissive personality traits.
http://mailchimp.com @ Rocket Science Group

Dominant and Submissive Interaction

People who describe themselves as "dominant" also tend to describe themselves as strong, assertive, aggressive, competitive, extroverted and self-confident. People who describe themselves as "submissive" also tend to describe themselves as weak, shy, timid, introverted and yielding (Reeves & Nass, 1998; Jordan, 2000). Language, content and manners can be used to communicate these personality traits in an interface or product.

The way products present information is a vital component of how that information is interpreted. For example, statements made in a certain and unambiguous fashion tend to be considered more dominant. Statements made in a more ambiguous way tend to be considered more submissive.

Language, content and manners can be used to communicate personality traits.

Remember, when it comes to conversation, you're looking to design a *complementary* personality. For example, a product that functions as an assistant should interact more passively while one that is functioning as an instructor should interact in a more dominant way. The dominant product might always go first, prompting the user, where a more submissive product would wait to be prompted, allowing the user to go first. As we mentioned in Chapter 4, when it comes to conversation, someone has to lead, and opposites attract.

The use of positive language is an example of a friendly interactive quality. An unfriendly interactive personality might use negative language that restricts the user from completing certain tasks. In an interesting twist on this idea, MailChimp chose a friendly-dominant personality for their mascot, but removed that personality from the actual workflow of the application. The MailChimp mascot (i.e., Freddie von Chimpenheimer the IVth) simply observes and makes humorous comments, rather than actually being involved in your work. However, the application itself is very usable and easy to converse with. With this mix of dominant and submissive qualities, the MailChimp interface is a great example of combining both masculine and feminine characteristics to create something that's both original and authentic.

The Manners of Interaction and Conversation

Basic rules of human etiquette also apply when designing products. Adding "manners" to products to help evoke emotions and build relationships doesn't require new technology—only a new way of thinking about design. It's often as easy as paying more attention to the emotional qualities evoked by the dialog between the user and the product in different situations.

Hello and Goodbye

Products should always greet a user when they arrive and ask permission or implicitly indicate they're leaving with words, a sound, a gesture, or a screen shift before they go (Reeves & Nass, 1998).

Greet the user when they arrive.

FIG. 5.29 Dashboard Greets User When Starting Car (Mazda 3)

@ Trevor van Gorp

Praise and Flattery

Products that offer flattery are preferred over those who offer no opinion at all. When we're praised, we're less motivated to distinguish between honesty and dishonesty, as praise makes us feel good. When evaluations are less positive, we often look for ways to dismiss them but still feel that they're true. Whether praise is warranted or not has no effect on what people think about the product that offers the praise (Reeves & Nass, 1998).

People will:

- Believe flattery provided by a product
- Like a product that flatters more than a product that says nothing
- Like a product that flatters more than a product that criticizes
  (Reeves & Nass, 1998, p. 54)

Flatter novices generously. Experts need more subtle and specific forms of flattery.

You can use praise to celebrate successes or encourage people to recover from a setback. Error messages and other negative signals often blame and criticize the user. Because people with less knowledge of a situation are more affected by their emotional responses, it's good to give novices more flattery. Experts need more subtle forms of flattery, focusing on more detailed actions. Almost everyone enjoys praise and dislikes criticism. Be careful not to offend.

Gender Stereotypes and Voice

Attributing gender to products is an automatic process, using the cues we perceive through aesthetics, interaction, and voice. Implicit in judgments of product personality is the perception of product gender. Such perceptions touch upon users' unconscious gender stereotypes. These stereotypes are associations that describe the appearance, attitudes, and behaviors of each sex and are used to anticipate how people (and products) will behave.

Stereotypes are associations that describe appearance, attitudes and behaviors.

According to Reeves and Nass (1998), praise from more masculine-sounding voices (whether they belong to a man or a woman) has more perceived weight than the same praise from voices that sound more feminine. Masculine-sounding voices are thought to possess greater skills in technical fields compared to feminine-sounding voices. Feminine-sounding voices, on the other hand, are perceived to know more about relationships, emotions and love.

People attribute:

- More drive to masculine voices than feminine voices
- More extroversion to masculine voices than feminine voices
- More willpower to masculine voices than feminine voices
- More persuasive ability to masculine voices than feminine voices
- More intelligence to masculine voices than feminine voices
- More weight to evaluations from masculine voices
  (Reeves & Nass, 1998)

The product's aesthetics, style of interaction and voice must work together to communicate a consistent expression of personality. Voices that conflict with the other elements of a product's personality will confuse and distract the user, destroying trust.

Apple's virtual assistant Siri is a good example of successfully combining both masculine and feminine traits. In North America, Siri has a feminine voice; in the United Kingdom, Siri has a masculine voice. The North American version is a good example of an authentic personality. Even with a more feminine voice, Siri's comments are both feisty and feminine.

Aesthetics, interaction, and voice must communicate a consistent personality.

Transact

When the user is satisfied that the aesthetic and interactive qualities of a product personality are consistent and the product reliably performs as expected, the product gains credibility and begins to earn the user's trust. The user is then more comfortable subscribing, providing contact information, or making a purchase. In other words, the user is comfortable making a commitment to the relationship in the form of a *Transaction*.

To build trust, a product's personality needs to be consistently expressed in all channels. When products express the many personalities of the people who designed them, users can become confused about the product's identity. An easily identifiable personality that is consistently expressed means that half your users will usually like it (Reeves & Nass, 1998). Characters that display inconsistent personalities are confusing and provoke negative emotions. This doesn't mean that your product's personality should avoid expressing different emotions in different kinds of situations. It means that the emotions you choose to express should be appropriate for the context of the design, as well as consistent with the personality your product expresses in other situations.

The personality of a product should be suited to the personality of the user group and the tasks and goals of the product. As we've mentioned, a product that functions as an assistant should be more submissive, while a product that is functioning as an instructor should be more dominant.

Inconsistent personalities are confusing and provoke negative emotions.

The Perception of Personality

The more clearly defined and homogenous your target audience, the easier it is to define the personality of your product. A dominant product might use higher contrast, highly saturated colors, sharp, angular forms and dominant language, and always be the first to initiate interaction. A submissive product would use lower contrast, low saturation colors and passive and submissive language, and always wait for the user to initiate interaction.

FIG. 5.30 Dominant and Submissive Designs

@ Trevor van Gorp

CONCLUSIONS

People respond to products in the same ways they respond to other people.

In this chapter, we've used the metaphor of human relationships to help describe the relationships we have with products. Thinking of product ownership and usage in this way frames every exchange between the product and the user as a social interaction that results in emotional reactions, experiences and relationships.

Before picking up this book, you might have dismissed the idea that people's emotional reactions to products, applications, and websites are the same as their reactions to other people. But in human-product interaction, perception has more influence than reality.

Even simple interfaces, like a screen with text, prompts reactions like those a person would elicit. People respond to products in the same ways they respond to other people. Like other people, products can demand our attention through both their aesthetics and manner of interaction. Products are not merely tools, but function more as living objects to whom we attribute personality and judge according to human social rules.

How do you design for emotion? You can't *not* design for emotion. All "uses of media lead people to allocate attention, assign personality, manage arousal, assess competence, organize information in memory, determine likes and dislikes, and experience physical changes in the body and brain" (Reeves & Nass, 1998, p. 253).

We perceive emotions in products and ascribe personality to them on the basis of aesthetic properties like language use, color, visual form, voice and gender. Whether it's a person or a product, once people perceive that an emotion has been expressed, they respond to those displays of emotion in a natural and automatic way (Fogg, 2003).

People like simplicity and predictability from both other people and from technology. To instill trust, any personality should be consistent within the product, its packaging and its marketing. If exchanges with the product have provided a positive impression, establishing trust and instilling confidence, the user will feel comfortable transacting with that personality. By designing products that conform to the rules we've learned by interacting with other people, we can help new and experienced technology users to form better relationships with products.

You can't *not* design for emotion.

In Chapter 2, we said that a good model:

- Is easy to understand, so that other people can enter the discussion and collaborate
- Helps predict what will occur so you can adjust your own actions accordingly
- Helps share and communicate ideas that are abstract and can't be seen or touched
- Is easy to apply in the context of the design process

When applied to design, the A.C.T. model helps you to understand both the users' requirements, and how the product itself interacts with the user to fulfill those requirements. It's easy to understand and apply in the design process, and helps in predicting design outcomes and communicating ideas. A.C.T. encompasses a number of different perspectives on the design of emotional products and services.

A.C.T. Model
Attract

- Processed unconsciously and automatically (Reptilian brain)
- Aesthetics of the product (i.e., sight, sound, smell, touch, movement, and color)
- Whether users' find the aesthetics appealing
- Pleasures and passions the aesthetics provide

Converse

- Processed unconsciously and automatically (Mammalian brain)
- How the product interacts and behaves (i.e., ease of use)
- Whether the product meets up to users' standards
- Benefits that come from use and the completion of tasks
- Feelings of intimacy and connection

Transact

- Processed consciously—can override unconscious (Neomammalian brain)
- Based on the attribution of personality communicated through the qualities of the aesthetics and interaction
- The product's contributions to our self-image and identity
- Benefits that come from the completion of goals
- Feelings of trust leading to commitment

Forge better relationships between people and the products they use.

The A.C.T. model helps practitioners to systematically address the requirements necessary to create successful relationships with products. By identifying the personality of your users, matching it to your product's personality, and then actually designing, marketing, advertising, and packaging the product with that personality in mind, you can help people forge better relationships with the products that they own and use, fostering product and brand loyalty.

In the end, it requires the skill and sensitivity of the designer, marketer and branding professional to make every interaction consistent, beautiful, authentic and appropriate for their target audience.

In Chapter 6, we feature interviews and case studies with some of the top design professionals currently applying emotion in their design process.

REFERENCES

Anderson, S. P. (2011). *Seductive Interaction Design. Creating Playful, Fun, and Effective User Experiences*, Berkeley: New Riders Press.

Csikszentmihalyi, M. (1990). *Flow: The psychology of optimal experience.* New York: Harper Perennial.

Desmet, P. R. (2002). *Designing emotions.* Delft: Pieter Desmet.

Fehrman, K. R., & Fehrman, C. (2000). *Color: The secret influence.* Saddle River, NJ: Prentice Hall, Inc.

Fogg, B. J. (2003). *Persuasive technology: Using computers to change what we think and do.* San Francisco: Morgan Kaufmann Publishers.

Foladare, I. S. (1969). A clarification of "ascribed status" and "achieved status." *The Sociological Quarterly*. Vol 10, Issue 1, p. 53–61, Jan., 1969.

Gibson, J. J. (1977). The theory of affordances. In R. Shaw and J. Bransford (Eds.), *Perceiving, Acting and Knowing.*

Hastings, Reed. (2011). An explanation and some reflections. Netflix blog. <http://blog .netflix.com/2011/09/explanation-and-some-reflections.html> Accessed 10.20.11.

Isaacson, W. (2011). *Steve Jobs.* New York: Simon & Schuster.

Jackson, R. (2011). Six things Jeff Bezos knew back in 1997 that made Amazon a gorilla. *Forbes.* <http://www.forbes.com/sites/ericjackson/2011/11/16/6-things-jeff-bezos-knew-back-in-1997-that-made-amazon-a-gorilla/> Accessed 12.17.11.

Jordan, P. W. (2000). *Designing pleasurable products.* London: Taylor & Francis.

Kemper, T. D. (1978). *A social interactional theory of emotions.* West Sussex: John Wiley & Sons Ltd.

Kissmetrics. (2009). Communicating color efficiently: Red & green. *Kissmetrics Blog.* <http://blog.kissmetrics.com/communicating-color-efficiently/> Accessed 11.20.11.

Lundholm, H. (1921). The affective tone of lines: Experimental researches. *Psychological Review, 28*(1), 43–60.

McLean, P. D. (1990). *The triune brain in evolution: Role in paleocerebral functions.* New York: Plenum Press.

Norman, D. (1999). Affordances, Conventions and Design. *Interactions 6*(3), 38–43.

Norman, D. A. (2004). *Emotional design: Why we love (or hate) everyday things.* New York: Basic Books.

Norman, D. (2007). Simplicity is highly overrated. *Interactions 14*(3). CACM. <http://www .jnd.org/dn.mss/simplicity_is_highly_overrated.html> Accessed 08.03.11.

Poffenberger, A. T., & Barrows, B. E. (1924). The feeling value of lines. *Journal of Applied Psychology, 8*, 187–205.

Reeves, B., & Nass, C. (1998). *The media equation: How people treat computers, television and new media like real people and places.* Cambridge: Cambridge University Press.

Rocket Science Group. (2011). *VoiceandTone.com.* <http://voiceandtone.com> Accessed 12.10.11.

Russell, J. A. (1980). A circumplex model of affect. *Journal of Personality and Social Psychology, 39*, 1161–1178.

Saari, T. (2005). Mind-based media and communications technologies. How the form of symbolical information influences felt meaning. In *Acta Universitatis Tamperensis*, 843. Tampere: Tampere University Press. <http://acta.uta.fi/pdf/951-44-5225-9.pdf> Accessed 06.14.05.

Saari, T., Ravaja, N., Laarni, J., Turpeinen, M., & Kallinen, K. (2004). Psychologically targeted persuasive advertising and product information in e-commerce. ACM International Conference Proceeding Series; Vol. 60. Proceedings of the 6th international conference on Electronic commerce. Delft, The Netherlands. <http://portal.acm.org/citation.cfm?id=1052220.1052252> Accessed 07.03.05.

Sanders, E. B. N. (1992, Fall). Converging perspectives: Product development research for the 1990s. *Design Management Journal, 3*(4), 49–54.

Sternberg, R. J. (1988). *The Triangle of Love: Intimacy, Passion, Commitment*. New York: Basic Books.

Thoits, P. A. (2004). Emotion norms, emotion work, and social order. *Feelings and emotions: The Amsterdam Symposium* (pp. 359–378). Cambridge: Cambridge University Press.

van Gorp, Trevor, J. (2010). *Design for Emotion and Flow*, IA Summit. ASIS&T, Phoenix. 2010.

Walter, A. (2011). *MailChimp Personality Traits*. <http://aarronwalter.com/design-personas/> Accessed 12.10.11.

Wellman, K., Bruder, R., & Oltersdorf, K. (2004). Gender designs: Aspects of gender found in the design of perfume bottles. In D. McDonagh & P. Hekkert (Eds.), *Design and emotion: The experience of everyday things*, New York: Taylor & Francis.

Wickens, C. D., & Hollands, J. G. (2000). *Engineering psychology and human performance* (3rd ed.). Upper Saddle River, N.J.: Prentice Hall.

Yerkes, R. M., & Dodson, J. D. (1908). The relation of strength of stimulus to rapidity of habit-formation. *Journal of Comparative Neurology and Psychology, 18*, 459–482.

Interviews and Case Studies

6

In Chapter 5, we introduced the A.C.T. model; a framework that describes how to design for the different stages of product relationships.

This chapter features interviews and case studies from some of the sharpest minds in the industry on the topic of designing for emotion. We've sought out interviews and case studies from people who've purposefully applied emotion in their design process to deliver practical results. Interviews and case studies in this chapter include.

Interviews:

An Interview with Patrick W. Jordan
An Interview with Stephen P. Anderson
An Interview with Aarron Walter
An Interview with Trish Miner on the Desirability Toolkit
An Interview with Marco van Hout on the LEMtool

Case Studies:

Windows Phone 7: Reference Designs for Metro UI
The Emotional Elements of PICO™

INTERVIEWS

An Interview with Patrick W. Jordan

Bio:

Pat Jordan is a specialist in user-centered design, branding and marketing. He holds honorary chairs at City University London and the University of Surrey, and has formerly held chairs at Carnegie Mellon University and the University of Leeds.

He is a consultant to many of the world's most successful companies, and to the third sector (charities and voluntary organizations). He was an advisor to the UK government from 2000 until 2010.

Some of his clients include: Starbucks, Microsoft, Samsung, Gillette, P&G, Unilever, Siemens, Philips Electronics, Nokia, Ferrari, Renault, Nissan, HSBC, Masterfoods and Sunbeam.

Interview

I felt that it was a very important part of fitting the product to the person.

TvG: What sparked your interest in designing for emotion?

PWJ: As a psychologist, I have always been interested in emotion. I was working as a human factors specialist for a consumer electronics company and became involved in a project that looked at how people responded to products emotionally. I felt that it was a very important part of fitting the product to the person.

TvG: Can you tell me a little more about what you mean by "fitting the product to the person"? In what respects should a product "fit" a person?

PWJ: It should fit them cognitively in the sense that they understand how it works and what it does. It should fit physically, in terms of them being able to use it and interact with it, and it should fit emotionally in the sense of them engaging with it and having positive feelings about it.

TvG: When we talk about emotions, it seems like we often confuse the word "emotion" with the simple experience of pleasure. Can you explain to me what the differences are between them?

PWJ: I think that pleasure is a broader term and that positive emotions are a subset of pleasure. Pleasure can include positive things that are not really emotions such as tactile or sensory things. In my work, I define pleasure as the "practical, emotional and hedonic benefits of product use," so it covers all the positive benefits that a product can bring.

TvG: In your book *Designing Pleasurable Products*, you mention the pleasure model of Lionel Tiger as a framework for understanding how to design better products. How much of an effect do you feel that providing pleasure has on the success of a product?

Providing pleasure is the biggest factor in determining a product's success.

PWJ: Aside from marketing and strategic factors such as pricing, advertising and retail channels, I would expect that providing pleasure is the biggest single factor that will determine a product's success. As people have become increasingly sophisticated, consumers are demanding the *wow* factor in products.

TvG: You mentioned the different types of benefits that people can derive from products as "practical, emotional and hedonic benefits". Can you give me an example of each type of benefit?

PWJ: Practical benefits would be the things that users can do with it, and how easy it is to use (i.e., functionality and usability). For example, being able to download music from iTunes, or being able to share images on Facebook. Emotional benefits are the feelings they get, for example pride in having a cool car. Hedonic benefits is the "catch all" for other positive things … enjoying the feel of a phone in the hand, for example.

TvG: So, would it be safe to assume that different types of products need to provide different types of benefits?

PWJ: Yes. And also that different users will prioritize different benefits in the same product, so it's important to have a good understanding of users and how they will use a particular product.

TvG: Apart from understanding your users, which is always important, how does a design team decide on and prioritize the types of benefits they should be providing in different products?

PWJ: This can vary from product to product and also depend on marketing strategy, etc.

TvG: Can you give me an example of how this has occurred on a project you've worked on?

PWJ: Generally, my clients and I usually start by identifying who will use the product and for what. We will then do a Four Pleasures analysis to see what kinds of pleasures the product could deliver under each of the four headings. We then discard the framework and put all the potential benefits in a single list.

The aim is to deliver as many of these benefits as possible, but we will pick two or three to highlight in the design and marketing of the product. These should be ones that connect with the users priorities.

> Different users will prioritize different benefits in the same product.

TvG: Can you explain to my readers what the Four Pleasures are?

PWJ: The four pleasures are:

Physio-pleasure is to do with the body—pleasures derived from the senses. In the context of products physio-pleasure would cover for example, tactile and olfactory properties as well as ergonomic issues.

Socio-pleasure is the enjoyment derived from relationships with others. Products and services may help to enhance or facilitate particular social situations and may confer social or cultural status on the user.

Psycho-pleasure refers to people's cognitive and emotional reactions, including their reactions to the design of products, services and marketing campaigns.

Ideo-pleasure concerns people's values. It is important that the values embodied in products and services are consistent with the values of those for who they are designed.

The aesthetics of a product can make it seem extrovert, quiet, aggressive, cute, etc.

TvG: You've advocated the view that products should be viewed as "living objects" with which people have relationships. How do you think that the pleasures and benefits relate to the different stages of a relationship? Are there certain benefits or pleasures that are more important to provide at the beginning of a relationship? As it progresses?

PWJ: That's a really great question. I think things like a visual or tactile wow can be really important at the beginning, whereas things like reliability and attention to detail are the things that cement the relationship in the longer term.

TvG: How do you think we perceive the expression of emotion, and by extension of personality, in the things that we use?

PWJ: I think in quite similar ways to how we might perceive it in a person, based on appearance and behavior. For example, the aesthetics of a product can make it seem extroverted, quiet, aggressive, cute, etc. Meanwhile how it "behaves" when you use it can make it seem dependable, stubborn, unreliable, hard-working, lazy, etc.

TvG: How important is it for a product to express a clear personality that carries through all of its elements? For example, the physical design, the user interface, etc.?

PWJ: I think consistency is vital. It is important to be clear about the benefits and personality that we are trying to communicate, and to put that at the center of all design and marketing communications aspects. If there is inconsistency, the message becomes blurred and the product (and the company making it) loses integrity.

Reference

Jordan, P. W. (2000). *Designing pleasurable products*. London: Taylor & Francis.

An Interview with Stephen P. Anderson

Bio

Stephen P. Anderson is an internationally recognized speaker and consultant based in Dallas, Texas. He created the *Mental Notes* card deck, a tool that's widely used by product teams to apply psychology to interaction design. He's also of the author of the book *Seductive Interaction Design*, which answers the question: "How do we get people to fall in love with our applications?"

Prior to venturing out on his own, Stephen spent more than a decade building and leading teams of information architects, interaction designers and UI developers. He's designed web applications for numerous technology startups as well as corporate clients like Nokia, Frito-Lay, Sabre Travel Network and Chesapeake Energy.

Between public speaking and project work, Stephen offers workshops and training to help organizations manage creative teams, make use of visual thinking, and design better customer experiences. He frequently tweets as @stephenanderson and occasionally updates his website (poetpainter.com).

Interview

TvG: How did you become interested in the more emotional side of visual and interactive design?

SPA: Actually, I think I've always been interested in the emotional side of design. I started off my design career as a graphic designer, where the focus tends to be on emotional reactions, more so than other considerations (I still love flipping through a good design annual and marveling at people's creativity).

It was only a couple of years in that I started to think a lot more about how people might actually want to interact with a website, which meant learning everything I could about things like usability, information architecture and programming. This background has given me an advantageous, though occasionally awkward, perspective. One that considers both the functional and emotional needs of the people we're designing for.

While much of the early usability versus design debate has died down, you still see a lot of people biased toward their own area of expertise. We still see smart developers and usability folks dismissing aesthetics as an afterthought to the "real job" of making something work well. Of course, the more we learn about the brain and how we come to make sense of new information has made it pretty clear that how we feel about something has a strong influence on our judgments and behaviors.

TvG: Why did you call your book *Seductive Interaction Design?*

SPA: The book began as a presentation entitled *The Art & Science of Seductive Interactions*. I had collected several examples of sites that did a great job engaging with me, from the very first encounter, but needed a good theme to tie it all together. Most of the examples used things like humorous language, visuals instead of text, unexpected surprises, or curiosity to keep me interested—all good examples of playful design.

Around this same time, Kathy Sierra had written a great post on "cognitive seduction" that helped form my initial musings on this topic. If I felt that "seduction" was too strong a word, that quickly changed. I began to think about first-time user experiences as a chance encounter between two people. Everything I wanted to talk about maps well to the dating analogy: initial attraction, romance and interest.

> If I felt that "seduction" was too strong a word, that quickly changed.

Most software and web apps still do a terrible job of sustaining people's interest. This can be seen in enterprise software that doesn't get adopted by employees, and web apps that can't get visitors to spend more than 15 seconds using them. If we think of these systems as people, rather than tools, you see a lot more opportunities to create meaningful (and seductive) interactions.

TvG: In my own work, I've seen a lot of enterprise products suffer from low adoption for those exact reasons. You mentioned the dating analogy of attraction, romance and continuing interest as one way to help increase adoption. Can you give me an example of how those stages might play out in a product or brand?

> **Everything maps well to the dating analogy: initial attraction, romance and interest.**

SPA: If you think about meeting a person for the first time, we form a lot of judgments about that person solely based on appearances. The same is true of the online tools we use. Research has shown that attractive visual design can influence everything from trust to perceived (and even actual) efficiency.

Then, you have the interactions. In the dating scenario, a charming person makes it nearly effortless to have a meaningful conversation. Nonconfrontational language, compliments, humorous jokes, a bit of flattery or flirtatious behavior—these things are very disarming. Contrast that with most business applications. These tools pretty much sit across from the table, silently staring, waiting to throw error messages at us when we can't figure out what they want!

A lot of what I mean by seduction is often just having good social graces—thinking of our systems as people with whom we interact. In fact, I encourage people to role-play with a browser prop, pretending to be the page being designed. This simple exercise is often a very illuminating way to see just how human (or inhuman) a screen can be.

The best examples of seductive interaction design use friendly (or at least human-sounding) language, train users through playful interactions, allow for self-expression, offer up pleasant surprises, convert through curiosity, and a host of other characteristics that are a lot like the initial stages of dating.

TvG: If seductive interactions are really about manners and social graces, wouldn't the nature of that seduction differ based on the target audience or user group you're designing for?

SPA: Oh certainly! This is something the gaming industry has figured out. In game design, you have competitive players, you have people who play games for social reasons, and you have those who love games with elements of discovery and exploration. Good game designers know how to build games that target each type of player.

> **A lot of what I mean by seduction is often just having good social graces.**

Similarly, in real-world encounters, we adjust our interactions based on individual personalities. We quickly figure out what conversation starters pique interest or turn people off. We adjust how we relate to different kinds of people (our language, use of stories or facts)—these are human traits that we all develop naturally.

Fortunately, we have some pretty good personality models we can build upon, like the Meyers Briggs Type Indicators or the Big Five Personality Dimensions.

At some point, I can see the systems we're building being adaptive enough to relate to individual personality styles. In the persuasion space, we're already seeing hints of this with persuasion profiling, where ecommerce sites will tailor their selling strategy based on your past buying behavior using a scarcity message with some people (e.g., "only 3 left!") or elements of social proof (e.g., "38 of your friends read this book") for others.

I'd add that what is seductive varies not only amongst individual personalities, but also by context. If I go to open a checking account at a bank, we'd all hope the teller will be friendly and hospitable—maybe even crack a few jokes, if deemed appropriate. However, if I return to that same bank a few months later because I've been a victim of identity theft, I'd expect that same teller to treat my circumstances seriously—so cracking jokes would not be appropriate under the circumstances.

All that said, I think just moving from purely functional systems to something more emotionally engaging is going to be a big step forward for many companies. As much as we know about different personalities, there are still plenty of common human traits that are shared across cultures and personality types.

TvG: If a company is considering making their product or service more emotionally engaging, what would be the best ways to gain an understanding of their audience so that they can create an appropriate personality for their product?

SPA: My impulse is to say tools such as personas would work. However, personas are far too often based on assumptions about users, created by the internal stakeholders who feel they can represent their customers. These "assumption personas" suffice where organizations need some basic internal alignment around who the user is. But when it comes to designing for emotions, or really any kind of exceptional user experience work, you need the keen insights that only come from user research (or firsthand experiences).

> **We adjust our interactions based on individual personalities.**

The most successful projects I've worked on started with a few such insights. Things like "quality, not quantity connections," "freedom and choice," or "a sense of power." Understanding the core motivations that sit behind the actions we observe is critical to great work. So, to answer your question; good ethnographic research and the insights that come from it, presented in whatever format is fitting. That's the best way to gain an understanding of your audience.

I do know there is a growing interest in tools that measure emotional reactions. These are good for informing or validating a design decision. However, I doubt any tool could ever be a substitute for empathy.

> **I doubt any tool could ever be a substitute for empathy.**

Your question does raise another interesting point to consider, though. To what extent should we tailor a (product) personality for different audiences? I believe it's critical that a company know its identity: who it is, why it exists, and what it stands for. Everything else flows from this core identity.

Just as we all have our own identities that we then adapt to different situations, the same is true, or should be true, of these digital interactions. If we go too far in the direction of creating personalities that appeal to every audience type and situation, the end results may be something negative—confused and distrustful customers.

I recall you investigated the effect of personality on different mobile phone UIs [user interfaces]. Some UIs were friendly, with a softer color palette and rounded corners. Others were more harsh or masculine, with higher contrast and sharp edges. One of the questions I walked away thinking about was whether a single company should offer all these different aesthetics in order to appeal to more people. Is the product about the functions or the manner in which those functions are handled?

I believe, if you look at top global brands like Coke, Apple, Virgin and so on—the different products or lines of service all act and behave in a manner consistent with their core identity. Apple may appeal to the novice and expert user alike, albeit in different ways, but both groups would still describe Apple in the same way.

TvG: When I created those UIs for my master's thesis, the initial idea was to allow the user to select the interface style that reflected their personal preferences. But even more so, I wanted to see whether it was possible to design a specific personality type that users could easily identify.

By deconstructing the visual and interactive cues that communicate gender and personality in people, I was able to use those same cues to specify personality through design. That made it obvious to me that a lot of what we perceive when we judge personality is based on unconscious judgments.

We seem hard-wired to anthropomorphize the things surrounding us.

I then began to wonder whether we could learn anything about creating better relationships between people and products by looking at relationships between people. How important do you think it is to design for a relationship when it comes to creating emotional products?

SPA: I'm not so sure it's something we can help—we naturally form relationships with sufficiently advanced products. Consider the fact that we can see "faces" in everyday objects, or that we scream at inanimate objects when they don't work. We seem hard-wired to anthropomorphize the things surrounding us.

Companies that recognize this can design intentional emotional bonds that elevate a functional product to something more significant. Take a simple Coca-Cola bottle—the trademarked contoured shape mimics feminine curves and suggests "health, vitality, sexiness, and femininity" (or so I've heard!).

To be clear, this doesn't mean we need to add a face or recognizable physical traits, but rather cues that are suggestive of human characteristics. At my house we have the Mint, a small robotic floor sweeper. What's fascinating to me is how we've named "him" Mo (after the frustrated maintenance robot in Wall-E) and read so much emotion into his little beeps and alerts. From an industrial design perspective, this is nothing more than a minimalist white rectangle. But, we affectionately talk about Mo as if he was a member of our family.

The upside of all this? We're likely to be more forgiving of products we find endearing. A friend recently commented on Apple's Siri, saying "her imperfections make her so cute!" Where else would we say that of what is essentially an error message?!

It's interesting to note the relationship isn't always that of another person. Researcher B. J. Fogg has observed that mobile devices are often perceived as an extension of ourselves (versus another being with whom with interact). This little insight changes a relationship from an interaction to something we nurture—no wonder we're so heartbroken when we drop and shatter the glass on our iPhones!

> **Mobile devices are often perceived as an extension of ourselves.**

TvG: One of the things I've found in my research is the need to design different types of emotional responses and personality traits at different points in the relationship. So when we first encounter "things," we want them to express a personality similar to our own. There's quite a bit of research in evolutionary psychology that backs up the idea of similarity driving initial attraction and mate choice. In other words, we're attracted to people who have similar attitudes, values, interests and personality.

Once interaction begins, however, the roles need to shift to be more complementary, with one person leading and the other following. So one person talks while another listens. This is the dialog or conversation, and this role can shift between individuals. Have you found that the way a product interacts needs to adjust over time as the relationship grows and evolves? If so, how?

SPA: A few years ago, I gave a presentation on "adaptive interfaces." At the time, I was thinking entirely about systems personalizing themselves based on your prior behaviors and knowledge accumulated about you. For example, if Google Maps knows I've lived for some time at the same address, why not skip the directions that get me out of my neighborhood—something I've hopefully figured out! I believe Google Maps does something like this now.

But, you have to be careful with how systems change over time, as we get used to things being "in their place" or behaving a certain way. All it takes is a look at how people react (negatively) to Facebook changes or the new Gmail aesthetics to see how uncomfortable change is. This is not, however, an argument for preserving the status quo, as we do also enjoy novelty and change—so long as our sense of control isn't threatened.

> **We get used to things being "in their place."**

To answer your question, though, I propose at least three kinds of systems:

Simple tools: These are often single-purpose utilities with which we don't really form a relationship, per se. They do what we need, when we need them.

A client tool for uploading images might be an example of this. I'm not so sure these tools need to evolve.

Complex systems that we figure out over time: In these cases our relationship with the product deepens as we gain mastery. Mastering a digital SLR camera is a good example of this. These tools are often difficult to use, and call for some determination if we are to learn all the ins and outs. This, by and large, is how software has been built for the last several decades.

Finally, there are **systems that lead us into mastery by slowing revealing features or adding functionality as deemed appropriate**. This has been the model used in game design for years, where players start off with limited capabilities and equipment, slowly leveling up throughout the game, until mastery is achieved.

> There's a lot of psychology around emotional engagement.

For traditional software design, there's a lot of psychology around emotional engagement, appropriate challenges, achievements, and similar gaming ideas that could certainly make a lot of software a little less daunting, or at least serve as an alternative to the help text and training that has been added to make up for unnecessarily difficult tools.

There is another dimension to this evolving relationship that is worth mentioning; perceptions of growth and support from the company. Even if we dread any changes to our most beloved products, we still want to know that the company is growing and evolving—that there is still support being offered. I may have found the best invoicing tool in the world, but if the group behind it offers no communications and no updates for over a year, it doesn't matter how perfectly that tool is working for me. There is a level of insecurity that will eventually affect usage of that tool. Psychologically, we want to know that something is going on, that we are still being attended to as we gain mastery.

Reference

Anderson, S. P. (2011). *Seductive Interaction Design: Creating Playful, Fun and Effective User Experiences*. Berkeley: New Riders Press.

An Interview with Aarron Walter

Bio

Aarron Walter is the lead user experience designer for MailChimp, where he socializes with primates and ponders ways to make interfaces more human. Aarron is the author of *Designing for Emotion*, the purple stripe in the rainbow of knowledge from *A Book Apart*. He lives with his wife and son in Athens, Georgia, and is a wannabe barista. He tweets about design under the moniker @aarron on Twitter.

Interview

TvG: What was it that sparked your interest in designing for emotion?

AW: This is a topic that I started to explore when I was hired at MailChimp about four years ago. But I've always been drawn to the brand. I was a MailChimp user before I was hired. At the time, I was also working as an academic professor teaching interface design courses.

Ben Chestnut, the CEO and cofounder of MailChimp, has always brought a certain personality to MailChimp that I found very interesting. It's kind of funny and layered, but it always comes across as very honest and I always very much appreciated that. When I was looking at ESPs [email service providers] to talk about in the classes I was teaching, MailChimp was the one that appealed to me the most, and it was mainly based on the brand.

It wasn't based on a feature set, because at that point, although the product had been around for a little while, it was still rather small and simple. When I was hired, we had a lot of conversation about brand and personality. I was an advocate for trying to take the brand personality further and was given a lot of freedom to experiment with that.

> I was an advocate for trying to take the brand personality further.

Over the course of the years, as we were working on the copy and the interaction patterns, we were also thinking about and discovering principles of psychology. Over time, I started to see some really interesting results. I started to see that if I used emotional design, I could shape a good customer experience, and not just directly through the interface, but with lots of other things too. It also has a profound effect on marketing, because you don't need to market people who are already infatuated with the product. They go and tell people how great you are.

In my research outside of MailChimp, looking at a lot at companies and products, I've found this is a common thread. A company like Wufoo basically doesn't have a marketing budget. They don't do a lot of active marketing, but they've got millions of users because people just love the experiences they have with the product.

That was one thing that I discovered that's a really cool outcome of emotional design. Creating a positive emotional experience for customers also influenced their interactions with customer service when they needed support. When a lot of our customers jump into live chat or send us an email, they crack jokes! And the reason they do that is because they see us cracking jokes. It creates a really positive, lighthearted exchange that makes it so much easier to help a customer who is confused.

> If I used emotional design, I could shape a good customer experience.

Being in a positive mood means they can listen and understand the instructions a lot better, too, so that's using a principle of psychology called "priming." Basically, we try to suggest a way of thinking based on the interactions that they have with the product itself. I think its really fascinating how you can touch on a lot of different aspects that we don't always consider in product design, web design, or design in general.

TvG: How much of an effect do you think communicating personality has on the success of an application or a site? One of the things we talk about a lot in this book is that all design communicates emotion and personality. But chances are, you're probably not communicating the right emotion or personality.

AW: Well, I see personality as not just an important part, but an essential part of what we're doing as designers. Personality is something that people are becoming more accustomed to expressing. We're merging our public and private lives together because we're communicating so much with each other on Facebook and Twitter. We change our voice and we change our tone depending on the context of the situation. I think that this influences our expectations of brands. We expect them to be as honest with us as we are with them.

I see personality as… an essential part of what we're doing as designers.

I think expressing personality can be scary for enterprises and big businesses. They may feel that having a personality and being honest about themselves feels a little weird. But it can be a really positive thing, not just for attracting people, but for filtering the people that you don't really want to do business with.

Most people think that business is focused on always trying to get more customers. But sometimes, when we get *more* customers, we get the *wrong* customers. Maybe they complain a lot, or are really confused because the technical background that's required to use the product or service is beyond them. In short, you may wind up with a customer base that costing you more than you're gaining from these people as customers.

In the real world, you may meet a person and just be attracted to them instantly. They've got similar mannerisms, a similar way of thinking, similar background, a similar sense of humor, similar value systems, and there's just this magnetism that connects you with them. You want to do everything you can to connect with them more. And that's the Holy Grail for brands; to create this real human connection with their customers.

They've got similar mannerisms, similar background, a similar sense of humor, similar value systems.

When we first meet certain personalities that are different or the opposite of us, they often rub us the wrong way. You don't want to have anything to do with them because their values are different. They just don't get you. You run away from them. It's a really positive thing to make sure you're talking to the right people, instead of talking to everyone.

TvG: One of the things that I've written about on Boxes and Arrows, and that you've written about in your book, is the distinction between dominant and submissive personalities. Given the idea of creating attraction through similar values, goals and lifestyle, how did you decide what the appropriate personality traits of Freddie and the MailChimp app should be? For example, how did you decide that Freddie should be more dominant rather than more submissive?

AW: Well, I'd like to say that we sat down and were very methodic about defining the personality traits and so forth, but it didn't really work out that way. There was already a great personality present when I was hired as the UX lead, and I was afforded the opportunity to try and push that further. There was already a pretty clear voice present as well.

At the time, we were a relatively small company. We've grown considerably bigger now, but we were facing the challenge of being a small company looking to build a customer base. We were basically these funny, goofy people with a chimp for a mascot. You walk the line there on coming across as juvenile, as not serious enough, or not sophisticated enough. People might look at your feature set and they might think "nice feature set, but it just doesn't seem professional. It seems a little goofy." That has sometimes hurt us. But I think in the long run, it's helped us stand out in the marketplace tremendously.

We use the personality of Freddie von Chimpenheimer the Fourth to make little jokes at the top of every page. The rules are that he will not give you feedback. He doesn't tell you the stats of your email campaigns. He doesn't say where you are and he doesn't give you navigation feedback because he's not functional. He's only there to add a sense of humor and convey our personality.

We did it that way because of Clippy. We're all familiar with Clippy, the hated office assistant. There are a few reasons why Clippy was so hated, and one was that it was a personality that was injected at the wrong time. He basically showed up when you didn't want him there, always offering help. It's one thing to offer help, but it's another thing to offer help when it's not needed and break the workflow.

TvG: It always seemed to me that Clippy failed to follow common social rules. He would interrupt you while you were working.

AW: It's my understanding that the execution of Clippy was not exactly true to the original designer's intent.

TvG: That's my understanding as well.

AW: I think they abused it when it was being implemented. I'm not sure who it was who made the final decision. In the past, Microsoft hasn't always made the best decisions in terms of user experience. In theory, that could be a really cool thing if it were done well. Clippy is the anti-aspiration for Freddy. The idea was that Freddy would offer a sense of humor and he would say things that would be a little bit pithy and a little bit witty, but not goofy.

Clippy is kind of the anti-aspiration for Freddy.

As our work grew organically, we defined our brand traits and created a design persona, which is what you're referring to with the dominant and passive traits. The voice was already clear. It was a just a matter of nailing that down. Now, he says stuff like, "Why am I smiling? Because I'm not wearing any pants," which is light and pushes the balance a bit.

TvG: It's a little edgy, which is good.

AW: Yeah, it's edgy and it really appeals to people. They're like, "Oh my god I can't believe it! That's hilarious!" Some people don't really get it and they just look past it. But more often than not, it really has a strong impact on people. They take screenshots of it, they post on Flickr, they blog about the things he says, they tweet about it, post it on Facebook. So, a lot of mileage has come from that little experiment. It's become somewhat of a trademark element for us.

But in terms of shaping the voice and tone at any particular time, we've completed a project called VoiceandTone.com. Kate Keefer, who is our content strategist, was working on a style guide for how we write at MailChimp. As we discussed this more, we started to realize that we don't actually want the people writing for MailChimp to try and be funny. In fact, we don't want people to try to crack jokes if they're not naturally funny. We want them to just be themselves. But there are some things that are okay and some things that aren't and we wanted to define boundaries.

The way the MailChimp voice operates is tied to the emotional state of our users.

She was creating this big PDF document with a style guide, which is pretty typical of most companies. But as we talked about it more, what we landed on was that the way the MailChimp voice operates is directly tied to the emotional state of our users. So if they're looking at a knowledge base article because they're confused, the voice can remain the same but the tone needs to change. The tone of his little jokes depends on whether the user is viewing a success message or an error message.

People are going to be in different emotional states when they encounter these different pieces of content. VoiceandTone.com lists our content types, identifies the emotional state of users in each situation, and gives sample copy that shows how we would respond in that situation. We've also got this design persona that helps us shape personality, not only in terms of content, but also in design and interaction patterns. We try to define what feels in and out of bounds for MailChimp. Voice and Tone is our interactive style guide to help guide how we write.

TvG: It sounds like your team has put together some great tools for ensuring that Freddy and the MailChimp application are speaking with a consistent voice. What do you think are some of the dangers of communicating an inconsistent personality through a product or an application?

AW: It would be like being with someone who is extremely moody or has a difficult time compartmentalizing their emotions when they're interacting with you. Maybe they were in a car accident on their way to work and then they take it out on everyone around them. That's not a good experience. If your personality is all over the place, you basically dilute the potential benefits you could be getting from interaction. You can confuse people who don't really know how you're going to interact with them, and it certainly doesn't inspire trust.

When you communicate a personality... people feel a human connection with you.

I think one of the biggest things is that when you communicate a personality through design and content, people feel a human connection with you. When humans connect with one another, building trust is a natural part of that relationship. I trust someone because I understand their personality and I feel a bond to them. So if there's an inconsistent personality, it can definitely degrade the level of trust in the relationship.

TvG: How important do you think it is for a brand to make sure that the personality is consistent, not only within the design itself, but also across channels. So for example, web, print and television ads?

AW: I think it's very important and that's a part of what we were trying to do with VoiceandTone.com. For example, we want to be a bit more consistent with tweets. How do we speak in 140 characters? How is that different than when we're writing a blog post? Whenever you define that voice for different tone situations, you definitely need to think about these different channels. A tweet is read very quickly. A blog post is read as long form, so you can get deeper into stories. So, there might be different ways of communicating there. But I think it's par for the course at this point that people need to consider different channels.

TvG: In some of your other interviews you've mentioned that it's important to know your target users when creating or tailoring a personality. Other than the persona that you mentioned earlier, are there any other design research methods or models that you've used to determine what the best personality for your design would be?

AW: I love process. I love things that help us do our job better, but I'm also always very skeptical of dogma in process. I feel like having a very specific set of research methods is great if it helps you understand things. But, we also don't necessarily have to be tied to it.

I was talking to our content strategist about this the other day, and what we landed on was that the best thing you can do to shape personality is hire good people. Hire people that have the same value system as you, that think the way you do, that you've got some emotional bond with. The trick with communicating personality is if you're concocting it, it's going to come across as dishonest and your audience will recognize that. People can smell bullshit a mile away. So if it's concocted and dishonest, it's not going to work out well.

People can smell bullshit a mile away.

Design personas are a good tool for having a conversation with your colleagues and getting it down on paper to say "here's who we are." Doing research on our users is such an essential part of what we do as UX designers, but we rarely turn our gaze inward to discover *who we are* as a company. Creating that design persona is a really helpful process, but it's not going to be all that helpful if the hiring practices don't take into account the value system of a company. So, I think hiring is a great place to start.

TvG: Were there any methods that you tried while you were working on MailChimp that you wouldn't use again?

AW: Maybe not methods, but the execution of certain methods where we made mistakes. There was one little joke that we made. You know how MailChimp wears a little blue hat (i.e., a mail man's cap) and he says "does this hat make my bum look big?" We got a few people writing in and complaining that we were making fun of the size of their butt. And it's just because they brought certain "baggage" to the application.

Obviously, the comment wasn't directed at the size of their derrières. It was just a funny joke about Freddy. You can't even see his bottom with the way he's cropped. So that was a good lesson learned. You have to take into consideration the potential baggage that the audience brings to your personality. Your personality can be strong, but the delivery might set people off if you're not careful.

TvG: Were you able to do any actual testing with users to determine what emotions you were actually provoking?

Take into consideration the baggage that the audience brings to your personality.

AW: We haven't looked at particular emotions, but we have tons of data and feedback about how people respond to our brand. We have one interesting data point that I've been really fascinated by. We've had a few people that have said "I'm sick of all these jokes, I wish I could turn them off. I've got to show this to my client and it's really annoying." So we thought about it and we tried a little experiment where we made a checkbox in the central preferences that's called "Party Pooper Mode" If you check that box, it turns off the humor. Freddie goes away and it's all business. It's a totally functional, usable application without the layer of personality on top.

I was very curious because at first, I was very reluctant to do that on principle. I felt like "if they don't get us, then they don't get us. We're just not a good match." In the end, the stats tell us that only 0.0007 percent of our users check the Party Pooper Mode box. It's very rare for people to turn off the personality in the application. I also think it's pretty fascinating to see how rarely we get complaints and how frequently we get funny comments in support chats and funny emails sent to us. People from all over the world write us letters. People post on Twitter and Facebook and Flickr.

When we talk to our users and have meet ups, people tell us that they just love the way the product makes them feel. I think that's really cool because we're building stuff in an office, just trying to make a living and pay our bills. But because we're building an experience that people have such a strong attraction to, I feel like we're doing something that's making real human connections with people. That's meaningful and it goes beyond what we're doing as a business. I think it's really inspiring.

TvG: We've chatted a little bit about the idea of personality needing to emerge somewhat organically from the organization itself. What do you think about organizations that often project a more neutral personality? I'm thinking here of large government organizations or more formal institutions.

AW: Creating a neutral personality can sometimes be the best pathway. The IRS, for example, has a very neutral personality. In some ways, I think that's a bad thing for them because they come across as cold and robotic. They're fighting an uphill battle to begin with, because people dislike having to pay money to them. I do think there are situations where you don't want to be cracking jokes, like in a banking application. Personality in design is not always about being funny—sometimes it's really serious. But you can be serious and still be human.

There's an example in my book about a nonprofit organization that helps people who are suffering from AIDS and are also homeless. It's called HousingWorks. org. They just show these beautiful photos of people and they crop the photos close to the face.

They're using the faces principle of design, which says that if a photograph is cropped and shows just a face, we concentrate on the emotion and the thought process that's happening behind a person's eyes.

If you crop the photo to show the whole body, then we start to think about sensuality, what the person is wearing and a lot of other extraneous things. But this is a very serious organization. They're fighting homelessness and AIDS, but they're also making a real human emotional connection. You're seeing real people and it's not stock photography. You can tell that these are real people with real stories. I think that's a really powerful thing. An organization like the IRS could benefit greatly by showing a little more humanity in what they do.

TvG: Now that the MailChimp redesign has been deemed a success and attracted a lot of attention, what lessons would you say you've learned about designing personality? Are there any opportunities that you felt you missed? What would you do differently if you were starting now?

AW: I don't know about missed opportunities. I think we feel pretty good about what we did and it seemed to work out pretty well. Our customers have, on the whole, responded very positively. There was one negative thing we received out of the gate when we launched. Initially, we didn't have a giant Freddy on the home page and that threw some people. They were pretty upset. I guess that's one thing to keep in mind when designing personality. Once people create a really great emotional bond with your brand, you have to be careful with that bond. You can't just shift things around dramatically. You have to take stock of what people are really attached to. They might be attached to something that you really want to move or change. But now, we're never going to leave Freddy behind. Freddy is an expression of the collective personality of all of us as a company. So when he wasn't center stage, people complained. That was definitely one lesson we learned from the redesign.

You have to take stock of what people are really attached to.

I like that we now have this VoiceandTone.com reference to work with. I think that would have helped us in creating the content. On the whole, I think we feel really satisfied with what we did. It's not that we don't think that there are flaws, but we feel good about how things came out.

References

van Gorp, Trevor, J. (2010). *Emotional Design with A.C.T.* Boxes and Arrows. <http://www.boxesandarrows.com/view/emotional-design> Accessed 12.12.11.

Walter, A. (2011). *MailChimp Personality Traits*. <http://aarronwalter.com/design-personas/> Accessed 12.10.11.

An Interview with Trish Miner on the Desirability Toolkit

Bio

In 2002, Joey Benedek and Trish Miner, now a Senior UX Researcher at Microsoft Corporation, published a portion of their work on developing a Desirability Toolkit in the conference proceedings for the Usability Professional Association (UPA). Since that time, the Desirability Toolkit has become the foundation for the development of all kinds of methods for measuring emotional responses to interaction.

Interview

We wanted to go beyond the measure of "is it usable?"

EA: What is the Desirability Toolkit?

TM: It's a set of cards (with one word or phrase per card) that's used to elicit user feedback on the experience of a product.

EA: Why did you create it?

TM: The impetus for the Desirability Toolkit was a need to get user feedback on the intangibles that we thought were a part of product use. We wanted to go beyond the expected measure of "is it usable?" Joey had started to think about measuring fun, so that was our starting point. We had some ideas about what we wanted in a tool. It had to be easy to administer in a user research lab session and easy to analyze. It had to be open-ended enough that the user could bring up aspects of product usage that mattered to him or her.

We didn't want the predetermined response set that often results from using a Likert scale. We were concerned about scales because when asked, people give a rating, when the topic may not be important or relevant to them. The words we present on the cards and the questions we pose to users (i.e., why did you pick that word?) are the framework for identifying the themes that become prevalent for a particular group of users while interacting with product.

EA: How did you determine which cards became a part of the set?

Product Reaction Cards - Terms

Accessible	Creative	Fast	Meaningful	Slow
Advanced	Customizable	Flexible	Motivating	Sophisticated
Annoying	Cutting edge	Fragile	Not secure	Stable
Appealing	Dated	Fresh	Not valuable	Sterile
Approachable	Desirable	Friendly	Novel	Stimulating
Attractive	Difficult	Frustrating	Old	Straight forward
Boring	Disconnected	Fun	Optimistic	Stressful
Business-like	Disruptive	Gets in the way	Ordinary	Time-consuming
Busy	Distracting	Hard to use	Organized	Time-saving
Calm	Dull	Helpful	Overbearing	Too technical
Clean	Easy to use	High quality	Overwhelming	Trustworthy
Clear	Effective	Impersonal	Patronizing	Unapproachable
Collaborative	Efficient	Impressive	Personal	Uncontrollable
Comfortable	Effortless	Incomprehensible	Poor quality	Unconventional
Compatible	Empowering	Inconsistent	Powerful	Understandable
Compelling	Energetic	Ineffective	Predictable	Undesirable
Complex	Engaging	Innovative	Professional	Unpredictable
Comprehensive	Entertaining	Inspiring	Relevant	Unrefined
Confident	Enthusiastic	Integrated	Reliable	Usable
Confusing	Essential	Intimidating	Responsive	Useful
Connected	Exceptional	Intuitive	Rigid	Valuable
Consistent	Exciting	Inviting	Satisfying	
Controllable	Expected	Irrelevant	Secure	
Convenient	Familiar	Low maintenance	Simplistic	

FIG. 6.1 The Words of the Product Reaction Cards (Desirability Toolkit)

Adapted from (Benedek & Miner, 2002) Developed by and © 2002 Microsoft Corporation. All rights reserved. (Used with permission of Microsoft.)

TM: The word set includes positive, negative, and neutral words so that users are supported in expressing a range of feelings about the product experience. If you just show positive words, you only get positive feedback on the experience.

The words are used to describe how the product makes users feel. Getting users to talk about how a product makes them feel is the rarest kind of feedback. Probing with emotional words can help to get emotion in the response. It puts the user in a personal frame of mind. We didn't set out to make the words specific to interaction with technology, but they are in that realm.

> The word set includes positive, negative, and neutral words.

EA: How can a design team use the Desirability Toolkit?

TM: The design team can use the Toolkit to determine what they want to evoke in the experience of their design. Each team member selects cards that describe what they want the customer to feel, then they share the word cards they choose and the reason they chose those words. Then, themes can be identified by discussing why the words were chosen. The themes get the team on the same page in how they would like users to react to the product they are designing. The right sized set of themes is the number the team can successfully execute, given resource constraints. Typically, a manageable set is three to five themes as goals.

Going through the exercise of the Desirability Toolkit causes a conversation to happen that often otherwise wouldn't—getting the design team to imagine and discuss a user's emotions. Design teams can use the Toolkit to assess design alternatives with product users. Or they can use it to structure user feedback to compare short-term product use to long-term. One other way that a design team can use the Toolkit is assess progress toward goals in design iterations.

EA: Is the qualitative nature of the results generated by the Desirability Toolkit a strength or a weakness?

Think of "useful, usable, desirable" as a three-legged stool.

TM: You can follow up with quantitative measures, but getting the richness of the personal and emotional makes the qualitative experience metrics valid. Quantitative measures can validate the Toolkit's outcomes and keep the focus on desirability to counter the tendency (that often happens when a team is driven by a release date) to say "OK, that's done, onto the next problem."

EA: What is the role of desirability in product interaction? When is it important to assess desirability in the context of making things useful, usable, desirable?

TM: It can be helpful to think of "useful, usable, desirable" as a three-legged stool. If you leave out one leg of the stool, it will fall over. Useful is a given, or should be, for a consumer product. Making the product usable, minimizing the need for users to adapt and learn, is critical. Desirability is the point of differentiation between competing products. Your product has to nail it. If you ship the product and it doesn't sell because no one likes it, you have failed.

EA: How can the Desirability Toolkit be used to persuade a reluctant decision maker of the importance that emotional connection plays in the success of a product?

The emotional experience of the user needs to be made relevant.

TM: I would start by showing decision makers what users are saying about the product, and making a distinction between that and what the business, or the channel, or the purchase controllers are saying. The emotional experience of the user needs to be made relevant. It needs to be enticing for the business to imagine having a product that fosters a positive emotional connection for the user. When there is emotion, there is real connection with the user. Build on that. Then, the design team has to deliver even more than the decision makers ever anticipated.

EA: Looking ahead, what tools do designers still require to understand the impact of user emotions on the success of their designs? What is it that you want to know about users that you don't know how to uncover?

TM: I would love to get into peoples heads and hear their thoughts without biasing them. I would like to wave a magic wand and get user input without influencing outcome. Eye tracking software is a great tool to see where a user looks when interacting with an interface. The insights into preference, choices made and rejected and task flow from the user's perspective are powerful sources of feedback on a design. Could there be something like that for what a user is feeling?

Reference

Benedek, J; Miner, T. (2002). "Measuring Desirability: New Methods for Evaluating Desirability in a Usability Lab Setting." *Proceedings of UPA 2002 Conference*, Orlando, FL, July 8-12, 2002. UPA.

An Interview with Marco van Hout on the LEMtool

Bio

Marco thinks, writes, and speaks about emotional design and the intersection of psychology, design, and innovation. As the creative director of SusaGroup, he works with companies and organizations to include mindfulness, emotion and meaning in their products and services through deep questioning.

Marco is a board member of the International Design for Emotion Society and a frequent speaker and workshop facilitator. As a visiting lecturer, he teaches at the Design Academy Eindhoven, Willem de Kooning Academy, University of Twente, Hogeschool Utrecht, and Rotterdam University. In his spare time, Marco is an enthusiastic abstract painter.

You can read and view more at: http://www.marcovanhout.nl and http://www.design-emotion.com.

Interview

TvG: The website for the LEMtool describes it as "a unique and powerful evaluation tool to measure the emotional impact of your website by simply asking people. It combines an easy do-it-yourself online environment to set up experiments, with an intuitive evaluation interface for your test participants. LEMtool uses caricatured cartoons as test scale." What prompted you to create the LEMtool?

MvH: In 2002, I became familiar with the work of Pieter Desmet, who had just finished his PhD on the development of PrEmo (Product Emotion Measurement Tool), a nonverbal self report instrument that measured 14 distinct (product)

LEMtool uses caricatured cartoons as a test scale.

emotions. I loved its intuitive interface. The simple but effective concept and the results it generated were both really interesting.

At the time, I was mostly working in the field of interaction design and on the development of web-based applications. I had just finished a research project on how to measure emotions evoked by interactive products, and in the process I found that PrEmo was not completely suitable for this. It kept my mind occupied for a couple of years, while continuing to develop web applications.

At one point I decided to see if we could develop a tool that was similar to PrEmo, but suitable for both static and dynamic interface evaluations online. In 2006 we presented the initial concepts for the LEMtool at the Dutch CHI chapter biannual conference. It generated really great feedback and we decided to continue with development.

There were a couple of requirements that would make the development different from PrEmo and also more challenging. First, the LEMtool had to be able to work with live websites and online prototypes. Second, it would have to take less time to evaluate an interface, so as not to interfere with the interaction as much.

We investigated different approaches in 2007 (Capota, van Hout & van der Geest, 2007), and in 2008 (Huisman, & van Hout, 2008) the final concept was introduced. It included the development of a new cartoon character, LEM, who expressed eight distinct emotions that we found were most relevant to basic web interactions. It works as a layer on top of a static image or dynamic website. A user can activate LEM and drag around an area of "emotional interest." The eight emotions appear and the user selects one that applies to that area.

TvG: What types of companies have found the LEMtool to be the most useful? In other words, are there certain types of companies or websites that seem to benefit more from testing the emotional side of their designs?

More common usability evaluations don't give a complete picture.

MvH: Since the live version is only a year old, companies are still discovering the tool. A great variety of companies have shown interest, from large software corporations, to UX agencies, to large financial service providers. What the companies who have used the LEMtool or asked us to perform user research with it have in common is an obvious focus on the experiential impact of their interfaces and applications.

They've noticed that more common usability evaluations don't give a complete picture, especially in terms of experience. I believe the LEMtool can be suitable for evaluations of most types of interfaces or applications. We have measured normal websites, mobile app mockups, static images of advertisements, and visual designs of web and mobile app concepts. A rare situation in which I would see no need to use a tool such as the LEMtool is when a company is really only interested in having its users get from point A to point B.

In that case, they're not willing to pay any attention to the value of the journey in terms of experience. However, if getting from A to B could be a frustrating or pleasurable experience, which one would you aim for?

TvG: Given the way that emotions influence decision making, the answer seems pretty obvious to me. What have been some of the most eye-opening things your clients have discovered using the LEMtool?

MvH: Apart from users in the studies claiming LEMtool was fun to use? Seriously, though, this is a really important characteristic of the tool. It's fun for users to evaluate their emotional responses, give feedback and use LEM (i.e., the cartoon character) as an expression of the emotions they feel. It has increased participation rates to as high as 35 percent, which for online user research is a high number.

Another important finding is that LEMtool is able to give insight into the "perceived usability" of a website. This is where self-report in general and specifically LEMtool can be very helpful. It's not task-oriented and allows people to express their emotions freely. Users can decide to give feedback on parts of the website that cover usability, or aesthetics, or just related to things they like on a website. This very broad feedback is a result of the focus on emotions, and not merely the need to merely provide feedback on looks, information architecture and usability.

> **Users can decide to give feedback on parts of the website.**

The feedback is not "this is too dark." The feedback is "it makes me feel sad—probably because it is too dark." This may seem like a minor difference in definition, but to have the emotion as a central focus of the feedback is vital to making design changes and decisions in later stages, when you're ready to improve your concept by "designing for emotion." It is insights like this that have made clients appreciate the added value of LEMtool.

TvG: You mention that people using the LEMtool thought it was "fun" to use. In this book, Edie and I have talked about using both positive and negative emotions in design. We've mentioned the dangers of creating associations with negative experiences, but also how negative emotions can be used to signal that something needs correction.

How important do you think it is to foster a balance of positive and negative emotion through design? Have there been any tests you've conducted with the LEMtool where you've found negative emotional reactions to be useful?

MvH: I think it is important to have both in mind while designing. In a way, emotional design is definitely mostly about creating positive emotions, just as design for usability was mostly about preventing negative emotions and making it "usable." Nevertheless, just as you mention, I think there is a place for negative emotions in design.

I think there is a place for negative emotions in design.

In his paper for the 2010 Design & Emotion Conference, Steven Fokkinga of Delft University talks about how negative emotions can enrich experiences. Not only can negative emotions signal that something is wrong or not working, but they can also intensify certain achievements. Think of the time when it was raining and you convinced yourself to go out jogging.

At first, you will probably be swearing and cursing the rain. But once you arrive home, you will feel more positive about the achievement because you withstood the horrible weather and did something positive. Negative emotions can empower action and motivate us to actually act on something, which can work out positively for us in the end.

I think in an interactive environment such as a website, slightly negative emotions can motivate us to pursue positive and richer experiences. However, since attention and experience on web are also very fleeting, we should be very careful to monitor the dose of negative emotions. The Web is less able to hold someone's attention or call upon someone's perseverance. I think there should definitely be more research done on this side of emotional design, not only in preventing negative emotions, but also on how they can enrich a web experience when used wisely.

When we work with the LEMtool, we often find clusters of negative emotions around certain areas of an interface. It can prove to be the most valuable part of the whole test. It's good to know what works well with the design, but even better to know what doesn't. Because we ask users to indicate the appraisal behind the emotion (appraisals are cognitive evaluations that cause an emotion), we can get a lot of insight into how the negative emotion was elicited.

Users provide a lot more detail in their negative evaluations.

We relate the appraisal to a type of concern: a goal, standard, or attitude. Then we relate each emotion to a characteristic of the website: aesthetics, usability or liking. With negative emotional reactions, the insights are extra valuable. Negative appraisals often motivate users to provide a lot more detail than positive appraisals. It would be better if the amount of detail was more balanced, but in practice this is very common with user research. I guess people love to complain and have the feeling it will help to improve the product. Users don't necessarily indicate *more* negative emotions than positive ones. But they provide a lot more detail in their negative evaluations, so they're very useful.

In a recent project for a financial services provider, we found that even though it seemed that the negative emotions had the upper hand, in the end users were very positive about the experience of the interface. This also shows we shouldn't focus blindly on the negative reactions, but view them within the context of the total experience and then use them constructively.

TvG: How often do you see indications of people responding to sites as though they have personalities?

MvH: That's an interesting question! With all the knowledge that we have about how people relate to computers and interfaces, you would definitely expect this. People "screaming" *at* or "laughing" *with* a website. Who doesn't recognize the feeling of wanting to punch the screen because something is not working properly? But, in all honesty, we haven't encountered this yet in our tests with LEMtool.

I think there are two possible explanations for this. Because the tool itself requires interaction, it is possible that people "cool down" a bit and their emotions become less intense. Second, I'm not sure if people see websites as people or as just having human features. What we often see in LEMtool tests are that people see the brand behind the website as a person.

> **People see the brand behind the website as a person.**

For example, a user leaves a comment "why don't you help me out here?" with the emotion "dissatisfaction." You could think the person is directly addressing the website, because the site is not helping them out, perhaps in giving direction.

Nevertheless, in the context of the comments we see, this comment usually seems to be addressed to the brand or the people behind the website. People are aware they're in a test and sometimes use the test environment to leaves tips for the developers about improvements. Luckily, this doesn't happen that much, but there is room for improvement there.

We are currently investigating ways to help participants utilize the comments to explain why they feel the emotion, rather than focusing on solutions. It's something many psychologists encounter when a patient is with them for the first time. When the psychologist asks the patient how they feel and why, the patient tends to immediately answer by describing what they think they should change about their behavior to feel differently. But this wasn't what the psychologist asked. The LEMtool doesn't ask users to solve the problem for the designer. We only want to know how they feel and why.

I do think, however, that there has been a change in the personalities of websites. Nowadays, the presence of brands and developers is less obvious in many popular websites, which likely gives more room for website personality. Also, some websites are probably more able to show personality than others.

> **Some websites are probably more able to show personality than others.**

References

Capota, K., van Hout, M., & van der Geest, T. (2007). Measuring the emotional impact of websites: A study on combining a dimensional and discrete emotion approach in measuring visual appeal of university websites. In *DPPI 2007 conference*. Helsinki, Finland.

Huisman, G., & van Hout, M. (2008). The development of a graphical emotion measurement instrument using caricatured expressions: The LEMtool. HCI2008. Liverpool: John Moores University.

CASE STUDIES

Windows Phone 7 Reference Designs for Metro UI

In 2009–2010, as part of preparing for the launch of Windows Phone 7 for Microsoft, Moni Wolf led the development of industrial design references (with the support of Catherine Kim and the Minimal design team) to act as examples of the seamless blending of the Metro user interface with hardware.

Bio

Moni Wolf is a Principal User Experience Designer at Microsoft's Interactive Entertainment Business (IEB). Before joining Microsoft in 2009, Moni started her design career in the Consumer Electronics Industry with Motorola in 1995.

During her career, Moni has lead numerous international design teams in the United States, Latin America, and Italy, where she and her teams partnered with global industry leaders and manufacturers.

She obtained her bachelor degree in Industrial Design at the Fachhochschule in Schwaebisch Gmuend, Germany, and her Masters of Art in the United States with a major in Computer-Aided Design and Visual Perception.

Introduction

Our design team was tasked with developing an industrial design reference for Metro, the user interface of Windows Phone 7 (WP7). This project presented a fun and exciting opportunity for our industrial design team. The Metro user interface (UI) and graphic user interface (GUI) were loaded with innovation, and introduced a revolutionary new look and feel to the mobile phone market. Our design and development teams got emotionally attached to Metro, and we learned early on that critics and consumers were responding in a similar way.

Our design and development teams got emotionally attached to the Metro UI.

The goal was to translate the graphic design principles of the Metro UI/GUI into a physical product. Meeting that goal meant expressing emotion through the physical design. In other words, our task was to evoke the same emotions through the physical design that are expressed by the Metro UI/GUI. In our designs for WP7, it was important to capture the "soul" of the Metro UI/GUI and create a harmonious translation of aesthetics and device interaction from the software to the hardware.

A product's hardware design often times serves as its first introduction to the user. The hardware design is the attention-getter. Some people call the moment you encounter the product the "moment of truth." Perhaps you see it in a magazine, or while browsing online, or walk by it at the store. The design of a product can grab your attention in that moment.

How Does the Product Grab Attention?

The experience starts with the *excitement* that's created on first exposure to the product. Seeing the product causes the user to feel excitement. The product resonates with you and this causes you to want to connect with it. Ways that products can resonate, connect and communicate include:

Projecting and communicating innovation

Users may respond by saying things like "this is the smallest watch I have ever seen!" or "wow! it's made out of one piece of brushed aluminum!" or "this looks like it's very high quality."

Reflecting an appealing time

This is often done through simplicity, durability, or a certain style embodied in its geometry, colors, materials and finishes (e.g., "I love brushed aluminum").

Having compelling qualities that capture attention and speak to your desires

Users experience immediate gratification when they begin using the product. The learning curve is small, so you can quickly feel skilled and competent. With Windows Phone 7, this could include tasks like taking a picture, making a phone call, or sending a multimedia message with an image attached. At the end, the user

> **Some people call the moment you encounter the product the "moment of truth."**

FIG. 6.2 Windows Phone 7 Start Screen
(Used with permission of Microsoft.)

Dating and Metro	DATING	METRO
Excitement	++	+
Connection	+	++
Gratification	++	+
Loyalty	+	+

FIG. 6.3 Dating and the Experience of Using Metro

Dating progresses through multiple phases of interaction, as does the experience of using a device with the Metro UI.

(Used with permission of Microsoft.)

feels calm and satisfied and understands what has just happened. The relationship between interaction and feedback is transparent and the result is peace of mind.

The experience starts with the *excitement* that's created on first exposure.

For success in evoking deep emotions and forging honest, strong and long-lasting interest, the design needs to be mirrored and supported at all the touchpoints of the product, including branding and other mass communications. This also includes the in-store or online purchase, the service experience and the out-of-box experience.

Positive and consistent experiences across all of these touch points lead to trust and loyalty. Loyalty can be increased by the pleasant discoveries users make over time while using the product and reinforcement from peers in the social environment.

One way to think about the progression from excitement to loyalty is to think of it like dating.

The design needs to be mirrored and supported at all the touch-points of the product.

The Industrial Design team worked to derive and translate the initial set of design principles for the Metro UI/GUI into a set that was specifically relevant to the hardware design. In the industrial design of the physical product, these principles are expressed at three levels. In the first level, the product feels *light and simple*, but is already expressing personality and emotion. On the second level, it begins to feel *purposeful*, and by the third level, if feels *soulful and alive* through the addition and experience of the details.

Metro Reference Designs

Within each reference design, principles are expressed that shape the user's experience of the phone. For example, *light and simple* is a principle that is expressed through a dramatic reduction of design elements. *Light and simple* is also expressed through typography that is clear, readable, straightforward, and communicative.

The principle of *soulful and alive* is expressed through the performance aesthetic of elements that move, like the sliding screen. The motion and transitions of the screen of the phone from open to closed mirrors transitions between states in the UI/GUI.

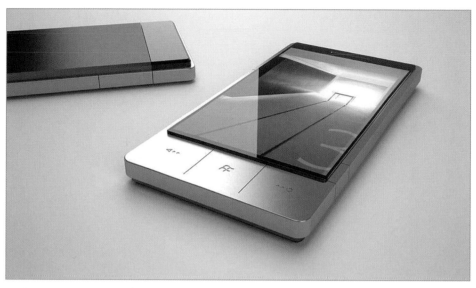

FIG. 6.4 Windows Phone 7 Design Reference: Plate

Plate is the expression of the design principle: light and simple. It expresses these qualities through a dramatic reduction of design elements.
(Used with permission of Microsoft.)

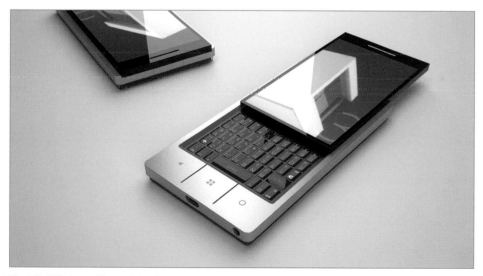

FIG. 6.5 Windows Phone 7 Design Reference: Plate (Open)

(Used by permission of Microsoft.)

FIG. 6.6 Window Phone 7 Design Reference: Extrude

Extrude expresses a friendly personality with its rounded edges and soft touch finish, which fit well into the hand.

(Used with permission of Microsoft.)

FIG. 6.7 Window Phone 7 Design Reference: Pouch (Front and Back)

Pouch provides an alternate implementation of the controls below the screen. Its soft, pillow-shaped back offers an inviting tactile experience for the user when holding the device.

(Used with permission of Microsoft.)

Soulful and alive describes the design elements that persist over the life of the product and encourage a deep sense of loyalty to the product. Soulful and alive expresses the personality of the product through colors, materials, finishes, and the tactility of the controls. It's a sprinkling of magical moments.

In Plate, the frameless glass, layout and geometries of the controls exemplify our attempts to provide a seamless integration of the phone's Industrial Design with Metro's GUI. The device's sliding mechanism has been fine-tuned to resemble the soulful and luxurious performance aesthetic of Metro. The device's body is composed of horizontal layers, with some of them sliding to expose the keypad. This relates the design of the phone to the motion of multiple layers in the Metro GUI.

The principle of soulful and alive is expressed through the feel of the product in the hand as the keyboard is exposed. As the screen slides, it progresses through deliberate movements designed to attract and satisfy the users' need for feedback. The acceleration and deceleration define the transitions from closed to open and communicate the personality of the product. The principle of timeless typography is expressed in the hardware controls, which take the same form as the distinct software tokens that are a part of the UI controls.

The main insight gained from the creation of the Metro Reference Design is that the designer needs to completely understand the "why" or the "soul" of the product. That is, he or she must know what the deeper purpose of the product is. This allows us to define product features and express the product's personality through its industrial design.

Soulful and *alive* expresses the personality of the product through colors, materials, finishes, and tactility.

The designer needs to completely understand the "why" or the "soul" of the product.

The Emotional Elements of PICO™

In this case study, we look at the development of a revolutionary medical product called PICO™.

Bios

Damian Smith and Chris Fryer are part of the New Product Development leadership team at Smith & Nephew's Advanced Wound Management division. Chris was the Project Lead on the development of PICO™ and has worked in the medical device industry for 10 years, with a background in engineering. Damian has worked in the medical device industry for 18 years, specializing in the design and development of wound management products, and was responsible for delivering the Human Factors for PICO™.

Matt Pattison is a Human Factors Specialist and cofounder of 7bn. He has worked for leading global innovation consultancies and has designed and run complex global and local innovation programs for Nokia, Smith & Nephew, Johnson & Johnson, Mercedes Benz and Philips. Matt specializes in understanding the needs of people based on behavioral analysis and in engaging designers, marketers and strategists in representing the human factor in design and innovation.

Shayal Chhibber is a Senior Design Researcher at Microsoft, working for the Interactive Entertainment Business. He specializes in ethnographic research and identifying patterns in consumer behavior that can inform future strategies. Prior to joining Microsoft, he worked alongside Matt at 7bn on projects for Smith & Nephew, Kohler and Coca-Cola.

Introduction

Our health has a direct effect on our emotional state.

The world of medical device design offers a rare and complex challenge when considering the role of human emotions in the design of a product. Our health has a direct effect on our emotional state and the relationships we seek with the healthcare products we use, in some cases, to keep us alive. Designing medical devices is made more complex by the fact that there are typically several stakeholders involved in buying, administering and using the product—each with her or his own emotional (and economic) needs that must be considered to develop a product that truly resonates.

Design Context

The world of chronic wound care is often seen as an unglamorous, complex and even 'dark art' within the clinical world. From small pressure ulcers (bed sores) that can last a few weeks, to complex vascular disease management or skin grafts that require specialist regimes, each wound is different and each patient requires a customized treatment regime.

The complexity around healing skin and soft tissue has led to the proliferation of many solutions, ranging from simple gauze dressings that cost a few dollars and primarily manage the symptoms, to high-priced dressings with active ingredients and specialist adhesives which actively treat the wound. At the high-tech end of this spectrum is a set of products known as Negative Pressure Wound Therapy (NPWT).

Traditionally, these devices are used for patients with severe chronic or complex surgical wounds that proved difficult to heal. In simple terms, the devices consist of a foam or gauze dressing (custom-made by the nurse at the wound site), a vacuum pump, a canister, and a length of medical tubing. The tubing runs from the pump to the porous dressing and allows the pump to draw out excess fluid, called

NPWT devices are typically large and can be a source of embarrassment, stigma, and loss of self-confidence.

exudate, from the wound bed and collect it in a canister. It's this application of negative pressure that aids in structural healing and encourages the growth of new tissue, often with impressive results.

NPWT devices are typically large, often leaving patients tethered to a bed. Drawing fluid and infectious material from the wound and collecting it in a transparent canister is a clear and visceral event for the patient; it clearly conveys that the machine is "doing something." But patients also report that it's an uncomfortable sensation, can produce strong odors (from draining fluid), and be a source of embarrassment, stigma and loss of self-confidence in many types of social scenarios. Larger devices provide excellent therapy for complex wounds, but their requirements can make them difficult to use outside of acute-care settings.

With a push for home treatment and a desire for patients to become more active, manufacturers developed portable battery powered Negative Pressure devices. Despite the reduced size, these devices still functioned in exactly the same way. While allowing some patient mobility, they don't offer the freedom of movement that patients desire. While decreasing the size, these initial, portable devices still did not provide the high level of discretion that patients both desire and require.

Introducing PICO™

In 2010, Smith & Nephew, a world-leading medical technology business, collaborated with 7bn, a design research and innovation consultancy, in order to better understand the complex human factors considerations that would be applicable to the portable NPWT device they had been seeking.

PICO™ (a mathematical term for very small) is a break-through product that is entirely is different than other products on the market. Its innovative design truly untethers patients. To promote further independence, the manufacturer worked alongside interaction designers at 7bn to develop a simple user interface for patients to operate the device. With minimal training, nurses could be confident that patients would be able to operate it independently.

When developing the product, the manufacturer started with one question- how do you make this therapy simpler at every stage: from application, through wear, to disposal? That question led to the first shift in thinking- why draw fluid away from the wound into a canister? Instead, they used a smaller vacuum which applied enough pressure to draw fluid into an intelligent dressing that allows fluid vapor to evaporate away from the dressing, while locking the exudate behind a one-way

Nurses could be confident that patients could operate it independently.

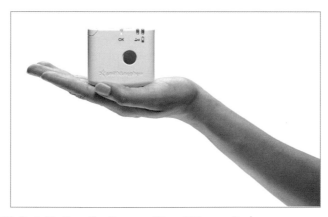

FIG. 6.8 **PICO™: Portable Negative Pressure Wound Therapy Device**

(Used with permission of Smith & Nephew Inc.)

membrane. This allowed the design team to produce a truly pocket-sized pump that was much smaller and more portable than its competitors. While it would not be a solution for the large, complex wounds that still require the more powerful drive of traditional NPWT devices, PICO™ is a perfect solution for the more common, simpler wound types that may not otherwise be treated with NPWT.

However, reducing the size did not lead to an automatic win. As fieldwork with patients and clinicians was to prove, this was merely the start of the challenge of meeting the emotional needs of all the stakeholders.

Wound care products are different than conventional consumer products. There are more stakeholder needs at play, and patients, those with the most to gain or lose, have the least choice in the process. To begin understanding the emotional needs of the different stakeholders, the team undertook a series of ethnographic site visits, observing and talking to surgeons, nurses, patients, and others involved in using the traditional systems.

Emotional Considerations

Stakeholders involved near the beginning of the product's journey (i.e., surgeons and purchasers) were often driven by performance (i.e., does it do the job?) and the economic viability of the product. Confidence in the engineering and core principles that formed the foundation of the product were proven in tests on wounds, and by meeting the requirements of global standards.

To understand the emotional needs of stakeholders, the team undertook ethnographic site visits.

However, the research found that the emotional needs of nurses and patients were much more nuanced and more difficult to satisfy. Although time-consuming, the process employed by nurses to dress wounds and set existing Negative Pressure devices was more akin to the process employed by a skilled artisan.

While often taking up to 45 minutes, the nurses saw the complexity of the process as a reflection on the level of care they gave their patients, and they drew a tangible sense of pride from building the intricate dressing and ensuring that the device was working properly. Working properly generally meant that when the machine was turned on, there were no beeping alarms indicating a problem with the seal over the wound.

The application process is complicated and customized for the often-challenging topography of the human body. Multiple components, body nooks and folds all lead to difficulty in getting the all-important airtight seal, which allows the NPWT to work. There is often a good degree of collaboration between patient and clinician during this application process, and both share a very genuine sense of anxiety in anticipating whether the port, tubing, and device are attached properly, so that the device is able to create a vacuum seal the on first attempt. Improper application of the dressing and other NPWT components can lead to leaks in the seal, which renders the pump unable to deliver therapy.

Quite often, the NPWT fails to seal, and the clinician has to locate the leak and make adjustments. This leads to more manipulation of the dressing (and the wound), which can be painful for the patient and laborious for the clinician. In worst-case scenarios, it results in a team of clinicians gathered around a patient, prodding, poking, and chasing the leak, while all grow increasingly frustrated.

Patient and clinician both share a sense of anxiety in anticipating whether the machine is attached properly.

Design Solution

In contrast, PICO™ is a simple system that can be applied to a wound in a couple of minutes. Many of the potential "leak points" associated with traditional NPWT products are addressed by having the tubing and port in place. Although this made the process much quicker and simpler, it may have been perceived by nurses as undermining the value of their skills. The design team explored the trade-offs with nurses by developing a range of dressings. In the end, they were able to offer a more flexible system that leveraged the skills of nurses, while also optimizing the use of the product across a broad range of wounds. Nurses were excited by its ease of use and the potential to make this treatment accessible to a broader range of wounds than was currently feasible.

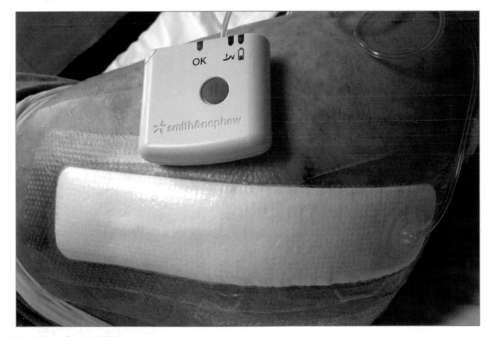

FIG. 6.9 Using PICO™

(Used with permission of Smith & Nephew Inc.)

Nurses were excited by its ease of use.

Patients' emotional needs were complex and varied. The increased mobility and discreteness of PICO™ was a clear benefit, but it lost the visceral associations that had come with the older products, which clearly looked like they were doing something to heal the wound. The power of portability and subtlety, however, were perceived advantages. In the early months following the release of PICO™ in the United Kingdom, positive news stories flooded in. From the testimonial of a young man, who was able to wrap PICO™ in a leg bandage so that he could visit a music festival, to others who could go to their local Elders Club for the Christmas party, the PICO™ made places that had been out of reach in previous years accessible again.

The user interfaces of existing NPWT products were multi-faceted. Homecare nurses frequently recounted tales of late-night calls from patients who didn't know whether the device was working or not, confused by the array of information that it was giving them. It was often observed that even some nurses couldn't decipher or decode the meaning of the various and inconsistent icons used by manufacturers to indicate leaks, power state, etc. Often, clinicians would refer to "the third light along" instead of "the leak indicator," for example.

To give nurses and patients more confidence in the device's ease of use while ensuring that it still offered the appropriate level of control and feedback, the team developed a simplified user interface. This UI used a markedly reduced set of controls and icons to convey critical states to the patient, rather than overwhelming them with constant feedback on performance. The simple form and interface immediately resonated with nurses and patients.

CONCLUSIONS

To give nurses and patients more confidence, the team developed a simplified user interface.

Smith & Nephew Advanced Wound Management's goal is to reduce the human and economic costs of wounds. With PICO™, they used the constraints of simplicity, accessibility and usability to drive advancement in technology and user experience. The low price of this therapy helps to make it appropriate for a broader range of wounds than traditional NPWT. By focusing on the core needs of users, this accessible device creates an emotional connection by reducing stigma and being accessible, understandable and consumer-driven.

A medical publisher in the United Kingdom recently told the 7bn team, "it's the only medical device I've ever wanted to own." Community nurses in Sweden are lobbying for PICO™ as the only truly accessible and cost effective way to bring NPWT devices to the masses, helping many more people in need.

By considering both the human and economic costs of wounds from the start, and creating a development program with emotion and human factors at its heart, PICO's innovations have satisfied both the economic and critical emotional needs of people living with a wound.

™Trademark of Smith & Nephew

Trademarks

Amazon.com® is a *registered trademark* of Amazon.com, Inc.

Back To the Future® is a *registered trademark* of Universal Studios, Inc.

Batman® *and Batmobile*® are *registered trademarks* of DC COMICS.

Barbie® is a *registered trademark* of Mattel Inc.

Bing®, *Clippy*®, *Intellimouse Explorer*®, *Kinect*®, *Live Search*®, *Metro UI*®, *Natural Keyboard Elite*®, *and WindowsPhone*® are *registered trademarks* of the Microsoft Corporation.

Clicky™ is a *trademark* of Roxr Software Ltd.

Comcast® is a *registered trademark* of Comcast Corporation.

Coca-Cola® is a *registered trademark* of the Coca-Cola Company.

Deadliest Catch® is a *registered trademark* of the Discovery Channel.

DeLorean™ is a *trademark* of the DeLorean Motor Company (Texas).

Dornbracht Tara™ is a *trademark* of Dornbracht Americas Inc.

DreamHost® is a *registered trademark* of New Dream Network, LLC.

Empire Avenue™ is a *trademark* of Empire Avenue Inc.

ETS Trip Planner™ is a *trademark* of Edmonton Transit System.

Facebook® is a *registered trademark* of Facebook, Inc.

foursquare® is a *registered trademark* of Foursquare Labs, Inc.

Gmail™ is a *trademark* of Google Inc.

Google® is a *registered trademark* of Google Inc.

Google Maps™ is a *trademark* of Google Inc.

Instagram™ is *trademark* of Burbn Inc.

iPhone®, *iPhone 4S*®, *iPod*®, *iPod Touch*®, *iPod Nano*®, *iTunes*®, *MacBook Pro*®, *Macintosh*®, *Mac OS X*®, *and Siri*® are *registered trademarks* of Apple Inc.

Journey to the Wild Divine™ is a *trademark* of Wild Divine Inc.

Johnson & Johnson® is a *registered trademark* of Johnson and Johnson Inc.

Kohler® is a *registered trademark* of Kohler Co.

Leica® is a *registered trademark of Leica.*

MailChimp® is a *registered trademark* of Rocket Science Group.

McDonald's® is a *registered trademark* of the McDonald's Corp.

Mercedes-Benz is a *registered trademark* of Mercedes-Benz AG.

Mint™ is a *trademark* of Evolution Robotics, Inc.

Mr. Yuk™ is a *trademark* of the Children's Hospital of Pittsburgh.

Nokia® is a *registered trademark* of Nokia Corporation,

Philips® is a *registered trademark* of Koninklijke Philips Electronics N.V.

PICO™ is a *trademark* of Smith & Nephew.

Porsche® is a *registered trademark* of Porsche Dr. Ing. h.c. F. Porsche AG and Porsche Cars North America.

Rachael Ray™ is a *trademark* of Rachael Ray Digital LLC.

Scrivener™ is a *trademark* of Literature & Latte Ltd.

Seattle Children's® is a *registered trademark* and trade name of Seattle Children's Healthcare System.

Sharpie® is a *registered trademark* of Sanford Corporation.

Smith & Nephew® is a *registered trademark* of Smith & Nephew, Inc.

Star Wars® is a *registered trademark* of Lucasfilm Ltd. and/or its affiliates.

The Bachelor® is a *registered trademark* of ABC.

The Dukes of Hazzard® and *General Lee*® are *registered trademarks* of Warner Bros. Entertainment Inc.

The Original Angelic Sole® is a *registered trademark* of John Fluevog Shoes Inc.

Twitter® is a *registered trademark* of Twitter Inc.

Virgin Mobile® is a *registered trademark* of Virgin Mobile, Inc.

VoiceandTone.com™ is a *trademark* of Rocket Science Group.

Volvo® is a *registered trademark* of Ford Motor Company, AB Volvo, or Volvo Cars North America.

Wall-E® is a *registered trademark* of the Walt Disney Company.

Werther's® and *Werther's Original*® are *registered trademarks* of August Storck KG.

Wufoo™ is a *trademark* of SurveyMonkey.com LLC.

Index

Page numbers followed by *f* indicates a figure and *t* indicates a table.

A

Achieved status, 162
Acoustic recognition software, 22
Adaptive interfaces, 183
Adoption, 61
Aesthetics, 4, 86-89, 130-132
  attract users, 88
  attractive babies, 104
  desirable, 130-131
  interaction and, 86-89
  of personality, 152-155
  of product, 178
    personality, 147
  quality of, 88
Affective design, 19
Affective states, 6, 7, 45, 46f
Affordances, 148-149
Ambitious, 109
Anxiety, 42, 42f
Appraisal
  process, 33f
  theory, 32
Arousal, 31, 34-39, 35f, 43, 43f, 53, 66, 67f, 79
  affects motivation, 54f
  emotional, 143-144
  guidelines for, 144-145
  line, 156
  motivation and, 69-70
Ascribed status, 162
Association and meaning, 54-55
Attention, 11-12, 39-41, 39f, 52, 59f, 61f
  emotion and, 66
  goals and, 57-58
  limits of, 61-62
  measuring, 60-61
  senses and, 62-66
  types of, 58-60
Attention Economy, The (Davenport and Beck), 57
Attract, converse, and transact (A.C.T.), 129
  model, 134f, 138f
    comparison, 134f
    interaction, 133, 133f
    persuasion with, 137

    seductive interactions, 133
    using, 138-141
Attraction, 61, 133, 135, 149
  aesthetics of personality, 152-155
  color, 153-155
  guidelines for, 152
  image
    distance in, 159, 159f
    size, 156-157, 157f
  line and form, 155-156
  motion, 159-160
  principles, 151f
  scene changes, 160-161
  screen size, 157-158
Attractiveness, 103-105
Auditory sense, 65-66
Awareness, 60

B

Behavior, 43-45, 44f, 51, 152f
  emotion and, 67
Boredom, 42, 42f
Broken heart syndrome, 63

C

Cell phone, driver on, 60f
Character, 47
Clippy, 187
Cognitive seduction, 179
Color
  definition, 122-123
  unconscious color associations, 121-123
Commitment, useful function, 96, 132
Companionate love, 99
Conscious emotion, 26-28
Conscious neomammalian brain, 30
Consistent experiences, 202
Consummate love, 99
Content strategy, 164
Continuous feedback loop, 31
Continuous partial attention, 61-62
Conversation, 133, 161
  dominant and submissive interaction, 166-167

Conversation (*Cont'd*)
  guidelines for, 164
  and interaction, manners, 167–168
  power, 162, 163*f*
  status, 162–164, 163*f*
  stereotypes, gender, 168
  voice, gender, 168
Credibility, 107
Cultural status, 106

D

Decision making, emotion and, 9–10
Design, 22
  for emotion cover, 27*f*
  goals, 131*f*
    defining, 140–141
  models, 91–94
  useful, usable, and desirable, 1–4
Designers, 2
Designing Pleasurable Products (Jordan), 176
Desirability Toolkit, 192–195
Desirable aesthetics, passion for, 130–131
Desmet
  agents level, 132
  events level, 132
  object level, 131
Dialog interaction, 133, 133*f*
Discomfort demands users' attention, 62
Distress, 38–39
Divided attention, 59–60, 64
Dominance hierarchy, 115
Dominant interaction, 166–167
Dominant *versus* submissive characteristics, 153*f*

E

Emoticon, 130*f*
Emotion, 4–15
  and advertisements, 10
  aggressive behavior, 117
  association and, 14–15
  attention, 66
    and information, 39–41, 39*f*
    and memory, 11–12
  and behavior, 67
  benefits, 92–93
  conscious and unconscious, 26–28
  creation of meaning, 4–15
  and decision making, 9–10
  design models, 91–94
  designing, interviews with
    Anderson, Stephen P., 178–184
  Jordan, Patrick W., 175–199
    Miner, Trish, 192–195
    van Hout, Macro, 195–199
    Walter, Aarron, 184–192
  evolution of, 115–124
  experiencing, 21–22
  expression of, 22–23, 120
  and flow, 71–79
    contributes to, 41–43
  human relationships, love, 95, 97–99
  mental and physical, 31–39
  moods, sentiments and personality traits, 45–47
  motivation and behavior, 43–45
  negative, 198
  objects displaying, 13*f*
  originate, parts of brain, 28
  perception of, 85–86
  personality, forms relationships, and
    meaning, 12–14
  personality traits, 84
    design and, 101–109
  positive, 176, 198
  processing, levels of, 91–92
  reasons to design, 6–14
  reptilian brain, 28–31
  responses, experiences, and relationships, 89–101
  unconscious emotional responses, 25
  understanding, 21–25
Emotional affect, 7, 39–41, 45
Emotional arousal, 53, 143–144
Emotional benefits, 92–93
Emotional design, principles of, 19, 51
Emotional engagement, 60
Emotional experiences, 90, 90*f*
Emotional meaning, 53–54
Emotional needs, prioritize, 3–4
Emotional processing
  behavioral level, 92
  reflective level, 92
  visceral level, 91
Emotional relationships, 90, 90*f*
Emotional responses, 51, 90, 90*f*
Emotional states, 19, 35*f*, 45
Emotional traits, 47
Emotional trends, 36*f*
Empathy, 108
Entertainment-oriented media, 38
Eustress, 38–39
Evolutionary terms, 41
Excitement, 201
Experienced users, 76
External stimuli, 22

F

Feelings, 22–23, 45, 62
Feminine stereotypes, 110–113
Fire alarm, 25f, 38
Flattery, 10
Floor sweeper, 33, 34f
Flow
    attention and, 57–62
    causes, characteristics, and consequences,
        72–79
    emotion and, 71–79
    emotion contributes to, 41–43
    experience, 53
    measuring success through, 53–56
Focus of attention, 57–59
Four Pleasures, 177
Foveal vision, 64, 157
Freddy, 191
Frustration, 43
Furious, 156f

G

Genders
    in products, 113–114
    stereotypes, 109–114, 168
Genie effect, 161
Geographic maps, 24
Goal-directed use vs. experiential use, 76
Goal-oriented activities, 53
Graphic user interface (GUI), 200
Guidelines, A.C.T.
    for arousal, 144–145
    attraction, 133, 135, 149, 152
        aesthetics of personality, 152–155
        color, 153–155
        image, 156–157, 157f, 159, 159f
        line and form, 155–156
        motion, 159–160
        principles, 151f
        scene changes, 160–161
        screen size, 157–158
    conversation, 161, 164
        dominant and submissive interaction,
            166–167
        and interaction, manners, 167–168
        power, 162, 163f
        status, 162–164, 163f
        stereotypes, gender, 168
        voice, gender, 168
    transaction, 169
    for value, 142–143

H

Homunculus, 63, 63f
Human relationships, love
    forms of, 95, 98f
    types of, 97–99, 98f

I

Ideo-pleasure, 177
Illusory love, 98–99
Intelligence, 107
Intention, 44f
    affect by value, 68f
    behavior, 152f
    and motivation, 67
Interaction, 86–89, 133
    and conversation, manners, 167–168
    dialog, 133, 133f
    dominant and submissive, 166–167
    seductive, 133
Internal stimuli, 22
Intimacy, 96
Investment, 61
iPhone keyboard feedback, 65f

J

Jargon
    desirable aesthetics, passion for, 130–131
    usable interaction, intimacy of, 132
    useful function, 132
Jordan
    emotional benefits, 132
    hedonic benefits, 92, 131
    practical benefits, 132

L

Law of Hedonic Asymmetry, 141
LEMtool, 195–199
Light and simple, 202
Longer-term goal, 54

M

Macrosuasion, 137
MailChimp, 79f, 88, 185, 188, 190
    personality traits, 140f
        dominant and submissive
            interaction, 166f, 167
Mammalian brain, 29–30, 90, 135
Masculine, 110–113
    product characteristics, 147

Material status, 55–56, 106
Memory, 11–12
Mental models, 23–25
Mental/emotional state, 41
Metro reference designs, 202–205
Metro user interface (UI), 200–205
    dating and experience, 202*f*
Microsoft IntelliMouse Explorer, 55*f*
Microsoft Natural Keyboard, 74, 74*f*
Microsuasive goals, 137
    defining, 140, 141
Mid brain *see* Mammalian brain
Mixed emotions, 31
Moods, 46
Motion, 159–160
Motivation, 43–45, 44*f*
    and arousal, 69–70
        affects, 54*f*, 70*f*
        behavior, 152*f*
        intention and, 67
MP3 players, 88
Multisensory experiences, 11–12

N

Negative affect, 67, 68
    balancing, 69
Negative emotion, 11
Negative emotional, 20
    affect, 40
Negative experiences, 11, 141–142
Negative Pressure Wound Therapy (NPWT)
        device, 206, 207*f*, 208
Negative stimuli, 69
Neomammalian brain, 30–31, 90
Norman
    behavioral level, 132
    reflective level, 132
    visceral level, 131
Novice users, 76
NPWT device *see* Negative Pressure Wound
        Therapy device

O

Old brain *see* Reptilian brain

P

Party Pooper Mode, 208
Passion, 95
Personality, 4–15, 146*f*, 147, 170*f*, 186
    aesthetics, 152–155

and interaction, 86–89
evolution of
    dominance and friendliness, 116–117,
        119–120
    submissive behavior, 117–118
identity and, 85
objects displaying, 13*f*
perceiving emotion and, 85–86
perception of, 169
Personality traits, 13, 14, 47, 84
    design and, 101–109
        ambitious, 109
        attractiveness, 103–105
        empathy and exciting, 108
        intelligence, 107
        social status, 106
        trustworthiness, 107
Persuasion, A.C.T., 137
Physiological arousal, 145
    saturation level, 154
Physiological goals, 54
Physio-pleasure, 177
Pico, 209*f*
    emotional elements, 205–210
Pleasure, 176
Positive affect, 67–68
    balancing, 69
Positive emotional affect, 40
Positive emotional experience, 185
Positive emotions, 176, 198
Positive experiences, 11, 202
Positive memories, 12
Practical benefits, 92
Primary appraisals, 32
Primitive visual cues
    image size, 156–157
    line and form, 155–156
Product Emotion Measurement (PrEmo) Tool, 195
Products
    personality, 83–86
        aesthetics, 88
        perception of, 86
        75 emotions relevant to, 37, 37*f*
Psychic energy *see* Attention
Psychological goals, 54
Psycho-pleasure, 177

R

Reality model, 24
Reptilian brain, 28–31, 90, 135
Romantic love, 98

S

Searchlight of attention, 64
Seatbelt buckle, 20f
Secondary appraisals, 32
Seductive Interaction Design (Anderson), 179
Seductive interactions, 133
Selective attention, 59, 64
Senses and attention, 62–66
Sensory homunculus, 63, 63f
Sentiments, 46
Short-term goals, 54
Social hierarchy, 115
Social ranking system, 29
Social status, 106
Socio-pleasure, 177
Soulful and alive, 202, 205
Sounds, 65
Spotlight of attention, 65
Status, 162–164
Stereotypes
    gender in, 109–114, 168
    masculine and feminine, 110–113
Stress, 38, 43
Submissive behavior, 117–118
Submissive interaction, 166–167

T

Tactility, 63–64
Takotsubo cardiomyopathy *see* Broken heart
        syndrome
Target user group, 139
Task-oriented media, 38
Touch, 63–64
Transaction, 133, 136–137, 169

Triune brain, 29f
    theory, 28
Trustworthiness, 107

U

Unconscious
    emotion, 26–28
    emotional responses, 25
Usable interaction, intimacy of, 132
Useful function, commitment to, 132
User benefits, types of, 92–93
User experience, 53
User interface (UI), 182

V

Valence *see* Value
Value, 32–33, 32f, 35f, 36
    affects, 43
        choice, 66f
    good *versus* bad, 141–142
    guidelines for, 142–143
    judgments, 32–33
    and meaning, 55–56
Visual attention, 60, 64–65
VoiceandTone.com, 188
Voices, 168

W

Windows Phone 7 reference designs, 200–205

Y

Yerkes-Dodson law, 38, 38f, 70, 71f, 144f